THE INNER WORLD OF QOHELET

Frank Zimmermann

(with translation and commentary)

KTAV PUBLISHING HOUSE, INC.

NEW YORK

1973

SBN 87068-181-8

LIBRARY OF CONGRESS CATALOG CARD NUMBER: 72-5823

MANUFACTURED IN THE UNITED STATES OF AMERICA

For Rebecca and Judy and Warren.

Table of Contents

It would be a good thing if man concerned himself more with the history of his nature than with the history of his deeds.

—Hebbel.

If all the dreams which men dreamed during a particular period were written down, they would give an accurate notion of the spirit which prevails at that time.

—Hegel.

Preface

The objective of the present book is two-fold: to provide the student of Qohelet with an insight into his character and personality in the light of psychological knowledge, and to show how the discordant type of book that he wrote is a mirror of the chain of neuroses that afflicted him; and secondly, to indicate that the language in which he wrote the book was Aramaic and not the Hebrew that we know today.

The psychiatrist or analyst will find nothing new in these pages: here is but another example of the sufferer unburdening himself to his therapist. I wish the evidence were more ample: that I could have spoken with Qohelet face to face, seen his emotion as he told his story, noted the tone of his voice, where he smiled or was tearful, whether he was hesitating or agitated, silent or effusive, have him repeat his tale, and note the variations, what he added and what he suppressed, what were his conflicts and his dreams especially, what associations, and perhaps more expansively the relations between his mother/sister, the other members of his family, and himself. The portrait presented here may be something like a painting done from a photograph. Nonetheless, something of Qohelet's personality comes through to illumine much of the book he wrote.

Some writers have classified me as Freudian (e.g., Erwin R. Goodenough, *Jewish Symbols in the Greco-Roman Period*, VI, 142, 143) but I am not entirely so. I have nothing but admiration for the guide and teacher Sigmund Freud, and this book, page after page, is indebted to his researches, and to those of Wilhelm Stekel in his monumental ten-volume series, *Disorders of the Instincts and the Emotions* (available in English). But I have been influenced by—to mention but a few of the older pioneers—the theories of Otto Rank, Carl Jung, and Alfred Adler, and by the moderns too; yet I have kept an open mind and reserved my own judgment.

Part of this book is devoted to the linguistic evidence for the proof of translation, of Aramaic into Hebrew. The idea that Qohelet is a translation only came slowly after years of work in the Septuagint, the Apocrypha, and the Pseudepigrapha, which made retroversion second nature to me. The surprise is that although proof of Semitic origins in the Apocrypha and Pseudepigrapha in many instances was limited to a meager half-dozen, in Qohelet there is the rich harvest of over seventy-five examples of translation and mistranslation.

There was a problem of method in dealing with the material. For example 3.3, "There is a time to murder," contains within itself the following elements: Qohelet's compulsions, his aggressive thoughts and criminal tendencies, the antithetic character in which he frames his thoughts, and his persistent doubts, as well as a discussion of a reading in stich b. It was thought best to ally all the verses that pertain to one question and one topic even though there be some repetition. A complete analysis and discussion of many problems regrettably could not be included. Throughout, to cut the Gordian knot, I have simply expressed my opinion. I trust it will not sound dogmatic. It was not intended so. The two parts of the book, the psychological and the philological, are quite interrelated. Scholars, of course, will betake themselves to the latter part for the discussion and evidence. The general reader will find, hopefully, enough of interest and stimulation.

In a number of instances, I have given my own translation of a verse to point up a difficulty *ad hoc* rather than give a standard translation. A new translation, however, was given at the last based upon the newly conceived character of Qohelet as well as the restored underlying Aramaic. The commentary in brief form furnishes the evidence. It should be emphasized that the commentary is not a full-blown exposition where the temptation was strong to include much more. It was thought best to limit the commentary severely to point out the Aramaic substratum of the Hebrew as well as the psychological implications of the verse(s) for understanding Qohelet's personality. For this contribution it is hoped the book will have served its purpose.

It is a pleasant duty to acknowledge my thanks to Doctor Ira Eisenstein, President of the Reconstructionist Rabbinical College, Philadelphia, who read the manuscript, to a psychoanalyst friend who encouraged me in my theories about Qohelet, but who modestly wishes to remain anonymous, and to Mr. I. Berger for his painstaking editing, as well as to Mr. Bernard Scharfstein for his careful attention to printing details. Lastly, gratitude to my wife Rebecca, whose devotion and encouragement can hardly be expressed in these lines.

New York, December, 1972.

A man is infinitely more complicated than his thoughts.

—Valery.

Introduction

In contemporary literature a new technique, a new treatment of an author and his writings, which critics were not aware of in the preceding centuries, has gained recognition and acceptance with men of letters. When Freud and his associates and disciples initiated a new methodology in the treatment of mental disorders, their insights and discoveries were so fruitful that specialists in other fields, even remote from clinical analysis, found the advances in the new knowledge rewarding and stimulating. A host of investigators in anthropology, mythology, folklore, and culture patterns invigorated whole systems of thinking with discoveries and new interpretations. Freud himself, aside from his technical studies in psychoanalysis, was a pioneer in other areas as well.[1] Other scholars such as E. Jones, T. Reik, O. Rank, G. Roheim have made similar outstanding contributions by means of the psychoanalytic technique.[2]

In literary criticism, too, a new era has opened up. Critics will now deal in depth interpretation: of the unconscious operating in the author's work, the correspondence between the external events and inner motivation, of frustration and guilt, anxiety and neurosis, repression and symbolism. Countless monographs have appeared on Edgar Allan Poe, Mark Twain, Shakespeare, Lewis Carroll, Thomas Mann, Dostoievski, Goethe, to enumerate a few at random and to say nothing of modern authors themselves (e.g., James Joyce) who have made use of the new insights in their writings. Most critics take the position however that much of his personality and the kind of nature an author has is disclosed in his writing as if he had composed a complete dossier on himself, as e.g. Henry James unwittingly reveals himself on every page, as Leon Edel avers. A book is a mirror of its

XI

creator, and symbols are but signals from the author's unconscious. That is to say, the symbols that he employs may bear interpretation on two levels: what the author purports to have the symbol signify; and, no less interesting, what he means by the symbol in his unconscious self. Or he may relate an experience to convey one idea when he means something else entirely—discernible to his alert interpreter. In the case of Qohelet, unsparing energy and erudition have been deployed to explain what the text says, through investigations in etymology, word meanings, philology and syntax; through studies of the Hebrew text with the ancient Greek versions, the Peshitta, the Vulgate and the Targums; and through the combing of cognate Semitic languages for the enrichment of our understanding of the Hebrew language. Now the questions that must be probed are: Can we understand now more comprehensively, more penetratingly the personality of the author of Qohelet? How is it that he wrote this peculiar patchy type of book? Is it possible to understand more comprehensively the sentiments and significance of what he had to say? Why is his book replete with truths, half-truths, and contradictions? How is it that he articulates a peculiar farrago of ideas, alien to Jewish tradition? He never mentions Abraham, Isaac and Jacob, nor the covenant Yahweh made with them, nor the nation of Israel, nor the Torah with its statutes and ordinances; he never offers a prayer nor cries out to God for mercy though he suffered much; he does not speak of the holidays nor the Sabbath. It is difficult to focus him in time and place. He seems to have no relationship with people, with family (except his wife and son in distant negative terms) nor with his father or mother. He is not a philosopher nor does he have a philosophical system.

The usual explanation of Qohelet's style and personality, to bring the book into some semblance of unity and concordance of the leading ideas, is to assume that there were minimally five different editors, two epilogists, and two apologists, plus a number of glossators who took a hand in its composition. Appealing as this is to a rationalist so that propositions and their antinomies get pegged in logical pigeon-holes, the hypothesis of nine contributors or more is regarded as unfortunate and improbable.[3] Others take the view that this "amazingly contradictory book" stems from the personality of one who kept a journal or notebook in which he registered his thoughts as they came to him without too much regard or concern for concinnity. Still others rearrange and displace verses to conform with their conception of the author's thought.

The labor that students have expended on interpreting Qohelet has been extensive, fruitful, and informative. Words and their meanings have been redefined and amplified; textual and literary criticism have been judiciously advanced; dating the earlier and later elements of the Hebrew language has proceeded apace. Nevertheless, it must be confessed that Qohelet's personality has remained an enigma; we have not penetrated to the core of his complex persona.

To throw light on some of these problems, and to assess his personality, I have invoked the more assured results of the psychoanalytic method and discipline. What will this technique contribute to our understanding of Qohelet? In the first place, as in a musical composition by the Baroque masters, we shall not only listen to the main theme but to the counterpoint as well, which is not only a secondary accompaniment but a melody in its own right. Not only are the melodies played over and over again—Bach's Passacaglia and Fugue in D Minor will come to mind—but there are variations above and below as well; and on other occasions, the so-called counterpoint may swell to dominate the composition.

Thus the object of this study is to show that Qohelet's personality and thoughts are best explained by the complex neuroses that gripped and overpowered him, neuroses which he tried to ameliorate through a series of compulsive actions intended to drain off the pressure and the drives that surged within him. Even with a first reading of his book, it is easy to perceive in Qohelet the weariness of life, the lack of zest and interest in living, the futility of planning for the future, the obsession with wasted time, and the foreboding that time is fleeing, the meaningless use of his activity, his withdrawal from the world, his detachment as a nonparticipating spectator, and the concurrent fear of death and the welcome to life's end which would finish it once and for all.

I take it that the book is a complete representation of Qohelet himself. As Leon Edel well says, "The very form he [i.e., the novelist] has given the tale, the manner in which he has related to history, the words he has used, his choice of phrase and color and above all his symbolic images are in the end symbols of himself, signature of his inner being."[4] There may be in the book a number of glosses to be considered, but on the whole relatively few. As will be seen, the representation of Qohelet comes through whether in the first, second or third person employed. Thus the beginning of the book is manifestly in the first person. Then the first person is dropped, and an impersonal style is adopted with the second person, suppositiously addressed to the reader (e.g., 5.1, "Be not rash with thy mouth, let thy heart be not hasty . . . "), and then anonymously in the third person through observations and aphorisms (e.g., 5.19). In all cases they are reflections of one and the same, Qohelet himself, searching, searching, for some relief and deliverance from obsessions, anxieties, and compulsions. Anatole France has said that it makes no difference whether a man writes about a fly or Julius Caesar, he is not writing so much about his subject as about himself.

If Freud exaggerated on occasion when he declared that everything is unconscious, the more moderate claim that the unconscious plays a large significant role cannot be gainsaid. Before psychoanalysis, Keats himself had declared that a poet's life is a continual allegory, and his works are the comments on it. Again harking back to midrashic times of the first century C.E., it is interesting to see how the talmudic authorities cut loose from the Hebrew text, and in what might be called psychologically "free association" sought explications of the text based upon intuitive discernments from a modern point of view, e.g., Qoh.10.18, "By sloth the rafters fall in, and through idleness of the hands the house leaks," where the Midrash explains that this refers to a woman careless of her impurity.[5] In brief, to discover the latent thought is to find the most significant thought. New meanings and interpretations on verses which I believe have hitherto defied satisfactory relevant exegesis will provide a synoptic explanation. We may be able to perceive a new universal import to the book's composition. It will be interesting as well to peer into Qohelet's imagination, to learn what motivated him to write the way he did, and perhaps offer some solution in many instances to the peculiar cast of his style and framework of his ideas.

Simply the thing I am shall make me live.
—Shakespeare

I
Vignette of the External Qohelet

Qohelet pretended at the beginning of his book that he was a king over Israel in Jerusalem. Very quickly, however, the mask is dropped and he assumes his own self, that of a court official. The attitude, for example, that he bears to authority reflects this position. His demeanor in the presence of the king is one of profound obeisance, as the word of the king is supreme, Qohelet says, and no one may remonstrate with him (8.4). In two verses before, he advises that one must watch the countenance (see Commentary) of the king. Or again, in 10.4 he urges that if the anger of the king rises against you, don't resign your office, for soothing will remove much offense. He notices how the ruler screams at the dunderheads at court. These and other verses betoken his presence at the royal court. The king, however, is a foreign ruler (*see* p. 123) and there is ambiguity in the terms that Qohelet employs: *melek*, "king" (1.12; 5.8; 8.2.4; 10.20), and *moshel*, Aramaic *shalit*, "ruler" (9.17;10.4). The royal government of the Seleucids had its seat at Antioch on the Orontes while the vice regent/heir apparent/crown prince, usually a Seleucid, co-ruled at Seleucia on the Tigris. The Seleucid heir apparent would by courtesy be called "king" very much as *basileus* was applied to the "son of a king, or chieftain, prince, a powerful rich or fortunate person"[6] similar to the Latin *rex* and the English "king," and indeed *melek* bears that signification as well, as for example in Josh. 13.21 where *nasi'* is read, though in the parallel passage in Num. 31.8 the word is *melek*. The whole section of 4.15 receives new illumination: it is the Seleucid king introducing his son or co-regent to the populace, perhaps even a portrayal of a coronation scene. (p. 130, 146 ff.) Moreover, through his intimate experience at the court, Qohelet was able to witness the sloth and debauchery of the nobles and bureaucrats carousing in the mornings and to recall nostalgically how the king in another reign was independent and officials served conscientiously. (10.16–17).

1

Qohelet nevertheless was quite in awe of the king with his absolute power and authority. He held himself in strict accountability to the ruler to carry through his orders punctiliously (8.5), not from any sense of duty or loyalty but, as we shall see, from an apprehension stemming from the old situation of an austere father-son relationship.

Qohelet consequently has great respect for the wealthy man, too, the tycoon who exercises immense power and authority. One should never curse the wealthy man even in the recesses of one's chamber (10.20). He similarly observes that fools occupy high places, but wealthy persons sit humiliated in the low seats (10.6). In line with his philosophy that nothing can be changed (3.14), Qohelet resignedly regards the wealthy man as an immutable phenomenon; there is nothing much that one can do about his rapacity, and though for the victims Qohelet has much sympathy (4.1) yet in his fantasy he would love to be one of the rich (2.4 *et seq.*).

That Qohelet was a poor man, or one of very moderate means at best (4.8;5.7;10.19), is reflected from the standpoint of his observations. A man works hard ('*amal*, "toil, trouble, pain"[7] is always used, never '*abodah*, "work"), and after unremitting industry leaves his property to someone else (2.21.22); or it is '*inyan*, "grievous work, pain"[8] that persons are obliged to undergo, labor at (2.22–23;2.26). What the poor man knows in the struggle against life (so substantially at 6.8; (*see* Commentary) obviously mirrors again not a plutocrat but one who knows the arduous demands of everyday living.

He recognizes that "the race is not to the swift nor the battle to the strong"; but Qohelet knows wistfully and only too well from his own strivings the unhappy condition of intellectuals deprived of food, favor, and fortune (9.11). The poor man, if intelligent, doesn't count (9.15), and only money answers everything (10.19). By "poor" is not meant that Qohelet was ground by poverty. He had, for example, a slave—one slave, however (7.21).

All the signs point to the fact that Qohelet was a married man and had a child, a son. R. Gordis has argued that he was a bachelor[9], but on the whole the evidence, both external and internal, seems to point up that Qohelet was married. Thus he will say that just as one cannot know how the spirit of life enters the burgeoning womb, in like fashion one cannot know about God's activity (ll.5). The burgeoning womb (*beṭen hammele 'ah*) is an experience and concept that will not occur to a bachelor but only to one who has lived with a wife for the gestation period of nine months and watched wonderingly how the womb and embryo become larger and larger. Nor does a bachelor think in terms of an abortion (6.3). Similarly the bitter denunciation of woman, described as one of fettering hands and entrapping spirit, could likewise only stem from one who has experienced marriage with that kind of wife. If one is favored by God, he will escape her (7.26). The evidence for "son" found at 5.13 will be discussed (see p. 35, 94, 148).

Qohelet suffered from ill health. He declares that a man's days are filled with pain and torment (2.23) and he eats his meals but complainingly (so according to the recovered text from the Aramaic [5.16]). He knows that overindulgence makes one sleepless (5.11). More importantly, there is his mental distress. He is upset, restless, agitated (2.22). He dreams a good deal although he tries to minimize their significance. Fear God and you are safe (5.6). Qohelet's imagination conjures up nothing but ill, and terrifying mortal diseases for the old (c.12).

The epilogist of Qohelet portrays him as a lecturer (12.9–10), and one who cast into aphoristic frames many sayings based upon genuine experience, written honestly and with some style (12.10). If so, it must have been at considerable cost and struggle for Qohelet to present to the world an outward demeanor of composure for forensic delivery (10.9). He probably excelled in the composition of proverbs, where a more lengthy discourse, as his book shows, would be spotty in expression and style, abrupt in the introduction of subjects, with puzzling breaks in thought. His nearest congener, Ben Sira, is much more skillfull in that regard.

It is quite evident too that Qohelet knew at first hand, and participated actively in, life's larger experiences. He seems to have had some military experience (see p. 61). He has allusions to agriculture. Everyone including the king is dependent ultimately on agricultural conditions (5.8); but watching the weather is a futile occupation; one must proceed with one's work (11.4), and be pursuant of it persistently, for one never knows about the success of one's enterprise (11.6). He is acquainted with the advantages of a business partnership; isolation is disastrous when affairs slip and go wrong (4.9ff.;5.13). One should not put all of one's resources into a single venture (11.1f).

As an observer at the royal court, Qohelet was in a position to comment on the changing political scene. Apparently he witnessed how the older king "introduced" the heir apparent to the populace with much eclat on occasions. Qohelet was well aware how at first the popular enthusiasm for the new ruler is all but universal, but he knows about the reaction that inevitably sets in (4.16), and subsequently he will mourn the fact that the young ruler is inexperienced and that the nobles, disregarding their duties, will dissipate themselves (10.16).

Such might be the superficial aspect of Qohelet to one who might encounter him for the first time. Qohelet, however, has left a record of himself of far more engrossing interest as a human being, as one caught up in a web of fate, which for his time he could not undo, and for which in those days there was but little help, for a study and a knowledge of the unconscious had not yet been born. It was the writing of his book, as we shall see, that saved him from complete disintegration.

No man sins unless a perverse impulse seizes him.
—Talmud.

*It is with trifles, and when he is off guard,
that a man best reveals his character.*
—Schopenhauer.

II
The Neuroses and Compulsions of Qohelet

Antonio in the *Merchant of Venice* says to Bassanio that the Devil can cite Scripture for his purpose. Certainly Satan could quote Qohelet as Scripture more appositely than any other book in the Bible. Because of the unorthodox opinions Qohelet holds, skeptics are delighted by his views so congruent to their own; on the other hand, they ignore or are vexed by the puzzling orthodox opinions that come through. Conversely, the orthodox are horrified by his questioning of all things hallowed, but are gratified by the sporadic affirmations of teachings that they hold dear. Qohelet is a paradox: hedonist yet abstemious (4.8), religious but with reservations, really a man of varying opinions from one end of the spectrum to the other, colored by his pessimism and skepticism. "It is very difficult to give an account of the contents of Ecclesiastes, which should be at once clear, brief and adequate. There is very little strict development of the thought, and the endless repetition which the writer sees in nature and life has its partial counterpart in his book. The difficulty is increased by the uncertainty as to interpolations and the exegesis of particular passages . . ."[10]

Relevant as these observations may be, they do not touch, appraise, or comprehend the full scope of Qohelet's problems with himself and with his inner turmoil. A careful reading of the book reveals that Qohelet is not only skeptical of ideas, and rebellious at conventions, but there is nothing that he suggests as a moral or maxim that he does not contradict elsewhere in his own writing, and peculiarly even in such instances where his hedonistic espousals are the most affirmative and vigorous that he is capable of advancing (e.g., eat, drink, and enjoy life, 2.24;3.12 and elsewhere). Constantly, there always seems to be an alternative, another perspective, a retreat, a reversal, a hesitation, a

5

doubt in what he advocates.

He may say that the wise man knows where he is going (has eyes in his head, 2.14) and that wisdom fortifies a wise man more than the wealth (see Commentary) of the officials in a city (7.19); that the wise man's words are more acceptable than those of a ruler who storms at his foolish underlings (9.17); that he, Qohelet, made it his life's endeavor to pursue ḥokma (8.16); that wisdom is more efficacious than brute strength or weapons of war (9.16.18); that everything he would strive to do should only be performed wisely, and through the instrumentality of wise procedure (1.13;2.3;7.3); and that no one compares with the wise man in understanding (8.1). But all this is as nothing. Qohelet's doubts about wisdom's value and effectiveness assail him. Seemingly, what he has built up he tears down. He asks, in view of man's end and annihilation, why did he himself acquire wisdom (2.15); why even the wise man can never succeed in fathoming the fundamental ultimate enigmas (8.17), and that at any rate wisdom is a vexation of spirit (1.18). One may even question whether wisdom is attainable altogether (7.23). Certainly the wisdom of the poor man is scorned (9.16) although this is contradicted characteristically by the poor but wise young man of 4.13; and yet again, in a bit of candid counsel, Qohelet admonishes not to be overwise (7.16). Thus Qohelet runs the whole gamut of extolling wisdom, from the apex of man's indispensable aid and guide downward to a complete deprecation of its substance and value. There is no superiority of the wise even to the fool (6.8).

Ḥokma, then, as a guide for living is diluted by Qohelet's doubts; however, on occasion he may affirm its espousal in his philosophy. Equally paramount with him is the enjoyment of life's goodness, as much as it is in one's power to do so. He formulates his credo with the simple and attractive proposition that one should eat, drink, and pamper oneself in physical pleasures, i.e., have a "good time" (2.24;5.17). This advice would seem to be unequivocal, unreserved. But again Qohelet hesitates, retracts, and gives vent to his doubts. When prosperity arrives, there are likewise many who consume its abundance (5.10). But what satisfaction can obtain for the one who eats except what his eyes can encompass (*ibid*)? Enjoyment is limited to the eye alone.

His correlative recommendation of *simḥa*, "merriment, hilarity," is no less ambivalent. He has praise for merriment (8.15); and a man should strive to be happy (2.10) from his work (3.13), i.e., in the gain he has from his work. This is the best a man can do to extract some sweetness from human existence. Is this then the summum bonum?

The mind of the wise is in the house of mourning, avers Qohelet, and we wait expectantly. Qohelet wavers: The mind of fools is in the house of mirth (7.4). Qohelet tried *simḥa* but it was futility (2.1); hilarity is a delusion and what does *simḥa* accomplish? (2.2). But this is not the end of his doubt either. With still another reservation, he asserts that the ability to be merry does not depend upon man, on his temperament or resource so to speak, but is a gift from God, (3.15). Nor does it depend upon man's moral qualities either, whether good or bad, but simply that *simḥa* is extended to a man who mysteriously wins God's favor *(ṭob lefanaw)* whereas the sinner is not so favored (2.26 and elsewhere).

One might conclude that as a minimum, one should pursue pleasure however one can. Enter, however, his doubts. Qohelet, detached, analyzing, raises the question: Who knows what good there is for man in life, in the number of days of his futile existence (6.12)?

Qohelet too has mixed thoughts about his strivings and toil. There can be hardly any question that a man must labor, but the better choice and the greater satisfaction would be to labor to some purpose, at work of some value and permanency, and if combined with pleasure (8.15), could provide some stimulation and satisfaction. But once more Qohelet has his qualms and hesitations. After expending considerable planning and exertion in building—which at the end proved to be of no satisfaction—Qohelet reversed himself, declaring that he hated work as it was futile (2.18); why should a man labor in vain (3.9), and the rich man, a slave to work with no end to all his activity and gain, deprive himself of all enjoyment? This is ridiculous. And so it would be quite proper to say that Qohelet ends with a query, a mirror of his persistent doubt: what benefit does a man gain with his toil and the striving of his mind at which he labors under the sun? For all his days are filled with pains, vexation and distress, and at night his heart is not at rest (2.23).

While Qohelet will repeat himself with the same queries three or four times on the problems pressing him (*see* below), occasionally he will state his opinion, albeit with his usual inconsistency and retraction. He hates life (2.17) and therefore ostensibly there should be no reason for going on living. But incongruously he will soliloquize: sweet is light (life), and it is good for the eyes to see the sun. Then again he will praise the dead and their condition (4.2) and yet counsel in 7.17: "Why die before your time?" Compare the significant passage in 11.8–10 with the advice to the young man to enjoy life and to follow his roving fancy. He thinks that the fetal abortion has the better of any, both living and dead, for he will not have experienced life's bitterness (6.5); on the

other hand, it is quite clear that Qohelet is much concerned with his
health (c.12). Or he may advise that you should enjoy life with the
woman you love (this from the *Gilgaamesh Epic* p. 69 f. though he draws
upon it approvingly). But on the other hand, he regards woman as more
bitter than death (7.26).

Our conclusions, as we understand at the outset, are that Qohelet is
more than a mere skeptic, or simply critical of an idea or doctrine, or at
variance with hallowed Jewish teaching. His doubts are not intellectu-
alized as a result of prolonged study. *He is a pathological doubter of*
everything, stemming from a drastic emotional experience, a psychic
disturbance. He is doubtful about himself as a person of worth and
character. He has no self-esteem or value of himself. His doubt has
destroyed all values. He is an inferior, of no account, and he demeans
himself constantly. His doubt comes from a parapathy, a disease of the
mind which he shares with many neurotics. Qohelet therefore exhibits
certain personality traits that require discussion and analysis from a
new perspective and understanding.

For a brief induction into the character and behavior of Qohelet, we
shall examine a connected passage (3.1–8) to ascertain the preliminary
conceptions of Qohelet's personality traits:

> To everything there is a season,
>   and a time for every purpose under the sun.
> A time to be born, and a time to die,
> A time to plant, and a time to pluck up that which is planted.
> A time to kill, and a time to refrain (see Commentary),
> A time to break down, and a time to build up.
> A time to weep, and a time to laugh,
> A time to mourn and a time to dance.
> A time to throw stones, and a time to gather stones.
> A time to embrace, and a time to refrain from embracing.
> A time to seek, and a time to lose;
> A time to conserve, and a time to throw away.
> A time to tear, and a time to sew.
> A time to keep silence and a time to speak.
> A time to love, and a time to hate.
> There is a time of war and a time of peace.

The rubric to the section—"a time to be born, and a time to die"—is
essentially an introduction to a secret and private "life plan" that
Qohelet describes from the beginning to the end of life, the whole arch

of human existence: to weep, to mourn, to laugh, to embrace, etc. If one were to think of life's goals and programs in modern terms, one would say that, in a life plan, one should educate oneself, prepare oneself for work, get married, have children, etc. If the program were conceived on a day-to-day basis (assuming that an individual has to make this plan which in itself is an aberration), then one would rise in the morning, get washed, eat, go off to work, and then in the evening rejoin one's family. Such a life plan would be modified by changes, additions, and subtractions, all variable with each temperament and personality. Suppose, now, someone should suggest a plan of his own and remark, "There is a time to kill, to murder," we should look at him with some curiosity, even with apprehension. A time for murder? What is in the mind of such a man? Nevertheless, this is what Qohelet says, "There is a time for murder." There may be some objection that the text is not correct, and that we should read *laharos* ("to destroy") for *la-harog* ("to kill"). But even if this reading were correct, "to destroy" would likewise be discordant and surprising for anyone to include such an activity in his life plan. In my view, *la-harog* ("to murder") is the correct reading (certified indeed by all the ancient versions) and entirely in keeping with Qohelet's personality, as will be indicated in the course of this study. Some argue, secondly, that Qohelet does not mean murder individually, but that there is in general a time for murder in the world, and a time for refraining. But any examination in this catalogue of time for doing things will show that they are intended and indeed reflect one's purely personal frame of reference, especially chosen by Qohelet himself: laugh, mourn, throw stones, dance, sew. An epilogist, more rational than Qohelet, with a wider perspective on human events, and realizing that there are epochs in history that may be divided into larger categories and contexts, added as a subscription: there is a time of war, and a time of peace. This is quite in contrast with Qohelet, with whom the actions are personal, whereas his glossator with war and peace envisages a larger scale and with people. Note, moreover, as an index of the epilogist the difference in language and syntax, Qohelet employing 'et with the infinitive throughout, conveying compulsion, the epilogist using 'et with the noun.

In his classification of life's activities, Qohelet advises another activity which arrests our attention. He says that there is a time for throwing stones (3.5). For throwing stones? Why should anyone spend time throwing stones? And against whom? Qohelet is to be taken at his word that this activity is not an allegory of some kind; otherwise there would be no end to speculation of this sort. If he throws stones he is protesting something very real, and quite strenuously too. Then, as a third example which piques our curiosity, Qohelet avers that there is a time to sew (3.7). But why should one set aside a time for sewing? If Qohelet were a tailor, it would be possible to say that his occupation looms so large in his consciousness, and that he spends so many hours in the day sewing, that there should be a place in his life plan, a need, for sewing. But we know that Qohelet is not a tailor but a petty official at the court and that sewing would be incongruous, even bizarre, in a daily activity.

These examples exhibit conclusively that there are elements in Qohelet's personality that require probing and elucidation. Other injunctions, too, about a time to seek (3.6), a time to embrace and a time to avoid embracing (3.5; how does one focalize a time for embracing or avoid embracing?) would also strike the ordinary person as something bizarre, out of character with experience.

Some *ad hoc* answers may be supplied, albeit superficially. As understood for the moment, a time for killing means that Qohelet has hostile, aggressive, criminal impulses in his makeup that would drive him to murder. Not that he ever murdered anyone; many doubt-filled neurotics who are compulsive harbor such murderous impulses which they rarely execute. Fundamentally they are too timorous for that, for in any enterprise their doubt enters and freezes them. The instinctual drives that infuse Qohelet are indeed repressed successfully but at the cost of the disintegration of his psyche. The idea that he has this impulse within him restrains him, horrifies him, and leads him to substitute compulsive actions, sometimes in lieu of his criminal intentions, at other times to prevent him from committing a criminal action. Compulsive acts are necessary to bring relief for the emergent released anxiety. Frequently these impulses are converted into more socially acceptable guises, as for example the man who mocks or teases to cover his aggressions.

Qohelet also has this drive to throw stones. In the Bible, the throwing of stones to punish an evildoer is found on a number of occasions: for cursing the name of God (Lev.24.23); for stealing tabooed objects, as in the case of Achan (Josh. 7.25); as an act of rebellion against the tax collector (I Kings 12.18); as well as those who beguile others to worship foreign gods (Deut. 13.11; 17.5). The paramount instance, however, that occurs to everyone in the casting of stones is the punishment for the adulterous act, in the case of the virgin who did not stain at her marriage, (Deut.22.20f.) or the promiscuous woman Ez.23.47; Jn.8.5. As we shall see, Qohelet suspected his wife of infidelity.

Qohelet also advocates a time for sewing. Why should a man advocate what is essentially a feminine occupation (Ez.13.18)? This too is a compulsive action, an index of the latent homosexuality of Qohelet.

A number of other associated problems now become manifest as we examine this category of compulsive actions conveyed to us in the Hebrew text. One might question *ab initio* whether such a series need be set down at all. What impels Qohelet to register these obligatory acts? Why is he so preoccupied with them? And note, moreover, the contrasting antitheses (to be discussed below), a reflection of his bipolar tension, in which these irrational but mandatory acts are cast.

The message that Qohelet unconsciously conveys is that in looking over his life and his life plan, he has had to undertake many actions that demanded repetition, were irrationally disturbing, petty in significance, meaningless in performance. We sense that he himself realizes that he has wasted his time, that his life has been a failure; his work and activities have been sterile; he has led a futile existence, of *hebel*. Actually it was the writing of his book that proved to be his salvation.

Before proceeding, however, with any further statement and analysis of Qohelet, it would be proper to explore a little more closely the scope and character of neuroses and compulsions as material that may shed relevant light on an understanding of Qohelet.

We boil at different temperatures.
                                   —Emerson.

III

Obsessions and Neuroses Form a Complex

Since neuroses may manifest themselves in a wide-ranging number of compulsions and symbolizations, the present chapter will deal with only those neurotic symptoms that Qohelet signalizes to us by his thought and behavior, and those compulsions that are particularly marked in Qohelet.[12]

By neurosis is meant generally a disorder of the psychic process which in severe instances freezes a patient from participating in social activity and/or from doing his daily work. The disorder may arise from tension, for example, between the drives of the unconscious (the id) on the one hand, and the prohibiting force of the conscience or the super ego. *A neurosis is rarely isolated but is part of a whole complex or a whole system.* As Stekel illustrates, a patient comes to be treated for one symptom, e.g., impotence, or for alarming dreams that prevent him from sleeping, or for phobias. Through analysis, the therapist discovers other links in the neurotic chain.[13] Qohelet, too, has a system, a configuration, a link-in-chain arrangement of neuroses and compulsions. His book clearly displays in the manifest and latent processes of his thought: the hopes and frustrations, fears and ideas, guilt and conscience, futility and strivings, a morbid sense of time, self-punishment, and death wishes.

Obsessional neuroses may be words, phrases, ideas, fragments of thoughts, melodies that seemingly stem out of nowhere and jut in the patient's mind against his inclination. Obsessional thinking is characterized by a number of marked features:

1. Because of his pathology, the obsessive person cannot control the stream of his associations. The conflicts that may arise on the surface may appear to be intellectual problems separated from his emotional disturbance. In the case of Qohelet, his sexual problem gets displaced by a philosophical one e.g. his pursuit of ḥokma, "wisdom".

2. There is a peculiar dichotomy in obsessive thinking, called "ambivalence" by Bleuler and Freud, "bipolarity" by Stekel. Freud has

12

pointed out that, merged in the unconscious, it is perfectly possible for the patient to have one and the opposite opinion at the same time. In Qohelet, the antithetic way in which he constantly presents his ideas is most pronounced.

3. While the patient thinks, a counterpoint thinking goes on: questioning, doubting, advancing but then retreating, retracting, changing the conclusions, pondering the alternatives, suppressing events or ideas leading to conclusions, reversing the premise to make it a conclusion, chopping up the logic, rearranging the thought structure, annihilating the syntax, making a subordinate clause a coordinating one. Linguistic and syntactical peculiarities are quite marked in Qohelet. Evidence for this will be found in the chapter on Vocabulary and Syntax.

4. The neurotic will share with children and primitives a belief in magic, e.g., lucky days, ominous encounters, unlucky numbers, zodiac signs. He believes also in the omnipotence of thought. Were he to curse someone, for example, he would be convinced that his curse would be mortally effective. As will be shown, Qohelet fears oaths and curses and believes in the omnipotence of thoughts.

While the average person will sublimate his emotions of hate and criminality more or less successfully, the compulsive neurotic finds it difficult to repress his criminal aggressions from occupying his thoughts. If they surface to consciousness, he is compelled to struggle against them with all the power and resources he can summon. They take the form of resolutions and oaths to himself, restrictive actions re-enforced with oaths, vows to himself interconnected and interspersed with magic formulas, and acts with self-denials. He must also perform a sequence of compulsive actions, e.g., fasting or mortifying himself so that his relative be not injured or die, or to remove guilt from himself. The struggle, however, is futile and without end. The neurotic is constantly in doubt whether he satisfactorily completed the routine he has scheduled for himself. Did he wash his hands enough? Did he count all the posts on the way home (like Samuel Johnson)? He deploys more strenuous endeavors, a more rigorous action, more resolute exertions—but all to no avail. The neurotic finds himself at the end in a cul-de-sac, a frustration, a defeat because he is struggling with nonreality, with the need to start the entire process all over again.

The compulsive act may be recognized by the patient himself as illogical and absurd; yet if he did not perform it he would be in a state of anxiety. Incestuous desires, for example, which he cannot repress successfully must be defused or discharged by the compulsive act. The origin of compulsive neuroses, while found in infancy and early childhood, stems, in the main, from around the onset of puberty (Stekel).

Compulsive neurotics may be quite gifted and highly intelligent but their emotional difficulties undermine their pinnings and confound them. Their abilities are misapplied; their intellectual life dissipated; their living is monotonous; their illness gives them an excuse for not achieving their objectives. The final results that are accomplished are thin and fragmentized. They have "achievements," though at a tremendous cost, through the media of daydreams, fantasies, obsessions, and compulsions. Obsessions, then, are not mere thoughts. They represent a whole psychological complex, a whole system, a psychological outlook on the world.

Investigators have found[14] that the compulsive neurotic finds all sorts of stratagems for wasting his time. He spends much time in evaluating trifles, giving them a mystical value which of course they do not have, and, per contra, paying no attention to matters of significance. His day is filled with "tremendous trifles." Actually they are framed by the patient to prevent "horror vacui," the terror of emptiness, lest he conceive of thoughts that he should not think or perform actions he should not undertake. Then certain details are scrutinized and acted upon to cover up and obliterate a certain remembrance which would be mortal or disastrous were he to recall that fateful episode with a head-on confrontation.

An imaginary life plan of the neurotic patient creates a world of fiction, of mythical facts and ideas in the place of the true world (so in 3.2f.). This displacement of the world's reality by one of fiction creates a falsification of the remembrance of things past. A patient when reporting an episode may very well give a substitute version for a repressed, i.e., an earlier embarrassing or traumatic experience ("screen recollection," as phrased by Freud[15]). He may have a fear of recollection, actually an experience of guilt. The therapist as a rule will understand that not all the facts are presented. Probably the most important events are omitted. Qohelet reiterates that there is no remembrance of men or events in the past (e.g., 2.16). Actually as a French proverb has it, "To want to forget something is to think of it."

Noteworthy is the neurotic's attitude toward time. It is meaningless to him because in the essay to annul a certain act in his memory and behave himself as if the event or experience never existed, he will withdraw himself from the usual succession of hours, night and day. Time exists only for what he has to do compulsively. What is automatic for the syntonic personality, in walking, washing, defecating, is for the compulsive, a complex detailed procedure requiring a careful execution and a minute fulfillment. Otherwise it would have to be repeated. This so occupies him that he is actually quite busy—about a pseudoactivity, about nothing. Really he may know that his time is wasted, still he can do nothing about it. He is listening to another drumbeat; he is determining his own tempo, out of step with the world of time.

Qohelet has a certain timelessness about him. He does not seem to have any roots, is withdrawn from the world. He is not related to anyone though he has relations (*see* p. 39). *Per contra*, he sought to tie his name to the great and famous, to royalty such as Solomon. He has no relation to historical incidents, nor any connection with named individuals, nor anything connected with world time: holidays, Sabbath, days of the week. If night is mentioned, it is only in connection with his pains and lack of sleep (c.2); or the profligacy of nobles who eat in the mornings (10.16), or to be industrious, if one is engaged in agriculture (11.6).

On the other hand, he is very much aware of the passage of time, which again he shares with many neurotics: how time ravages the body—his own and other persons—and thus gives him a fear of death.

Authority plays an important role in the conduct pattern of the neurotic's life. His obedience or catering to parental authority is easily recognized to be false or hypocritical. On the other hand, the shattering of parental authority can be highly significant. At a certain period in his life, a boy may pattern himself after his father as his hero, and he will consider his mother to be the fairest and most devoted. Were he to discover that his mother proved faithless to the father (or so he may *imagine*, e.g., as in a divorce), or were his father to commit a true breach of the moral law, his judgment would be most severe and condemnatory: You have been hypocritical about the principles you have taught me, you have betrayed them; therefore you shall receive the greater condemnation! This feeling of betrayal may underlie the contempt for all women and authority (compare the chapters on the biography of Solomon and Qohelet's identification with Solomon).

Should a neurotic commit himself with oaths and vows to himself, tying it in with a death clause, about his near relative, his mother or father, or even himself ("May I never live the day through," "May I drop dead"; in the Bible the frequent "May Yahweh do unto me and more also") and then fail to carry through the provisions of the vow, in his deficient fulfillment of the vow a grievous sense of guilt will overcome him. Should such a relative have an accident or die, he feels responsible, guilty of murder. Knowing the power of oath, a compulsive is apprehensive about giving oath in court.[16]

This commitment through a vow to oneself prevents many neurotics from achieving a sense of happiness. If early in life they have taken an oath linked with a death stipulation (if my father [my mother] would only die, I then would be happy) then guilt overwhelms them as they become older, and they contrastedly seek to preserve the life of that one against whom they originally had the death wish. Since in their earlier period their happiness was tied in with the wish of death, full enjoyment is always deferred and there is no happiness for the present. What right have you to be happy is seriously asked by G.K. Chesterton; many neurotics would say you cannot achieve a sense of happiness; others, you must never be happy.

Freud has posited that the neurotic has his own "private religion." This is eminently true. He obeys not the external laws but the drives of his own psyche. He has his own dictates; he has need of his own compulsions; he sets up and carries out his own activities. With regard to formal religion and creed, he is of two minds: he would like to be a true believer, a genuine *shomer mizvot*, a true observant. On the other hand, because of his doubts, he is an unbeliever, a skeptic, a blasphemer, even an apostate. "This often results in fear of entering a house of worship" (Gutheil). (Compare Qoh. 4.17: "watch your step when you go to the house of the Lord.")

The neurotic may indulge in self-reproaches; actually this originates from a sense of guilt. Qohelet broaches this when he employs the second form of address projectively as advice to "you." The suffering and pain the neurotic experiences is mingled, not without enjoyment and pleasure, because the self-reproaches represent, too, a merger, a collage of memories now repressed combined with a wish for repetion. Pains leading from obsessions are not given up. On the contrary, as asserted by Gutheil, they may frequently be a substitute for pain. A death clause may frequently be linked with pains although the patient may be completely unaware of the connection. The neurotic pact that he may have made with himself may run: As long as I suffer these pains, my relative (father, mother, sister) will be spared death, will be saved.

Like so many dreams reported by neurotics, Qohelet's inner disturbance is betrayed by the fact that the prime conflicts and perplexities of his life are repeated again and again. He is repetitive because these problems rule his consciousness; he would like to rid himself of these torments. Though they originate in past experience, they continue into the present. They harbor painful forebodings for the future. He lacks the means to solve these personal torments. He sets them down over and over again for he does not have the means to arrive at solutions for these afflictions.[17] Still he must ask and find out despite this inability to reach solutions. His recital of the difficulties are essentially hopes for deliverance, for salvation. But in the unending hope for his solution, Qohelet traverses the same vicious circle round and round, coming back to the inevitable starting point. This is one reason for Qohelet constantly "seeking" (8.17;9.1;3.6;7.25).

In his search for answers, for example, Qohelet mentions some seven times that the best in life for a man is to eat, drink, and enjoy himself (because, as we shall see, Qohelet could not allow himself by virtue of his neurosis to abandon himself to enjoyment [4.8;6.2.3]). He mentions five times that he is restless, agitated, full of aches and pains and cannot sleep at night. What is the reason he cannot sleep, he asks himself, and he is agitated and his thoughts keep him awake (8.16). He mentions at least five times that no satisfaction comes to a man for all the toil and trouble he experiences. Why cannot he secure some satisfaction? More than four times he refers to the judgment that hangs over man (i.e., Qohelet himself). He declares there is no remembrance of things past (2.16; 9.5). What is he trying to hide? And yet, whatever was, will occur again (3.15;6.10;1.9), and the world, i.e., the human condition, is a bitter frustration for man to be afflicted with (1.13;3.10). He is obsessed by other problems: of the property and the moderate wealth that he has acquired, why indeed must he leave it to someone else (2.18.21;6.2); that one fate overtakes man, however superior or inferior (2.14.15;9.2); and if he does secure some pleasure, it is mysteriously a gift from God (2.24;5.18) who dispenses His bounty to those He favors; the luckless have to do without, and even get punished for their pains (2.26;7.26). He mentions once (7.1) but implies twice that the day of death is better than the day of birth; that there is a perversion of Divine morality wherein the wicked receive reward as if they were the righteous, and the righteous the villainous retribution (8.14; 9.2.3). Because a penal sentence is not pronounced quickly, the minds of men are large with evil machinations (8.11;9.3). He dreads oaths (5.3.4;8.1f.) and curses (7.21;10.20) for their power. Man has a portion (fate) that he cannot escape (5.17;9.6–9) and yet who can forewarn a man what is in store for him? And afterward, after death, what then (6.12;8.7;10.14)? He repeats constantly because he cannot find the answers.

It should also be observed that as a mark of Qohelet's emotional rather than intellectual distress are the aphoristic utterances which on examination are but innocuous platitudes and banalities, and not pieces of wisdom at all. They are trite to dullness. For example, we read in 11.3, "if a tree fall in the south, or in the north, in that place where the tree falls, there shall it be." One turns away from the text with a feeling of mystification: of course, where the tree will fall, there it will lie. What is the lesson of this observation? Or of the first part of the verse, if the clouds fill up, they will pour water on the earth. Well, yes and no; anyway, what is the significance of that remark? Or 1.15: "That which is crooked cannot be made straight." Or the latter part of the verse: "that which is lacking cannot be counted." In the main the same judgment applies. The point seems ordinary or middling. It is obvious that Qohelet's apothegms do not have the directness, the pith, the acerbity—yes, the wisdom—that is found in the Book of Proverbs. They are trite without even the usage of well-worn sagacity. To Qohelet, however, these observations based upon neurotic experience and drive, had quite an impact on him, and if innocent to us, set bells ringing in his head and gave a mortal significance to his being. We shall consider this relevance in the course of this study.

There are other marks, too, of Qohelet's disorder: the general disorganization of the book, the lack of any sustained coherence, the flitting from subject to subject and round again, his special vocabulary, the disorder of the syntax, the special meanings and neologisms that a neurotic might employ, the lack of coherence even within the verses proper—all are a further reflection of the disharmony in Qohelet's mind. The special vocabulary of Qohelet, a further mark of his neurosis, will be found in a separate section.

When a man dies, he does not just die
of the disease he has; he dies of his whole life.
—Charles Pierre Peguy.

IV
Qohelet's Sexual Impotence: First Symptoms

In chapter twelve of our book, a poignant description of an old man with his declining physical powers is graphically set forth. The imagery in some cases seems obscure, but the general outlines are quite recognizable, mounting to a crescendo in the finale, which distressingly points to the futility of utilizing aphrodasiacs to remedy his ills. It will be noticed, as in so many poetic flights universally, that the text lends itself to a number of stratiform interpretations. Justification for the translation will be found in the commentary: the passage runs as follows:

1. Be mindful of your health in the days of your youth, before the days of illness arrive, and the years have caught up wherein you say, "I do not desire them anymore";

2. Before the sun goes a-glimmering, and the moon and the stars fade, and the clouds return after the rain,

3. At the time when the guardians of the house become unsteady, and the strong men become gnarled, and the grinders become useless because they are few, and the viewers at the windows be dimmed,

4. Ere the two doors to the outside are stopped, and the ease of grinding flags, ere the twit of a bird become faint, and musical notes decline;

5. Before one is terrified of a height, and fearful of pitfalls while walking, and one shall despise almonds, and caperbuds will be noisome, and the caperberry be useless; for man has set out on the road to his long, long home, and the mourners will turn round and round in the streets,

6. Before the silver cord is snapped, and the golden bowl is shattered; and ere the pitcher is broken at the fountain, and the wheel falls broken into the well;

7. And the dust return to the earth as it once was, and the spirit to God who gave it!

19

The symbols in this passage have been much discussed. See R. Gordis, *Koheleth and his World,*[2] 1955. H.L. Ginsberg, *Qohelet* (Hebrew), Tel-Aviv, 1961; and R. Pfeiffer, *Introduction to the Old Testament,* and O. Eissfeldt, *The Old Testament,* transl. P.A. Ackroyd for further literature. Opinions of my own are set forth briefly on the *manifest* content first:

1. When a man becomes old, the sun, the moon and the stars that are darkened, components that are "overhead," i.e., found in the man's (Qohelet) head, become slowed and dimmed. Man's "illumination" has been darkened; this signifies that man's insight, thinking, power of intelligence, quickness of perception, capability of speech—these "constellations" of the senses become noticeably "clouded." For other levels of interpretation, *see* p. 21.

2. "The clouds return after the rain" portrays the perennial malaise of the old man. While Tobit (3.22, Vulgate) may declare that "After the storm, Thou makest the calm," whence the proverb "After the rain comes the sunlight," Qohelet in his despondency only perceives more illness—more clouds will only gather.

3. "House" is a well known figure for "body." "Keepers of the house" must be the protective hands: nevertheless, in old age they tremble. "The strong men shall be bent" are the fingers on the hand, vigorous, capable, and in constant movement. They become, however, gnarled and bent in old age.

4. "The two doors to the street are closed." The surface meaning signifies that when the mill stops droning at the end of the day, the only noise for many villagers during a summer day (Charles, A. Doughty, *Travels in Arabia Deserta,* ed. T.E. Lawrence, II, 200), the doors on to the street are closed, and it is *night.* Symbolically, the old man suffers from constipation, and also prostatitis: he urinates but with difficulty (Rashi, Barton). "Grinding" means ability to digest (Jastrow, *Dictionary* 356a). The old man has difficulty with his digestion, too. The verse is to be taken co-ordinately[18]: the two doors close and the ease of digestion declines.

"The voice of the bird becomes faint" (emended, *see* Commentary) signifies that in old age a man becomes hard of hearing so that he cannot hear the twittering of a bird; on the other hand, the higher musical notes that at one time he was able to sing ("the daughters of song" are the notes in the musical scale) now become impossible for him. His voice cracks.

5. He is likewise afraid of an uphill climb because he becomes short of breath and his heart pounds, and a declivity in the road gives him

apprehension.

He comes to the core of his frustration and disillusion, though written from the standpoint of his middle age: that he has lost sexual potency, and aphrodisiacs are unavailing (repeated three times with different wording). He pretends to despise almonds, the caper blossom, and the caper berry because they do not help him.

The final collapse comes through in vv. 6–7. The precious things of life, *hebel and gullah*, qualified by silver and gold: silver placed first as it was considered more precious in ancient times (but see further p.125) are burst asunder. The *hebel* or cord is the connective link with life, and the bowl is the heart, the container of the life force. The pitcher that is carried to the fountain of life to draw and carry the living waters finally is shattered too, and the wheel (possibly "bowl," so Dahood, cited by Ginsberg on the basis of the Ugaritic) is dashed at the well.

Such are the manifest physical signs of man's aging process. Superficially his bodily functions, and the various members of his body severally, falter in their vigor. The psychological dissolution needs now to be considered and it points in one direction.

II

When we remark on the various symbols depicted in this flight of imagination, we see that they represent disguised sexual symbols as well. Before Freud, commentators entirely innocent of the psychoanalytic method (as for example Ibn Janah, in his *Book of Roots*, ed. W. Bacher, 142, Rashi, Ibn Ezra in their commentaries, H. Graetz, *Kohelet*, 1871) had seen in 12.5 erotic symbols. Freud has taught us additionally that in the dream (and so in any poetic flight) the different parts of the body may serve as a mask or substitute for the genital parts. I give the references most conveniently from the *Basic Writings of Sigmund Freud*, New York, 1938, Modern Library Edition. The reader may likewise be referred to the studies of C.G. Jung, *Symbols of Transformation*, Bollingen Series XX, vol. 5, Index; W. Stekel *Interpretation of Dreams*, 1967, p. 14; A. Garma, *Psychoanalysis of Dreams*, 1967, p. 218; E.A. Gutheil, *Handbook of Dream Analysis*, 1966, Chapter III.

The most clear cut symbols are:

arms, fingers: "The genitals may be represented in dreams by other parts of the body; the male member by hand or foot..." (p. 375).

teeth: The loss of teeth in a dream is a well-known symbol of the (patient's feeling of the) loss of potency. (Compare 388–89 for the whole discussion by Freud.) It should be noticed that tied in with the anxiety of losing teeth is the fear of getting old–fear of death (Gutheil, *Handbook*, p. 217).

eyes: In Oedipal dreams, the eye appears as a sexual symbol. "The blinding of the eye in the Oedipus legend and elsewhere is a substitute for castration" (*ibid*, p. 393, n.1.).

the doors: a familiar sexual signification. "Anyone who has had experience in the translating of dreams will, of course, at once be reminded the penetration into narrow spaces and the opening of locked doors are among the commonest of sexual symbols..." (*ibid*, p. 392).

bird: a very frequent symbol (*ibid* p. 390. Compare the winged *phalloi* of the ancients).

voice: i.e., the daughters of music in the parallel gives the sense that it is the musical sound. The voice often appears as a sign of potency. (Compare T. Reik, *Ritual* p. 263).

way: "travelling, journeying, alighting, getting out of bed equals sexual intercourse" (Freud, p. 397.n.).

height: a familiar conception and disguise of coition. "Steep inclines, ladders, stairs, and going up and down them are symbolic representations of the sexual act" (p. 372).

grinding: Grinding represents the crushing of the wheat kernels by the millstones (see presently). "All complicated machines, weapons and tools are as a rule the male genitals" (p. 373, condensed). Other investigators have added to our knowledge. Compare Garma, *op. cit.* Index).

The Hebrew language, as would be expected and relevantly to Qohelet, supplies similar symbols of imagery and sexuality. Thus, *basar*, meaning "body, flesh," is employed metonymically for penis, e.g., Lev. 15.2: "If a man have a flux from his flesh...". *yarek*, "thigh," is used similarly: Gen. 42.2; 47.29: "Put thy hand underneath my thigh" (Abraham to Eliezer; Rashi: the place of his circumcision); *yarek*, of course, and like all these symbols is bisexual.[19] *'Eber*, "limb," also "bird's wing," is employed for penis; similarly, *'ezba*, "finger" is employed metonymically for the male gland, e.g., Pes. 112b: "Not all fingers are the same"; in the same way *'ammah*, "finger," although the Talmud is uncertain which of the five fingers is meant (Men.31a) but again is deployed in the meaning of penis. The word *bait* means not only "house," "body" but also the vulva. In the rabbinic literature, *shimmshah 'et beita* means "she had sexual intercourse"; *kibbdah 'et beita*, "she washed her house or body," i.e., she washed her vulva.

delet: "door" is found naturally as a symbol for the womb. Compare

Job 3.10. In the Qohelet passage, the *delataim* as a dual signifies the two labia of the vagina. "Voice" (Heb., *qol*) has a sexual signification and overtone. Compare Berak. 24a,—*qol be'ishah 'erwah*, "Voice in woman is sexual."

derek: "way" has a sexual association. Thus Gen. 6.12: "And God saw the earth and behold it was corrupt; for all flesh had corrupted their *way* upon the earth" is interpreted by the Rabbis in a sexual sense.[20] So too, the well-known phrase, "The way of a man with a maid," based upon Prov. 30.19, where *derek* again is used ("an act of adultery," Ibn Ezra).

tahanah: The Hebrew root "grind" has a very definite connotation of sexuality. Thus Samson was employed as a grinder in prison because of his great strength (Judg. 16.21), but the talmudic scholars fancifully comment that the Philistine brought their wives to be impregnated by him. Compare semantically the Greek *mule* = mill and *mullas* = prostitute; *mullos* = a cake in the shape of *pudenda muliebria* Liddell and Scott, *Dictionary*, 1152b. The fallen hero could not simply be a grinder. Note also the significant verse in Job. 31. 9–10:

> If mine heart had been deceived by a woman,
> Or if I had laid wait at my neighbor's door [!]
> Then let my wife grind *(tahan)* unto another
> And let others bow down upon her![21]

The millstones mentioned in v.3 bore in postbiblical times names of obvious sexual signification, for the upper millstone was called *rekeb*, "the rider," and the nether stone was called *shekeb*, "the lier under." And similarly, the association in the Targum of Jonathan which translates the words *rekeb, reihayyim* in Deut. 24.26 as "bridegrooms, brides." *Shaqed*, "almonds," have fecundative power. "In Phrygian cosmogony, an almond figures as the father of all things, and in the myth of Attis, Nana conceived him by putting a ripe almond in her bosom, or by eating an almond."[22] Similarly we are told by E.A. Westermarck,[23] "To increase sexual power, a man eats almonds three successive mornings before breakfast...which produces a lasting effect."

caper: the blossoms and berries of the caper, specifically *capparis spinosa*, are a stimulant to the sexual appetite, *'abiyonah* being specially mentioned as arousing desire (Compare Jastrow s.v. and article *caper-berry*, *Dictionary of the Bible*, ed. James Hastings, I, 350).

hebel: the rope or cord (note association with *kesef,* root *ksf,* one meaning of which is "desire") with its connotation of binding and connection has a phallic significance. *Habal,* "bind," may be associated with *ḥebla,* "pain," especially of birthpangs (Brown, Driver, Briggs, Oxford Lexicon, 286) i.e., binding pains. Compare likewise *filium,* thread, cord ("thread" being another phallic symbol because "to thread" in folklore means to have intercourse), *vide* Stith Thompson, *Motif-Index of Folk Literature* VI, p. 790 (thread entering needle, J86;Z186) which bears the signification of figure and shape (of a woman) and is undoubtedly connected with *filius, filia* "son, daughter." Similarly the Greek *mitos*=thread which in Orphic speech stands for "semen," C.G. Jung, *Symbols of Transformation,* 127. For a final analogy from Latin, we may refer to *funiculus,* a diminutive of *funis,* "rope," and employed (compare Webster's International Dictionary, 3rd edition) for umbilical cord, spermatic cord.

gullat: bowl, or a sort of bowl, with which a semantic *kad,* "pitcher," may be compared as a sexual symbol masculine in concept. And so Rashi, "This means the penis" *(zeh ha-'ammah)* (cf. Josh. 15.19: Jud. 1.15). *Galgal,* too, as the wheel by which the bucket is raised or lowered in the well, is likewise a well-known phallic symbol (Jung, *op. cit.* 203; Gutheil, *Handbook, Bor,* "pit," more likely "well," is a symbol employed by the Bible itself: "Drink water from your own well" (Prov. 5.15) = have intercourse only with your own wife. In slang, too, the bottomless pit=female pudend, Partridge, *Dictionary of Slang,* 48.

The verbs that are employed in this section—tremble, be bent, be few, be darkend, be closed, decline, be faint, sink down, be fearful—all betoken and comprehend one characteristic: a process of failing, failing, failing, and a forecast of the end. In brief, the first part of c.12, seemingly a poetic soaring of the heights, comprehends a content of significant sexual experience. By means of paraphrase, the section may be understood as follows, with some passages additionally carrying a latent polyphonic meaning:

Be mindful of your health while you are young before the days of weakness come when you shall say, "I have no [sexual] pleasure in them."

Before your hands, fingers, teeth, and eyes fail, your life is darkened by the loss of sexual powers, and the failure of this life instinct weakens the instinct for life (Qohelet forecasts his end by the description of the funeral and the mourners). The female doors have closed because the "grinding" has faltered (the impotent Qohelet cannot penetrate the vagina because he fails in erection), the voice of the bird gets thin, and the music (music and dancing are well-known symbols for the enjoyment of life) falters, and he is afraid of pitfalls on the road (he is now afraid of the sexual act because of his repeated failures, and he pretends to despise aphrodisiacs because they are unavailing anyway).

The loss of potency, however, did not come of a sudden to Qohelet. He had both a wife and son; he had, moreover, periodic spells of awakened sexuality. When the realization came to him that he was impotent, however, it was shocking and demoralizing. The sense of inadequacy, of noncompetence, the failure to measure up sexually is the first signal to us of his futility, of his pessimism, and of his despair. The significant dysfunction of the life force seriously forecasts a decline and end.

A number of other verses in Qohelet manifest themselves chainlike as further evidence of Qohelet's impotence. The symbols do not run either seriatim or consecutively as in C.12, but are quite identifiable. One verse reads:

Because of sloth, the rafter sinks,
And because of laziness, the house leaks (10.18).

There is no connection in this passage between the verses fore and aft. It is interesting that in the "free association" of this verse, as interpreted by Rabbi Kohen in the Midrash to Qohelet on this passage, the allusion here is to a woman. According to this scholar, dire consequences follow when she does not examine herself properly for blood flux and impurity. This association is also apparent in the statement of Innocent III, *De Contemptu Mundi*, III, 1.18: There are three things that do not let a man stay at home: smoke (a smoky chimney), dripping (a leaky roof) and an evil wife. Note the latter collocation of the words. The symbols employed in the Qohelet verse are readily suggestive and identifiable. *Yad*, "hand," is a well-known symbol for the *phallos*; the lowering of the hands means the flaccidity of the penis; "house" is the symbol for "body" (Garma). Similarly in the first part of the verse, the beam in the roof (penis) droops through slackness. Like all symbols, the passage admits of a merger of interpretations. As all symbols are bisexual, "house" may represent "wife," a well-known symbol in Jewish tradition (*beito zeh ishto*: the scriptural "his house" [Lev. 16.6.11 compare Rashi] means "his wife"), or here generally marriage. The verse has the significance that through "neglect" (the original meaning of *'azlut*, so the dictionaries) and the incapability to respond to the wife's desire, Qohelet's failure to arouse his wife to orgasmic excitement will break up the marriage. Moreoever, "roof" implies Qohelet's head; his mind is preoccupied with his sense of failure at which he feels enervated, and experiences a decline in life's exuberance and a desire for living. Actually his thoughts are elsewhere, as we shall see on another "love object," and it is this projection on someone else that dampens his ardor for his wife.

In 6.7 the verse reads:

All man's striving is for his mouth

And yet desire is not satisfied.

On the surface, the passage simply states that a man works but to eat, but nevertheless the appetite is not filled. The passage implies more. "Mouth," by the familiar substitution of below to above, means the genitalia. The Hebrew *peh*, for example, is employed with the anus and with the womb, e.g., *peh shel 'aqarot*, "womb of the childless," *pi hattabb'at*, "mouth of the ring [anus]," Jastrow, *Dictionary*, 1138 for further exx. and Prov. 30.20: so is the way of the adulterous woman: she eats and wipes her mouth. . . . In our passage, Qohelet clearly implies that though a man work ever so hard, still most deeply and basically it is for his sexual fulfillment and happiness, and yet for him there is not satisfaction for his longing. Again, Qohelet reflects his traumatic parapathic experience.

There is likewise another enigmatic verse (in 6.9) which has hitherto defied a satisfying explanation:

Tob mar'eh 'einayim mehalok nefesh

Gam zeh hebel ur'ut ruaḥ.

The usual translation runs:

Better is seeing with the eyes than the wandering of desire.

This also is vanity and a striving after wind.

It is agreed on all counts that the verse is obscure: "wandering of desire" is certainly peculiar, and why "seeing" with the eyes is better than "wandering of desire" is difficult to say. The verse, from our view, should be interpreted as follows: seeing with the eyes is simply to be interpreted as another term for the sexual experience as given in the exposition below. The active verb *halak* means "go, depart," and in one of its associated meanings, "be lost, die" (compare the Oxford lexicon, s.v. *halak*). The expression then of *halok nefesh* signifies the loss of desire, the death of longing. The verse is therefore a genuine description of Qohelet's human quandary. To have some sexual experience in life is better than the loss of desire altogether. Qohelet's experience in that regard is restricted to his compulsive acts, each one really but a partial and pale substitute for an original primary act, and a cathexis of his libidinous discharge. His sexual emissions are for the wrong reason, i.e., not an assertion of the primal life force. Consequently, he concludes in the latter part of the verse that such substitute sexual experiences (including his homosexual tendencies) are a frustration and a futility.

In 4.5 there is a different theme: "The fool folds his hands and consumes his body."

The surface meaning is that a fool by being indolent consumes his flesh. This is in line with ancient Hebrew thought that fatness of the body was a sign of good health (Deut. 32.15). The passage, however, is not a general reflection about fools but of Qohelet himself. The "fool" represents the counterego of Qohelet, and the malign drive within. Ḥobeq is a word for "love, embrace" (e.g., for a wife, compare Jastrow, *Dictionary*, s.v.); *yad, yadaim,* "hands," represent the genitals. We have here a masturbation fantasy. Qohelet felt that his autoeroticism was consuming his body, a widespread idea,[25] and incidentally a reflection of Qohelet's fears about the wasting away of his body (p. 25, 46). The next verse reads conventionally: "Better a handful of quietness than both hands full of labor and striving after wind." The meaning seems quite obvious as a continuation of the previous verse. Better one act of sexual satisfaction and self-fulfillment than two acts of frustration and vexation. Conjoined with Qohelet's disturbance and impotence is his homosexual tendency. Mention was made of Qohelet's description of his own behavior at 3.7: "There is a time to sew." "Sewing" is associated with sexuality as "sew" in English slang means "impregnate a woman" (Partridge).

Another verse in this association which mirrors Qohelet's resignation in the blind alley that he finds himself is found at 11.3:

If the clouds be full of rain,
they empty themselves upon the earth,
and if a tree falls in the south or in the north,
in the place where the tree falls, there it shall be.

This is one of the verses referred to previously; it is pointless, known to all, and not the remark of a sage. True, storm clouds do give rain, but not necessarily. In Qohelet's unconscious, the observation is quite meaningful. When his gonads fill up, inevitably he experiences an emission (Garma, pp. 99,219: rain=ejaculation). And yet when the tree, a familiar symbol of erection, a striking symbol of power, once falls[26] it lies there prone and inert, and Qohelet's potency is not aroused even by proximity to a woman (7.26.28).

And finally, 7.2.3 may be cited as another example of Qohelet's unhappy situation: "It is better to go to the house of mourning than to go to a feast, for there you see the end of man, and it will arrest your attention. Better is anxiety [ka'as=Aramaic *rugza*=Angst] than laughter, for melancholy can relieve the mind."

Going to a party is a familiar symbol in dreams and signifies the enjoyment of life and coital satisfaction. Since Qohelet is impotent, he has no sense of happiness. He cannot let himself go to a party. He prevents himself from going. His abnormality, he fears, will become known to others. Also, as part of his psychosis, since his sexual instinct suffers inhibition and suppression, the opposing death instinct comes to the fore (it is better to go to the house of mourning). He would rather go to the house of mourning (and this is the meaning that the verse bears) since he cannot enjoy himself, yet his bipolar tension on the other hand supplies him with some satisfaction in that he is not the corpse "lying in state."

We have become aware of the first signs of Qohelet's disturbance through a number of verses that latently betray his impotence. We address ourselves now to the question: is it possible to track down the origin or cause of this failure?

Say unto Wisdom 'Thou art my sister'.
—Prov. 7.4.

Nobody can misunderstand a boy like his own mother.
—Douglas

V

Qohelet and *Hokma*

Impotence is only one symptom, one link in the chain of Qohelet's neuroses. The next direction of our inquiry will be: what is the source of Qohelet's lack of potency?

A pivotal verse, significant in implication for our understanding of Qohelet's impotence, is found at 7.26, where he declares:

"And I find more bitter than death the woman, because her heart is snares and traps, whose hands are chains; one favored by God will escape her, but the unlucky will be trapped by her"*(see* Commentary). Verse 28 follows through with this observation:

"My soul yearns continually, but does not find . . . one man among a thousand I was able to find, but one woman in all that number I could not find."[27]

Verse 26 condemns all women. The latter part of the verse however, clearly speaks of one woman: her heart . . . her hands . . . escape from her . . . be trapped by her. Even if it be contended that the verse deals with womankind in general, nevertheless one will reach the conclusion, anyway, with Remy de Gourmont that "Most men who rail against women are railing at one woman only." Qohelet's hostility to woman could stem only from one primal source: the unwholesome, hostile relationship with his mother which is in the background of the text. The hatred which was directed against women (at first his mother, then his wife) enlarges, and then is leveled against all womankind.[28] We must therefore conclude that *'issah* in the text means "his wife" who has built a wall around her husband, and confined him (or so he thinks) by every manner of chain and barrier. Qohelet, however, projects unconscious death wishes with regard to her ("she is more bitter than death") and he would certainly like to have her out of the way. To translate his thought: if this wife of mine were dead, I would be

29

free of her and her chains. This wish, however, is an intolerable transgression against law, custom, and morality. That Qohelet should harbor such thoughts strikes at his conscience and saddles him with a crushing sense of guilt. His strong desire to put her out of the way repetitively recurs ("I could kill her!"); the restraining inhibitions of civil law and Divine morality give him an acute anxiety feeling. In numerous instances, whether a man has committed murder or not—such is the belief in the omnipotence of thoughts—the crime and its penalty hang over his head as if he actually committed the deed and deserved to be punished for it. The repeated thoughts and "horrible imaginings" only intensify his guilt feelings.

With this woman, too, he is sexually impotent. But this was not always so. At one time in pubescence or adolescence, and this is in the nature of the case, he was quite sexually potent *but with someone else.* However, some traumatic experience seared him and destroyed his normal heterosexual relationships with women. What kind of experience was this? Here our material does not supply us with an answer directly, although there are clues in Qohelet that lead to a number of surmises.

However, it is easily possible to hypothesize from the plethora of evidence elsewhere how Qohelet as a lad experienced such trauma. Let us take the most common ordinary experience of modern times. A father dies or is divorced and the mother in the course of a year's time marries. This is most incomprehensible and agitating to an adolescent boy. He is at that period of his life when in his idealistic fervor he dreams of great adventures, of great sacrifices for his people, or a great crusade in which he is naturally the leader or general, and of a great undying love for a dream maiden, to whom he swears eternal fidelity despite all suffering and anguish. He will undergo the ordeals of fire and water to rescue her.

And now the mother says to her son that although she loved his father, now dead or divorced, she now loves this new man, and it is perfectly all right to share the same bed with the new husband "whom you now should consider as your new father," as she hopefully urges. All this is most bewildering: how can his mother who had sworn faithfulness and love to his father be now fondled by another man? His adolescent fervent idealism provokes him to a harsh immoderate condemnation: he berates his mother for fickleness; she has broken a sacred troth; her devotion was a sham; he hates her for betraying the love of his father. His conclusion: she is a dissolute woman who will give away her love, her charms to anyone who comes along. He may vow that he will never marry.[29] Of course, there is a primal feeling as well that he should take precedence and the new father is an interloper. He hates the new father as well.

While this might be a typical instance, there are quite a number of variations on this theme and situation. His mother may have been deserted by her husband, yet the boy censures her. Then to compound the wrongdoing, the mother remarries. Or it may be that in coming home one day, with his father away for a length of time, he finds his mother in an act of infidelity, in the arms of another man. His conclusion may well be that all men are not to be trusted and "all women are no good." Stekel calls this the shattering of moral authority.[30]

Other common circumstances could equally disturb Qohelet. Suppose that he, in common with many children throughout the world, sleeps in the same room with his parents and he hears erotic cries and disturbances that unsettle him. Or let us hypothesize that he slept with his sisters and brothers on the floor or on an improvised mattress in the same room, and as a pubescent boy clung to his sister night after night, and she did not object to exploratory sex play. He then experienced his first seminal emission. It is almost a fundamental law that one's first sensual contact is not forgotten, and the memory of the first sexual arousement and experience, not forgotten, may become fixed on the first love object. His wife now is not the substitute for his sister (or whomever). His potency can only be exercised and excited by this first love object.

We may formulate the progression of Qohelet's neuroses as follows: His incestuous desire for the love object (say for a sister) persisted to torment and plague him. It should be understood that *mutatis mutandis* he may have slept as a pubescent boy in his mother's bed. He had to repress his desire, which intermittently he did, successfully and unsuccessfully. He may or may not have developed hatred for his love object. In his frustration, what he could not possess he may have hated.[31] However that may be, because he has fear of the overpowering impulse now, he becomes burdened with anxiety. His behavior takes the form of compulsive actions in order to replace the original action of the pleasurable contact (in an older youth defloration of his sister, intercourse, sex play) and at the same time to throw off anxious feelings and prevent an immoral action.

Whatever the circumstances that led to Qohelet's impotence[32] it is highly probable that his sister or his mother was the origin and cause. If a "normal" man marries and the marriage ends in disaster, a man may

marry again. This apparently is not the case with Qohelet. Because of
his experience with his mother/sister, and tormented by recurring
doubt, he thinks his wife faithless, adulterous (3.5). He has ceased
relations with her and he yearns for a new attachment (7.28).

Qohelet repeatedly asserts that he is seeking someone or something:
"There is a time to seek" (3.6); "and I turned about to seek wisdom"
[hokma] (7.25); ". . . because though a man labor to seek it out, [i.e.,
the meaning of Life] yet he will not find it" (8.17); and the illuminating
passage just referred to at 7.28 "but not a woman did I find." Compare
such other passages as 1.13.17;2.3.10;8.16.17;9.1.

Is there now a love object that he constantly seeks and does not find,
an eternal quest unsatisfied, a quid pro quo experience he sensed once,
still apparently quite alive in his psyche? We are again confronted by
Qohelet's bipolarity and doubt. He could not find a single satisfying
tender, solicitous woman; yet his heart ever continued on a secret
quest.

Now a recurrent word in Qohelet's little book is hokma, "wisdom." It
is quite elusive in meaning, so that one is sometimes at a loss what
Qohelet purports to signify by it. Thus he will say, "my mind possessed
the insight of much hokma and da'at [knowledge]" (1.16); in the next
verse he will say, "I set my heart to know (!) hokma" (and so in 8.16); in
1.16 they are separated by "and"; on the other hand, in 7.12 they form a
construct (*but see* Commentary). Qohelet never actually defines what
this hokma is in contrast, say, to Proverbs: The beginning of wisdom is
the fear of the Lord; or the beginning of wisdom is to acquire wisdom
(4.7;9.10). We know further that through hokma he rescued a town
(9.15); that his hokma stood him in good stead as he experimented to
discover a Golden Rule of Life (2.9). He performs actions only through
hokma (1.13;7.23). Then, to the contrary, he will aver in essence that he
tried to be a wise man, but wisdom eluded him: exceedingly profound
it is, and who can fathom it? (7.23). In verbal and nominal formations
"be wise/wisdom" occurs some forty-nine times and five times where
he longingly seeks it (1.13.17;2.12;7.23.25).

The surrogate for the mother is this hokma. The word is feminine
and is personified in Prov. c. 8 and 9 (*Sophia* in Greek, *Sapientia* in
Latin), and quite early the word had close feminine associations: "Say
of Wisdom, Thou art my sister and call understanding thy kinswoman"
(Prov. 7.4). It is noteworthy how the general identification of
hokma=woman proliferated in other synonyms and related ideas as
well. Thus in the verse in Qohelet 9.9, "Enjoy life with the woman thou
lovest," the Qohelet Midrash on the verse offers the interpretation that

one should acquire Torah.[33] In 7.29, similarly, woman=Torah. The Torah is likewise designated as a bride.[34] In the ninth chapter of the tractate *Berakot* (folios 55-57), we have a series of dreams, common to every man, with their melioristic interpretations on the part of the talmudic authorities to mitigate the dreamer's feelings of guilt and sin:

He who has dreams that he had intercourse with his mother may expect to acquire understanding, with reference to Prov. 2.3 reading homiletically *'em*, "mother," for *'im*. He who dreams that he had intercourse with a betrothed woman may expect to acquire Torah, citing Deut. 33.4 with the homiletic play on *morasha*, "inheritance," and *m'orasah*, "betrothed." He who dreams that he has had intercourse with his sister may expect to acquire wisdom, as it is written:"Say unto Wisdom,'Thou art my sister'" (Prov. 7.4). He who dreams that he had sexual relations with a married woman may rest assured that he will gain entry into the next world. An explanatory comment in the Germara states that this circumstance is indicated only if he is not acquainted with her, or has not been thinking of her in the daytime. Rashi adds that such a man receives a double allotment: his own and that of his friend in the (future) Garden of Eden, which in effect is symbolic of a married woman.

In the continuing discussion it is remarked that he who sees a goose in a dream may expect to acquire wisdom, Prov. 1.20 (!), and he who has sexual congress with wisdom becomes the head of the Academy. R. 'Ashi stated, "I had intercourse with her, and I became the head of the Academy." This statement is a bit surprising, the metaphor bold, granting the rhetorical language. One commentator [35] remarked that in all other instances (of a score of more) the formula merely consists of one who has had a dream wherein he sees grapes, olives, an elephant, a donkey or whatever, and on the seeing alone, in the dream, a man may expect to realize an escalation of knowledge, recognition, or position. There is a concomitant support of a biblical verse. In the present instance, the commentator continues, it would have been sufficient for R. 'Ashi to declare: I saw a goose, or whatever, and the seeing of itself would have been sufficient warranty and prophecy that he would have been elevated to the presidency. Why does R. 'Ashi say that "I have performed an act; I have had sexual congress with wisdom and so I rose to the presidency?"

It must be clear, I think, that R. 'Ashi's remark is more than rhetorical; that an actual experience lurks behind his statement: that *Hokma*=Torah represented for him a reality of some substance. Whatever it was, the graphic *ba'ti 'aleiha*, "I lay with her," a remembrance, an echo, though unconscious, of a palpable experience persisted from his youth.

With Qohelet and his absorption with, and his quest, and need for, and his continual reference to ḥokma, a good deal may be supplied in the same vein. If *Hokma* is elusive and one can never attain it, in the background is the shadowy figure of an unknown woman, his lost beloved. There can hardly be any question that Qohelet's woes, his rootlessness, his lack of sleep, the pains in his body, his forlorn hopes, his self-denial, his sense of futility, the pointlessness of his striving and activity are all tied up with this woman, with this loss of the prime sexual object. In common with neurotic articulation of other neurotic formulas elsewhere, he may have unconsciously vowed to himself in this fashion: If I cannot have my sexually satisfying love to complete my life, I will deny myself the goodness that life offers. His body bears the full force of punishment. Illness, pain, lack of sleep, restlessness, frustration provide the "Iron Maiden" in which his body is being tormented.

Qohelet does not tell us what his primary sexual experience was and how it transpired. He probably could not, as he was quite young, and in the light of his later moral consciousness undoubtedly repressed his experience, whether with his mother or sister, the woman closest to him. If he "forgot" in adulthood his transgression, and would not ever admit to this violation of the moral code, other manifestations and attitudes toward memory show that this fixation on one member of the family persisted. It is quite clear that he wishes to blot out some experience that would be most painful for him to be exposed to and confront. He generalizes this by saying projectively, "Everything is forgotten. Everyone's deeds are forgotten. No one remembers anything with the passage of the years". All this means: "I hope no one will remember me in those years and what I did!" Thus in 9.5 he will say, "the dead don't know anything for their memory is forgotten", or "there is no memory either of the wise man or the fool" (2.16). A remarkable key passage throwing light on the preceding, which demonstrates the desire of Qohelet to suppress the past in the most absolute ferocious fashion, is found at 1.11: "There is no remembrance of them in ancient times; and of those that come after them there will be no remembrance, even those who are at the very last." Now this is demonstrably against experience, and the statement is one of the half-truths that Qohelet articulates a number of times in his book. So obsessed is Qohelet with the fear of his unconscious memory of something that may break forth—his mortal sin—that he emphasizes in the most determined fashion that there is no memory of anything by anyone, at any time, past, present or future. He may say, to the contrary, in the two preceding verses that whatever was will be, whatever happened will happen again because in the life that stretches out before him, one year, one month, one day, will be just a replica of his preceding years. And this is true—his time within will proceed with the same monotonous schedule. Nevertheless, a certain old, old memory, unresolved has to remain a white blur within him, *(Compulsion and Doubt, p. 288)* a blank, for the punishment entailed in this memory is dire and annihilating—death itself for illicit relation. Since with some patients suicidal impulses are always present, were they confronted with that primary transgression, they would take their lives (Stekel).

In his endeavor to handle a most painful episode, a neurotic patient may resort not only to repression to expunge the unpleasantness, but in addition may make use of the less frequent device of annulment. It is a form of amnesia, except that the latter is a scotoma of a complete period of time and space. Annulment is the expunging of a single experience, or act, or idea. The patient acts as if they did not or have never existed. A man may have a wife, for instance, and act as if he did not have one. As the psychiatrist J.A. Brussel says[36], "A man may be psychologically single even though he is ostensibly married. A lack of sexual gratification can result not only from inability or unwillingness to go after it as a single man but also in a married man's case from having his wife refuse him." He reports that his patient Albert was psychologically single, floundering in precisely "the kind of sex trouble that can afflict a single man."

It is quite apparent that on a number of occasions Qohelet annulled some unpleasant facts of his existence. In one instance, the collocation of words at 5.13, "a bad venture and he begets a son," show that he considered his son a bad venture, i.e., in the progression of his thought, the bad venture reminded him of his son, who is never referred to again in the succeeding verses at all, a problem indeed for commentators. On other occasions, Qohelet annuls his son's existence by complaining, "why should I leave the profit of that labor to a man who comes after me" (2.18.21) In 6.2 his heir-designate becomes "a strange man." Pertinent too is the instance where Qohelet incorporates in his own strain a small segment of the Gilgamesh Epic (see below for the text p. 69 f.), which predicates that one should love one's wife, keep one's clothes fresh and clean, etc.; yet Qohelet omits the striking phrase, "Pay heed to the little one that holds on to thy hand." As analysts have emphasized, it is important for us to know what persons or events have been left out of the dream (in a family situation) even in more measure than to pay attention only to personages who appear again and again to crowd the dream.[37]

Another example of annulment is evident at 4.8 where Qohelet nullifies his wife's existence by saying, "There is a man, and there is no *second*" which Ibn Ezra rightly interprets as his wife. The whole verse seems to be a categorical *annulment* of Qohelet's whole family, which neurotics frequently do[38] with their families, and yet the succeeding verses in Qohelet relate wistfully of the pleasure and the delightful blessing of a family circle.

The key text, in sum, at 7.28 manifests a morose, adverse hostility toward women specifically in the hapless alliance with Qohelet's wife. The first feminine relationships in his life with his mother/sister, on the other hand, fixated a love which he yearned to find again but could not under society's rule of morality and law. Qohelet deflected his ardor and potency for one who became impossible to aspire to or attain. In his maturity Qohelet apparently recognized this hopeless situation, but the unconscious refused to be denied and he continually yearned for a long lost love.

*I am not a well-arranged book,
but a human being, full of contradictions.*
—Konrad F. Meyer.

VI
More Links in the Chain

It will be understood that the depth of an impulse or drive or instinct, its power and the means to repress it, to channel it, or discipline it will vary from individual to individual. One person will go through life in comparative calm experiencing deprivations and enduring traumas, and yet no disturbing mark will be left on his psyche. In another, one traumatic experience, one disappointment in love, one scar condemns him to a life of neuroses and compulsions. As Emerson remarked, we boil at different temperatures. Moreover, neuroses are like infections: they spread and form into a system, through symbolization and fusion, very much as a taboo object will make another object taboo.[39] If a patient, for example, has a neurosis about red blood, it becomes transferred to red blankets, red signs, etc.[40]

One effect that agitates a neurotic quite markedly are vows and oaths—technically oath clauses, and co-ordinately the so-called "death clauses." We know how seriously oaths and vows were considered in biblical times. It is recounted in the Book of Judges (11.30 f.) that Jephthah, to ensure victory over the Ammonites, vowed that "whoever comes forth from the doors of my house to meet me, when I return victorious from the Ammonites, shall be the Lord's and I will offer him up for a burnt offering." When Jephthah came home victorious, "behold, his daughter came out to meet him with tambourines and dancing! She was his one and only child; besides her he had neither son nor daughter. Upon seeing her, he rent his clothes, and said, Alas my daughter, you have crushed me! You have dealt me a mortal blow! For I made a vow unto the Lord, and I cannot retract it! My father, she said, since you have made a vow to the Lord, do to me as you have spoken. . . . She went with her companions to mourn for her maidenhood on the mountains and at the end of two months she returned to her father, who did to her what he had vowed, and she one who had never any intercourse with a man" (11.39).

His daughter was sacrificed to the tribal god Yahweh. Could not this vow have been resolved? Was there no way out? Jephthah's adherence to his vow is not atypical (he lived about 1000 B.C.E.) Later documents as in the Priestly Code (ca. fifth century B.C.E.) tried to allow for a resolution: a husband or father could annul the vow of a wife or daughter (Num. 30.3-5.9). Vows, however, continued much in force. According to the Mishna (third century C.E.), if a man betroths a woman on the condition that she is without vows, and it was discovered she was under vows, then the betrothal is of no effect.[41] If he wed her without conditions, and she were found to be with vows that she is obligated to comply with and carry out, he divorces her without her marriage settlement (Mishna *Ketubot* 7.7). In *Ketubot* folio 71a, a man divorces his wife because she vexes him with her continual vowing. In rabbinic times, and indeed extending to the modern period, a vow/oath can be annulled by a scholar or three laymen. Vow annulment has persisted to modern days even in the liturgy, when on the eve of the solemn fast of the Day of Atonement, the recitation of the awe-inspiring Kol Nidrei "All religious vows, prohibitions, oaths, bans, penalties, and even substitutes thereof that we have taken on ourselves shall be null [varying texts: that we *shall* take upon ourselves shall be null]" is chanted.

What impels a person to take oaths, to make vows to himself? According to Freud, Stekel and others, the primary spur to the making of vows originates in masturbation. The parents of a child pay less attention to his aggressive or even criminal actions than to any sexual misconduct. They consider his masturbatory acts very seriously and warn the child with threats of dire punishment. They may actually harm him bodily. With these warnings, and knowing the disapprobation of society as a whole, the pubescent boy may promise himself very earnestly, vow by the life of his father, his mother, that he will not practice any sexual misdeed. He may become very "religious," pray to God for help, bind himself with successive vows and oaths, sworn again by the life of his father and mother.[42] The guilt feelings persist; each vow as it is broken intensifies his guilt feeling. If he has a tendency to neuroticism, he may need relief desperately. As he grows up, and his father dies through accident, illness, or before his time (and it is always before his time: "He could have lived yet"), the son feels that he is the murderer of his father. In modern days, he goes to a psychiatrist for relief, or goes to Confession, or prays, or "forgets" by annulment.

Stekel, for example, reports of one who was on the firing line at the front, who took an oath that if he ever got out alive, he would abstain from immoral sexual activity. He did survive the war. In time the man married and found that he was impotent. Analysis disclosed that he was unconscious of the fact that his vow clause was hanging over his head and prevented him from consummating the sexual act.

The neurotic who knows the binding power of vows, their imperious compulsion, their fearsome domination of his life is very much afraid of vows and oaths. Nothing terrifies a neurotic so much, Stekel notes, as when he has to take an oath in court. It should be emphasized that there is not one compulsion but a complex, a chain of vows. Each vow may have a countervow, each oath the counter false oath. The oath or vow that the neurotic has taken in the past is still very much in force in the present, and casts its ominous potency for the future as well. Vows are the most severe form of compulsion and control.

This horror of vows is quite marked in Qohelet. Everyone has the same mortal fate, he says in 9.2, the saint and the sinner, the good and the wicked, the worshipper and the nonworshipper. Other readers may add the rich and the poor, the powerful and the weak, the great and the little. To this category, however, Qohelet adds an anomalous example: anyone who binds himself with an oath, and one who is apprehensive of oaths. Why is this so significant? And why should this be included in the classification of those who suffer the fate of all? Giving an oath or refraining from an oath—is this on a par with the wicked or the righteous, the worshipper or the nonworshipper, a mark and character of man's life? To Qohelet, however, with his neurotic makeup, the importance of taking an oath/vow rules the dynamics of his thought and action. Making an oath, and fulfilling the obligation of the self for oneself, is not the equivalent of performing some meritorious deed or *mizvah* but a great victory for Qohelet's whole personality.

Pertinent, too, is the second example at 5.3f. Note that Qohelet in his isolating symptoms (4.8) shows no relationship with the Jewish people, nor with the land of Judea (except for the grand pretence of the royal residence at Jerusalem); nor does he know of Abraham, Isaac, and Jacob, and the covenant of God with them, nor the Sabbath, nor the festivals. Of the commandments, he knows but one. If we were to assume arbitrarily that there are 613 commandments in the Pentateuch, as the later rabbinic tradition artificially summed them up (Exodus Rabbah, sec. 32), it is surprising that Qohelet should single out only one of the 613: the making of a vow. Whereas the passage in the Pentateuch (Deut. 23.22f. which Qohelet has in mind and copies almost verbatim in 5.3) sets off an alternative in the sundry laws exposited at length that the nonfulfillment of a vow is serious ("and you shall have a sin"), and there is a vague threat of some penalty but which could be presumably offset by the offering of some sacrifice, for Qohelet the remissness is mortal and is certain to draw the Divine wrath and the destruction of one's work and worldly goods. God will surely punish you even if you say it was a case of forgetfullness (shegagah=shelutha in Aramaic "forgetfullness."[43] *See* Commentary). While the Priestly Code allowed for the forgiveness of a trespass done unwittingly (e.g., Num. 15.25: it shall be forgiven them because it was done in error), Qohelet is so self-punishing that no margin for error is allowed.

Similarly, in 8.2 where the first part of the verse should read: Watch the king's countenance; however in the matter of a Divine oath do not be rash (*See* Commentary). The injunction is clear: Do not rush to bind yourself in an oath to God, indicating again Qohelet's apprehension of taking an oath. Another interpretation would be that '*elohim* here would mean as one would say "a tremendous oath" since '*elohim* in Hebrew may bear the meaning of "immense, colossal, horrendous," and the like (Jon. 3.3). If so, this would only confirm again Qohelet's unmitigated dread of taking an oath.

Another characteristic of a neurotic's obsession is his conviction about the so-called "omnipotence of thoughts."[44] The neurotic believes that by his thought he may control the destiny of others. If he should so wish the death of another, it is quite probable and reasonable to his mind that such a person may suffer such a fate. Quite a number of neurotics feel responsible for the deaths of others. Conversely, he is very suspicious that others may have designs against him. This notion that others may harm him is quite widespread, and not only among obsessionists and paranoiacs. Millions of persons believe in the Evil Eye, for example, and protect themselves by wearing amulets and beads; others, by pronouncing God's name, or by an outburst of "Jesus Christ" to frighten away evil spirits ("the demons are subject to us at the mention of your name" [Luke 10.17]; "to cast out demons in the name of Jesus" [Mark 9.38]), still others by prayers and incantations, or by consulting horoscopes.

The Bible is well aware of this power of thought that may be translated into action: "My eye looks upon my enemies" (Ps. 92.12), i.e., to destroy them. The psalmist prays to Yahweh to save him from wicked men who "think evil in their hearts" (Ps. 140.3), "who think to trip him, to make his footsteps slip"; (v.5). "God makes null and void the thought of the crafty" (Job 5.15). In rabbinic literature examples abound. To cite but one: "Ninety nine persons die of an evil eye as against one(!) in natural course" (b. *Baba Meẓia* 107b)—exaggerated, of course.

Folklore is replete with instances of the power of thought that may change, influence or dominate other persons. Thus California Indians believe that the chief can read a visitor's thoughts. Or by magic knowledge in Irish myths one can acquire another's thoughts. Or friends can read each others thoughts.[45]

Qohelet is quite aware and skittish about this omnipotence of thought. Of course, one should not conceive of anything untoward against God. One's words should be few (5.1). A word uttered obviously cannot be called back. Don't let your mouth condemn your body (5.5: See Commentary). Of particular interest is that one should not curse the king, even in one's *thought*, and in the recesses of one's chamber one should not curse a rich man, for thoughts are like birds—"winged messengers"—and they will tell of the imprecation (10.20). Indirectly, this is a reflection of his position at court: He is afraid that someone will discern his evil thoughts.

Closely intertwined with the omnipotence of thoughts is the idea of the curse, regarded as being extraordinarily potent in the psychology of primitive peoples and neurotics. A curse, carried as if on a wave length, could do irreparable damage. The biblical tradition recognizes this full well (Jud. 9.57). The penalty for cursing was death. Such was the punishment for cursing a father and mother (Ex. 21.17), or the king (II Sam. 16.7;19.22), or one who cursed God's name (Lev. 24.23). The children of Israel who were quite fearful of the curses of Balaam, hired by Balak (Num. 22-24), and Nehemiah 13.2 almost a millennium later, still makes mention of them. When the Hebrews finally lay hands on Balaam they killed him (Num. 31.8; Josh.13.22). With the passage of centuries and the humanization of law and morality, the penalty and fear of the curse lessened (Prov.26.2). Nevertheless, the curse in whatever form—wishes can also kill—was looked upon with foreboding and anxiety for the power it possessed. Thus in the New Testament, Jesus curses the fig tree and it withers. In rabbinic times, a woman who cursed a man's parents in his presence was divorced without her marriage settlement (*Ket.* VII.6).

Curses play an important role among neurotics. For example, one neurotic woman, as reported by Stekel (*Compulsion and Doubt,* 27), had joined her brothers in a lawsuit against their father about a legacy. The father wrote a letter pronouncing a curse against her and her husband with the ostensible purpose of disinheriting her. "This curse made an important impression on her. She had always believed in the effectiveness of curses, and she wrote to her father many letters imploring him to retract the curse."

With regard to Qohelet, a conscious attempt is made to discount the potency of the curse. He advises you (himself) in 7.21: don't pay attention to all the conversation going on about you. Then follows an ellipsis, for if you do, you will hear your slave curse you. This would be quite impactive on Qohelet's psyche for fear that the imprecation could only come too true, too efficacious, and destroy him. But then he consoles himself with the idea: "don't forget how many times you have cursed others." This is whistling in the dark. Qohelet believes in curses, otherwise he would not have mentioned them. He has cursed others; he hopes that he does not hear the curse of slaves (Prov. 30.10). It is better to hide one's head in the sand. At least one would not know of the malediction.

Mention has been made of Qohelet's marked propensity for doubting. This doubting stems from the bipolar tension of Qohelet tinged with anxiety. This may originate, for example, in an infantile anxiety. As Freud illustrated with an obvious example, when a child is playfully (?) asked, "Whom do you love better, your father or your mother?", on the spur of the moment the child is bewildered. The unconscious flashes: if I say my mother, will my father be angry, antagonized? This may become a source of anxiety, of doubt. Suppose the child is really rejected by one or the other parent . . . or a younger brother or sister is favored over him . . . or he resides at home in traumatic conflict. . . . There are innumerable examples and extensions on this situation.

If an individual is in doubt, i.e., doubt about his whole being and ability, the psychic personality of this individual is bifurcated. His doubt always suggests an alternative, and this engenders antithetic thinking. One thought is always contrasted with another thought; one preference by another; one emotion by another; one egoistic fancy by another. In a similar fashion, as a variation on the antithetic motif, a patient will frame "either-or" situations.[46] His doubt freezes his ability to make a decision.

Qohelet amply betrays his persistent doubt by the frequent antithesis he frames throughout his book. The largest number, thirteen in all, manifest themselves in 3.1-8, e.g., "There is a time to plant; and a time to uproot the planted," etc. Then 2.19 phrases one of the typical antithetic questions prefaced by "who knows?": and who knows whether he will be wise or a fool?; (3.21) who knows whether the spirit of man goes upward and the spirit of the animal goes downward (to the earth (6.12); who knows what good a man should pursue in life, etc.; (8.1) who is like a wise man, and on the other hand who can know the real solution of anything? The latter verse is problematical in some details, but the antithetic character of the statement is obvious. Other passages are found at 11.5.6;6.8;9.1. This persistent manifestation of alternatives in Qohelet stems from his unresolved conflict, his indecision, his uncertainty—all told from the bifurcation in tension. This may be one of the reasons for Qohelet's inability to sleep. Antitheses indicate his inability to come to a decision.

Oaths, doubts, curses, the omnipotence of thoughts, vows, antitheses mark the troubled character and functioning of Qohelet. We shall consider now *time* and its meaning and relevance to him in the following section.

Wail my dear time's waste.
Shakespeare.

VII

Time Out of Mind

Time plays an important role in Qohelet's life. This time of his has nothing to do with the maturity of an individual, who applies himself assiduously to his work, who puts a premium on his time and does not wish to waste it, and who steadily pursues his goal (experiential time). With Qohelet, time is not something that one elects for good use or purpose. In the collocation of *'et,* "time," with other words in close association, in some instances through *hendiadys,* through contrast, through the climate and components of a situation, it is observable that *'et* carries with it a sense of fate, of tragic predestination, an inevitable decision fraught with a fatalistic sequel, of judgment against which there is no appeal. One may compare the identical roots in Arabic of *hiyn,* "time," and *hain,* meaning "death."

In 8.6 Qohelet declares that for everything there is a time and judgment, i.e., one will have to give an accounting at judgment (cf. 12.14). Moreover, as in 9.11 "time" implies the end-time of death, the fatal hour that overcomes both the one who has physical prowess and the man of intellect. This "time" (=fate) occurs of a sudden, without warning, as the snap of a trap for a bird, as Qohelet says, or as a fish in the mesh of a net; so does the "bitter time" (reading *'itto ra'ah see* Commentary) fall on man when he is least aware (9.12).

While on the one hand "time" has this connotation of impending doom, the *'et* in chapter three expresses differently Qohelet's sense of obligation, compulsion. For example, the idea that one is to seek out, and one is to destroy (verse 6) does not signify that at one time in one's life it is meet to perform these acts, or as the opportunity arises by chance that one should engage in these activities. On the contrary, these are continual diurnal practices that Qohelet is compelled to perform. For the Hebrew construction to express obligation, compare Ps.102.14;119.126;Hos.10.12.

We may revert with more understanding now to the needs, desires, and compulsions of Qohelet in chapter three, where *'et* figures so

44

prominently in the antitheses. The first verse reveals the perspective of his hopeless struggle: one must be born, and one must die. One thinks of the parallel in the Ethics of the Fathers, IV.22, ed.E.Travers Herford: against your will you have been born, against your will you continue to live, and in spite of yourself you die. Verse 2 continues with the very human cathexis of his compulsion by planting, and then when the plants do not grow well, or whatever, he must tear them out by the roots. But plants are well-known symbols of erection and sexual congress and are associated with children by meaning and symbol. [47] On the other hand, "to root out the planted" is in line with the other antitheses in this section, where refraining is the key meaning in the contrasting stitch to abstain from sexual intercourse. Note that *la'aqor*, "uproot," is associated as in the same root with *'iqqer*, "hamstring," *'aqar*, "the barren, impotent male." Here we may state provisionally how Qohelet articulates his hesitation about children. On the one hand, it is important to have sexual congress, naturally to have children. So the world says. But on the other hand, it would have been just as worthwhile and convenient not to have them. This is the significance of the verse as unconsciously revealed by Qohelet. As we shall see, Qohelet suspiciously considered that his son was not his own.

"There is a time to kill and a time to refrain" (a misreading on the part of the Hebrew translator of *'iddan lemirpe*) signifies that however aggressive thoughts crowd into one's mind and which give one the pleasure of idly fabricating designs against an enemy (wife) and to hate, one must put them out of mind nevertheless as they are a violation of societal morality. This latter verse is a psychological forecast of the next: there is a time in which one must destroy, and there is a time one must build up again. Interesting is his compulsion that there is a time one must weep, and a time to laugh, and then, substantially repeated further, that there is a time to mourn and a time to dance. What is so significant about having a time to laugh and a time to weep? A neurotic may have a strong impulse to misbehave inappropriately (to laugh) at a funeral. Inwardly he rejoices at the death of the deceased, and that he is not being buried himself. He cannot but smile inwardly at the solemnities and at the faces of the sober mourners. On the other hand, he is solemn and glum in the midst of merriment.[47a]

In 3.5, Qohelet's impulse for aggression comes again to the fore. He desires to throw stones at someone deserving of death, his wife as it turns out to be, probably because he suspects her of being unfaithful. But again reflecting his doubt, he may not have been completely sure

(9.9). The psychological repetition, registering the doubt as well, is found at 6cd. In the previous verse (5cd) Qohelet's doubt and inhibition about the sexual act are revealed: *habaq* here means the preliminary sex play different from verse 8, which means "to have affection for." Note sequentially the contrast "a time to hate." The antithesis in verse 6 "a time to seek out, and a time to lose," may refer to Qohelet's quandary in which he may have felt compelled to seek out his lost love object, e.g., his fixation on his sister, or, on the other hand, to give up the search as she is married, or that he himself is now married and has a wife and child. The idea, moreover, that there is a time to sew and a time to rip is a multiform symbol of a number of compulsions. First, blended with the act of sewing is this homosexual component[47b] (ut supra, see p. 27). His hatred for the female sex exposes his latent homosexual proclivity. Then at another level is the occupation that he must give his hands; in wrath he tears apart, a cathexis of his aggression and then ruefully looking back at the damage to a perhaps costly raiment has to sew them together again. Verse 7cd is tied in with the fear that Qohelet has in communicating with others, perhaps in pronouncing oaths for committing himself, or vows for self-punishment if he fails to carry out the provisions, or in general, that one should not talk too much because one may say the wrong or inappropriate thing.

All in all, it would follow from 3.1-8 that Qohelet had quite a number of compulsions, and had quite a routine for himself. Much of the activity would have been spurious really, a pseudo-activity and busyness, yet essentially not connected with the realities of life. The activities conceal much more primary action(s) and are only a deflection, a distraction—having no goal or direction.

We follow through with the question:Why is Qohelet so concerned and preoccupied with *time*? The answer seems to be that Qohelet, in common with many neurotics, mortally fears what time will do to him. He sees the old man (c.12), beclouded in his five senses (v.2), his hands trembling and his fingers gnarled (v.3), the teeth missing and the eyes failing (he cannot see or read); the voice of the bird becomes feeble, i.e., he is impotent (in the latter instance, he cannot sing the melody through). As the old man walks he drags his feeble limbs along. Looking with horror at old persons, Qohelet would keep time at a standstill if he could ("turn the clock back.")

Minkowski's researches show that in most psychotics space-and-time disorders lie at the root of their illnesses. The future is regarded as hopeless. Schizophrenics, as an extreme illustration, regard themselves as left behind in the tide of the world's activities. One individual described time in his immediate room as an hour behind in the next room. Another patient took aim at a clock with a pistol because he considered the clock his worst enemy. Still another talked about the rigid immobility of everything around him, and the mechanical routine he followed seemed to transform his future into a listless, witless duplication of the past (compare Qohelet). Still another patient, since he felt he could never achieve a worthwhile objective in life, tried to rid himself of the notion of time.

Interesting, moreover, are the cases cited by Fisher wherein his schizophrenic patients made the following complaints.: 1. One's head is like a clock. 2. Time has come to a standstill. 3. A prayer for the destruction of time. 4. Living in eternity. 5. A feeling of timelessness (on this last, compare Qohelet again). It should be remarked here, to correct any unintended impression, that Qohelet again is in no way to be considered schizophrenic. True, he has neuroses but he has not lost contact with reality; his personality has not disintegrated; he has no hallucinations or delusions. Yet from chapter nine and twelve and elsewere, it is plain to see *that he regards time as his nemesis.*

A. M. Merloo has found that the compulsive neurotic, on the other hand, is very aware of time, and is continually watchful of the passage of time. While he is apprehensive of what the passage of time might do to him "sans teeth, sans eyes, sans taste, sans everything," for him time is also life. Giving time to someone else signifies giving love to him. Giving of one's time and attention is giving of one's self. Time too (so Merloo) is found to be the very essence of love, an orgiastic experience. Time stops at that very moment.[48]

It should also be observed that in the same personality under changing conditions there are different rhythms of time, and also at different levels, conscious and unconscious. As a result, and so with Qohelet, we have different time concepts.[48] The syntonic personality is able to bring into harmony through the healthy and realistic contact with world time a proper synchronism, an orderly simultaneity in the whole ego system. Time in the constitution of the psyche demands memory, association, concentration, projection, contrasting, affirming, and negating. A reliable sequence measures out of the day life's experience, i.e., how further one has to fulfill one's needs and stimulate one for the enlargement and enrichment of life. The whole organization of time therefore, the whole time functioning, is a thermometer of the whole personality.

From the above we may summarize the crux of time in the overall personality of Qohelet. As he is apprehensive of time and its ravages on the body, he knows that he is powerless to stave off the assault, and the fell stroke of illness (9.11-12 *see* Commentary) frightens him as a forecast of sequential death.

The first concept of '*et*, then, is that time is doom, and in the futility of life (everything is *hebel*) Qohelet wishes its speedy termination, as he has nothing to live for. As Schiller said on one occasion, "The clock does not strike for the happy person."

The second significance that '*et* bears is the sense of the time that is required for performing compulsive acts. At certain stated times, not specified but implied, Qohelet has these impulses to kill, to destroy, to break through, to throw stones, to tear apart, to hate, to suppress his speech—all of which he must drain off (cathect). There are many neurotics who cannot start their day without performing one or more compulsive acts. These actions are only partly satisfactions and are either symbolical or derivative of the original (or proposed) act. The action is a waste and Qohelet, with many compulsives, senses this.

Qohelet is impelled to repeat these actions (to sew, to throw stones) because of his anagogic yearning, his good *yezer* (=impulse, *see below presently*) to better his life, to blot out the past (compare. 1.11: there will be no remembrance of things past), to secure a new and different objective. But all to no avail. The *bête-noire* of his life, parapathetic doubt, waylays him, and he founders helplessly. His doubts fall into a well-worn formula: Why should I continue to live? Why should I continue to work? What value or worth has it? Must this existence always be the same, meaningless and monotonous? He would gladly die. In neurotics suicidal impulses are always at hand. In Qohelet the forecast of his own death is constantly present, as evinced by his preoccupation with the death of others (4.2;6.3; *et seq.*).

Associated with '*et*, thirdly, are the attributes of judgment, decision, decree, both explicit and implied in the Hebrew text (compare particularly its collocation with *mishpaṭ* in 8.5 and the sense of evil and fateful decree in 9.11.12); compare similarly Arabic *fasl* and *qismat* meaning both "time" and "judgment." The word "judgment" carries pejorative overtones very much like the English "doom," which is derived from Old Norse *dömr* meaning "judgment, court, sentence." What contributed to the devolution of *dömr* to doom (cf. *din* "judgment," "punishment") was obviously the apprehension of litigants as to whether judgment would be decided against them. While this would naturally be the case with emotionally disturbed persons, there is an additional reason involved, and in many instances for a different reason altogether. A typical dream is reported by Stekel[49]: "I had to take an examination in canonical law," the patient related, "the examiner was a scriptor in the Royal Library. . . . I was very nervous. I thought it was impossible for me to pass the examination because it was so long since I had studied canonical law. . . ."

As Stekel interpreted the dream: many neurotics begin their analysis with a dream about an examination. Their apprehension is that the analyst might question them about their secret. In the present dream, analysis brought out that the patient had a terrible childhood experience, corrupted by an immoral, sexually uninhibited maid who played with his penis, performed fellatio on him, was discharged, but before that had the boy swear before a crucifix that he would eternally love her. Later in life he could not marry because of his oath to the discharged maid. When he tried marriage after a number of attempts, it failed. His illness was his secret[50] which he did not want to be disclosed, not only to his wife but to the analyst as well.

Qohelet mentions a number of times sentence and judgment (literally time-judgment 8.5) which he fears will be pronounced upon "you," meaning himself. Thus in 12.14 he or the epilogist declares that for every action, whether, hidden or not, God will bring "you" into judgment (8.5); the wise man is conscious of the judgment-time (8.6). Everything has a time and judgment (6.10); he cannot contend in judgment with one who is stronger than he is. Qohelet fears to be brought before the bar of judgment and inquiry for his secret sin might be discovered. What was this sin? Our material does not supply us with an answer but it must have been horrendous to him, either committed with his mother or sister when young, as has been suggested above. Inasmuch as Qohelet nowhere expresses a belief in an after world for judgment, the sin is going to be disclosed here on earth in the presence of everyone by the all-powerful God. It is of this that Qohelet is terror-stricken, not so much the punishment which he would accept as a proper desert as long as his secret sin with his sister/mother were not divulged in the Divine assize in the presence of everybody.

'Et, "time," for Qohelet is a foreboding, a dark portent of judgment-doom wherein he will have to divulge his secret of an incestous relationship in the past; the passage of time will forecast a weakened decaying body; time must be filled in with meaningless compulsive actions, all overcast by a fear of death, i.e., punishment, which may occur at any moment (9.12).

We cannot change the rules of the game (mathematics); we cannot ascertain whether the game is fair. We can only study the player at his game; not however with the detached attitude of a bystander, for we are watching our minds at play.
—T. Dantzig

VIII

Qohelet's Estimate of Himself

According to biblical tradition, a man can possess two "hearts"—a nature to do good and a nature to do evil. Gen. 8.21 speaks of the evil that is in man's nature from his youth. One who is perverse in heart is called *'iqqesh leb*, Prov. 11.20;17.20, while the antonym of "evil heart" is "straightforward in heart," *yeshar leb* Ps. 36.11;64.11. This recognition of the two impulses or inclinations is expressed even more graphically by the terms *yezer ha-tob* and *yezer ha-ra'*, almost a *terminus technicus* in rabbinic literature for the Good and Bad Inclination.

In reporting their dreams, neurotics frequently apply the symbol of the road leading to the right as the "right" road, the road of rectitude, truth, morality, correct conduct, while the road to the left or on the left leading to incest, immorality, perversion is immoral, improper, a violation of custom and law (compare Latin *sinister* "left"). Thus a student revealed in analysis that when he had extramarital intercourse, he said he performed the act with his left penis; on the other hand when he had intercourse with his wife, he performed the act with his right penis[51].

The figure of the right and the left in similarly employed by Qohelet. At first sight, the verse that runs that the heart of the wise man is to the right, but the heart of the fool is to the left (10.2), seems to be but another example of the antithetic structure in which Qohelet frames his doubts. However, "right" and "left" establish themselves as categories in their own right, with the overtones of moral judgments of right and wrong.

In a congruous classification Qohelet will also aver: "The wise man has eyes in his head, but the fool walks in darkness" (2.14). The question arises, however: who is this wise man that walks straightly and with circumspection, whereas the fool stumbles along in the darkness? It is curious that in the examples Qohelet gives of the contrasts between the wise man and the fool there is no indication (just as he does not define *ḥakam* elsewhere in the book) in what manner the wise man distinguishes himself as a wise man, and, *per contra*, how the fool denigrates himself. It is clear that Qohelet, in adopting the persona of another as he does in the case of Solomon (*see* chapter on Solomon), is persistently mirroring himself whether he utilizes the first person, the second person, or the third (*see* presently below). He consequently feels that when he acts purposively and does things that are worthwhile, he is acting as a *ḥakam*; on the other hand, when he acts compulsively without direction or reason, he is acting as a *kesil*. *Qohelet's ego and counterego then are the* ḥakam *and the* kesil *in the same person.* Qohelet laments the circumstance that at times he acts seemingly as a rational man, and at other times he behaves unwittingly and impulsively.

The split in the neurotic personality ranges wide over quite a number of opposites: part ego versus part ego form two hostile camps in which each holds the antagonists of the other side. Stekel illustrates this with the opposites of hero and coward, atheist and pietist, the legal fanatic and the criminal, skeptic and mystic, the chaste and the love neurotic, the pure and the impure, the cruel and the compassionate—all in the same person. Thus many compulsive neurotics are found as lawyers and philosophers (compare Qohelet as a "philosopher"). The dominant problem that preoccupies them is: "Is the true road to the right? Am I travelling on the right road to the truth?" Compulsive neurotics who study the law do so with the purpose of finding "the right way," though really wishing to defend their own criminal impulses! The philosopher, on the other hand, on his road to investigating the truth and antithetically arguing all sides of the question actually regresses from action to thought (inaction, and so Freud). Compare now Qohelet at 9.1:

"For all this I laid to my heart to make *clear* all of this: that (=how) the righteous and the wise and their actions are in the hand of God; how love and hate man does not know or why it comes; everything is as nothing before them" (*see* Commentary).

And at 8.16f.:

"When I applied my heart to know wisdom, and to see the sorry business that happens in the world—for neither day not night does a man enjoy sleep in his agony (*see* Commentary)—and I considered all the work of God and that man cannot find a solution to the enigma that transpires under the sun so that man should work with a purpose, no—he will not find it! And if a philosopher seeks to find the truth, he will not be able to find it!

One will be reminded, too, of all the passages cited above with the initial "Who knows . . ."—again, a part of Qohelet's philosophic quest, indicating again the constant debate of the philosopher to refrain from action. As we shall see in the case of Qohelet, relief was found in his dilemma and in the debate within himself by the composing and writing of his book.

A number of other psychological difficulties are revealed to us in the way Qohelet deploys unconsciously the first, second, and third person throughout the book, just alluded to. This process in formulating his observations originates in Qohelet's objectification of himself, his actions, and his whole situation. Remark should be made too, as Freud once observed, on the tendency of the compulsive to isolate himself.

One proof text that illustrates a number of these tendencies very well is found at 4.8: There is one that is alone (objectification), and there is not a second (annulment: he means his wife); and yes, he has neither son nor brother (withdrawal from the family); yet there is no end to all his labor (compulsion), neither is his eye satisfied with riches, "for whom then do I labor and deprive myself of pleasure?" This, then, is a futile and sorry business!

We may note, first of all, the attempt on the part of Qohelet to detach and objectify his circumstances as if he were a person on the outside looking in at a phenomenon remotely situated from himself; yet his own indignation and lament about himself breaks through in the first person that he works compulsively and unceasingly to gather wealth (but little as it turns out, see above, p. 2) and yet because of his apathy cannot permit himself to spend the money and enjoy it. In his distress and cry, he transits from the first part of the verse (impersonal) to the wrathful reproach of the second part: why do I deny myself pleasure? We may note also the isloating and withdrawing propensity wherein he seeks self-protection in his neurosis. Qohelet seems to be hanging in the air, unrelated, unaffiliated to family; nor does he know of ancestors.

In this standoff attempt to deal with himself as an observer apart so that painful inferences may be considered as belonging to someone else (*noli me tangere*), Qohelet's realization of himself, his imagined self-projection, becomes discernible in various *symbolizations*. On the one hand, his subconscious reflects what a worthless inferior being he is, and what in his eyes a futile striving all his life has been, and on the other hand, how grandiosely he dreams of identifying himself in royal pretension with King Solomon.

One index, among others, of how Qohelet deprecates himself is found in his attitude toward the rich man. For time immemorial slaves have cursed their masters. Not so Qohelet. He has such regard for the wealthy man, that one dare not even curse a rich man; he sets the wealthy man on the same footing with the king (10.20); and in 10.6, where folly is described as being enthroned on high places, and, contrasting one should await the phrase in the parallel stitch that the *wise* sit in a low place, Qohelet substitutes: "The wealthy sit in a low place." There is no need to emend the text, as scholars do. Qohelet is not only impressed but overawed by wealth. References are made to wealth six times (4.8;5.12;6.2;9.11;5.13;its loss in a bad venture is regarded as a calamity); to the rich man three times (10,20;5.11;10.6); to silver (money) 2.8;5.9 (bis); 7.12; 12.6; and to gold 2.8 (where he dreams in the persona of the grand monarch that he amasses silver and gold); the synonymous *hamon* [affluence, luxury] and *nekasim*, "property," and *'osher*, "wealth," in 5.8;6.2). For a small book such as Qohelet, these sixteen references to wealth and money are disproportionate; they loom large in Qohelet's mind; he looks up to the man of means. A concomitant observation would be that Qohelet's over-reverence for wealth comes from his respect for power that the wealthy man, equated with the king, possesses, and in whose hands life and death would be instantaneous. The plutocrat, masterful as he appears to Qohelet, gives him a sinking feeling of how weak and helpless he is.

Qohelet's deprecation of himself takes on further guises and forms. As he hates life because life has treated him shamefully and unkindly, making his existence a futility and his work a frustration, he wishes often enough that his life would end (7.8): Better the end of a thing than its beginning; and, —it is better to go to the house of mourning than to go to the house of feasting for that is the end of man: and, —better the day of death than the day of one's birth [7.2.1]. Just as pertinent is the symbolic way that Qohelet belittles himself in his writing, through varied identifications, as we shall now discuss: with the isolated lonely soul, with the disparaged dog, with the aborted infant, with the fool, with the poor man, with the evident deprecatory employment of *'adam* as a term for the ordinary man (cf. "person" in English as an inferior human being [*vide* Webster's International Unabridged Dictionary]), with *hote'* translated usually as "sinner" but in Qohelet "the ill favored one" (Siegfried, H.L.Ginsberg).

A man has a compulsion to work, for example (4.8), but Qohelet in his isolation wonders, breaking down to the first person mentioned previously, Why do I deny myself pleasure? Qohelet continues: Two are better than one [myself] for they have a mutual satisfaction in their work. For if one should fall sick [4.10f], the one will nurse the other. (*See* Commentary.) But if one [read:I] should fall sick, there is none else to nurse him back to health. The sequel wistfully continues on the benefits of a good compatible marriage: moreover, if two persons lie with each other, they have warmth, i.e., they have sexual enjoyment and experience. But how can one [read: I] have sexual satisfaction? If one gets overpowered [he will be mauled, ellipsis] if I get assaulted, who will assist me? Then he ends up in a proverb: Better yet the thrice twisted cord that will not easily be burst asunder [Ehrlich: husband, wife, and child]. This is the wistful yearning for domestic happiness where the familial bonds of shared joys and experiences are denied him. All this is a reflection of his isolation though Qohelet is formally married. The Hebrew *'ehad,* representing the Aramaic *hada'* (indefinite) and so the French usage *on,* will be recognized in these verses as reflecting the detachment and personality of Qohelet.

In 9.4 Qohelet avers that one who has still a hold on life (literally, has a connection, reading with the qere *yehubbar)* there is still hope (incidentally a contradiction with 4.2, "I praise the dead," characteristic of Qohelet's vacillation) for, he says, a live dog is better than a dead lion. Who is this dead lion, and who the live dog? Lion and dog of course are known as the two extremes of dignity and contempt. It is apparent that Qohelet must have seen the great king dead and inert (he speaks a number of times of the old king, senile [4.14], and hysterically shouting [9.17]). However solemn the exequies may have been with the old lion lying in state, Qohelet rejoiced that he was a live dog.[52] A dog, however, in the Near East is the most contemptible of creatures, an object of kicks and derision. Still Qohelet identifies with the dog. Observe too that the interpretation here may be multileveled. The dead lion here is the expired sexual prowess. The significance of the statement lies in this: Better to have a little life than to be dead altogether—better a little sexual satisfaction, however limited and incomplete, than none at all.

Qohelet's sense of hopelessness is perhaps no more acutely signalized than in 6.3. The Hebrew Bible makes use of *nefel,* "untimely birth, abortion," in two other instances: Ps. 58.9 where the Psalmist cursing the wicked in passionate, acerbic terms hopes that they may go lost from the uterus, and perish from the womb (v.4) and that God should break their teeth in their mouth (v.7), that they disappear like water that vanishes (v.8); like the worm that passes away in the slime, and like the untimely birth of a woman, let them not see the sun (v.9),—the strident language of a bitter crushed spirit is understandable. Similarly Job, who in his anguish of losing his children, his household and all his possessions, all seemingly without cause, should cry out (3.16); "Why was I not like the hidden misbirth . . .?", where undoubtedly the language is occasioned and sequential to "womb" (bis) and "uterus" (vv. 10-11). It must be confessed, however, that when Qohelet in 6.3 should say: if a man beget a hundred children, and live many years (and the days of his years be many, -a gloss)) and he has not enjoyed himself, I say that *an abortion is better than he,* it is with some sense of shock that the simile impacts on our consciousness. If a man has lived many years and has had a plethora of children, the two great blessings of the Hebrew people, (Job 42.16;Gen.25 and elsewhere) but did not enjoy himself, he is equatively like an abortion.(!) Second thoughts, however, in considering Qohelet's despair about life makes the phrasing understandable. In the words of one neurotic who kept a diary, "I have not begun to live yet, but I wish my life were over." Qohelet thinks of himself as one who should have been stifled at birth. Yes, even if he had lived two thousand years (6.6) and did not enjoy himself, life would have been in vain. He is like an abortion that people look upon with horror and nausea, and so he considers himself an object of loathing, for nobody values him, and therefore he does not value himself. He has not experienced the love that one human being bears for another. Conversely, he canot love anyone for no one has ever loved him. Life extends far into the future, Qohelet implies, for two thousand years, for an eternity in meaningless monotony.

To be associated in this connection is Qohelet's observation that it is better to remain in the womb (4.2.3) than to be still living or to have already died. This desire to be in the womb, i.e., to return to the womb, is praised by Qohelet by the word *ṭob* (good), also *naḥat* "gratification, satisfaction" (said about the aborted one). In addition, Qohelet laments the circumstance that if one has not enjoyed life, *and has not been buried* (this is at another level than cited above) that is has not been returned to Mother Earth, to the darkness and security of the womb, then his life [my life] has been lived in vain. The association of womb and grave is well known—in the womb where there is no fetus, no life; and so the grave—and has already been noticed by the Midrash to Qohelet (Soncino Ed. p. 75) which remarks on the juxtaposition in Prov. 30.16, "The grave and the barren womb." The Hebrew *qeber* = 1) grave, 2) womb.

In the system of doubts about himself, Qohelet identifies with one whom he calls *hote'*, usually translated as "sinner." The contrast of this word with *tob*, "good" (7.26;9.2.18;2.26), seems to postulate by adversative meaning the sense of "the ill-favored, the luckless." Either this meaning arose through a mistranslation of the underlying Aramaic *seriah* meaning 1) ill-favored, ill-savored or 2) to sin, or else this usage is part of the peculiar language of Qohelet who as a person with a disturbed psyche invents neologisms of his own in common with other neurotics. (See the full chapter on Qohelet's vocabulary.) Thus the passage in 7.26 becomes understandable in the light of this definition, in the context of the shrewish entrapping woman, that one who is favored (*tob*) before God escapes her; but the *hote'* "the luckless," is ensnared by her (similarly H.L.Ginsberg). But knowing Qohelet's personality as we do, *hote'* means something more. Qohelet does not regard himself as luckless alone but punishable. His criminal aggressive thoughts, his scarcely controlled instincts, that seek an outlet but are checked through the restraint of morality and law, the surging id intermittently controlled by the ego, overwhelms Qohelet with guilt feelings which have to be atoned for by punishment. He therefore punishes himself, and although his compulsions relieve his anxieties for a spell, he anticipates more punishments since he never considers he has had punishment enough. God the father is ever on the watch to punish him. *Hote'* in Qohelet is therefore one who is deserving of punishment for a misdeed, more imaginary than real as it turns out. He is a condemned man with no redress. *Het'* indeed via the same psychological process with a parallel Aramaic *hab* bears the similar signification of "sin" and "punishment" (Lev. 22.9;Num. 18.22.32). Compare similarly the Hebrew *'asham* meaning "sin" and "punishment."

Through this use of *hote'* we find another reflection of Qohelet's mental process and state of mind at 2.26: For the man who is favored before him *(tob)*, he gave wisdom and knowledge, but to the *hote'* (Qohelet) he has given an *'inyan* (compulsion: see chapter on Q's vocabulary) to gather and amass wealth; and then he must turn it over to the one favored of God (2.18.26;6.2). Why? He does not know.

9.18, while a little obscure syntactically, provides another instance of Qohelet's disconcerted opinion of himself: Wisdom is better than weapons of war. But then the latter part of the verse has not ostensible connection with the first: one "sinner" *(hote')* destroys much good. It is obvious that *hote'* must have a different signification here in the original sense of the Hebrew verb of "missing the target." The verse now bears the signification: while wisdom (intelligence, good strategy) is superior to armaments, yet if a man should miss the target, much good could be lost. The verse still unconsciously refers to Qohelet and his problems: if you miss your aim in life, much of life's zest is lost to you, and ennui and *horror vacui* characteristic of many psychoneurotic persons, take over for years and years of meaningless activity.

As Qohelet is, as indicated, a poor man his sympathies are with the poor. He is distressed by their tears, and enraged by their despoliation at the hands of their oppressors; the poor have no relief (4.1). This is not the point of view again of an affluent man. More characteristic of Qohelet is that he identifies himself with the unfortunate poor man who cannot cope with life's problems. What superiority does the intelligent man (Qohelet again) have over the fool if the wise man is poor and has to struggle unendingly against life (6.8)? Noteworthy in passing is the fact that Qohelet employs the word *'ani* in disparaging self-identification but on the other hand associates himself with *misken*, similar to the Akkadian sense of the word as "middle class man, burgher," in a meliorisitic sense. (See Driver and Miles, *The Babylonian Laws*, II p. 152 for the discussion on *misken.)*

In a number of instances, the word *'adam*, "man," used impersonally serves as a mask for Qohelet. The most clearcut instance would seem to be in 2.21: where the preceding verses in the chapter are nearly all in the first person which he then discards, but continues impersonally:

I hated life. . . . and I hated my work . . I changed my mind, falling into dejection about the work I labored at. Because there is a man (=Qohelet) whose work is with intelligence, knowledge and skill. . . . .But what does a man (=Qohelet) have for all his labor and concentration wherein he labors under the sun (2.17-22 condensed). Similarly vv. 24-25:

There is nothing better for a man (Qohelet, see v.25 *fine*) than that he should eat, drink, indulge himself for his labor. This also was from the hand of God. For who will eat (and who will drink, *see* Commentary) *and who will enjoy if not I?* Similarly 6.7: A man only labors for his mouth but the appetite is never filled. Obviously this can only come from personal experience. Other examples from personal observation are: 1.3;6.12 ("who can tell a man what will be after him under the sun") 9.3;12.5 ("For the man is going to his everlasting resting place . . .") cf. 6.1; 8.6.17.

Unusual on a number of counts is the passage at 8.8. On the surface the translation would run: no man has power over the wind to restrain it, and none has control over the day of death; there is no divesting of armor in the day of battle (*see* Commentary); nor does wickedness allow its perpetrators to escape. Disjointed as these ideas seem to be, in Qohelet's chain of neuroses all these statements actually hang together. The verse should be interpreted as follows: 'adam, first of all, is Qohelet himself. He finds that he cannot govern and hold in check the overriding drives of his instincts ($ruah$="spirit," "whim", "drive"). Tossing him hither and yon, they carry him headlong to death, the punishment that is inevitable, and always threateningly near; in this conflict, there is no letup ("battle," a familiar symbol is the conflict of the instincts: the ego and the counterego, the conscious and the unconscious, the id and the ego/superego in Qohelet's psyche); there is never any divesting of one's armor for a respite in this struggle: (Qohelet never has any inner peace); and finally criminality (criminal thoughts) never allows the unfortunate Qohelet to escape (agitation, forebodings of punishment, compulsions).

This last proposition, regarded by some commentators as antagonistic to the spirit of Qohelet, pietistic, a piece of moral theology, is rather one of the most characteristic indices of Qohelet's obsession. His hostile antisocial impulses for aggression that he strives to surmount (repress) with resolutions, oaths, imperatives to the self, compulsions, vows to one's ego, and death clauses only embroil and commit him again and again, and chain him with firmer fetters which Qohelet cannot burst and free himself.

Qohelet is paralyzed by a number of fears which centers around his inner core. The book repeatedly enjoins that one should fear God (5.6;12.13) and only the one who fears God will achieve salvation (7.18;8.12). Moreover, one must be careful of uttering too many words before God (lest unseemly words of defiance burst through). More worthy of attention, however, is 4.17, a key passage in the phobia nexus of Qohelet. The gist of the passage is: Watch your step when you go to the House of the Lord; and it is better to keep your mouth shut than to give a sacrifice that fools give; for they do not know what an evil action really consists of. Why should one be wary when one goes to the House of the Lord? Why is it dangerous? Contrast the Psalmist who encourages his brethren to go to the House of the Lord in throngs. It is clear that Qohelet knows that in coming within the precincts of the Temple that danger and mortal injury may lurk there. What is it that terrifies Qohelet? The answer is not far to seek. It must be the fear of the terrible punishment that God would inflict upon him for the heinous thoughts and criminal aggressions which he may have harbored within himself: death wishes for his wife, and/or the incestuous desires that he had for his sister, and/or the murderous thoughts to kill his own father—all these awesome crimes, one or all three, freighted with the most dire punishment that society has imposed from time immemorial——gave Qohelet the most crushing sensations about himself. It has been pointed out that the neurotic may be as much conscience stricken by his fantasies as if he actually committed the misdeed. He now looks for punishment; he feels that he deserves it; but as a parapathetic doubter he never knows whether he has adequately atoned and compensated for his crime. What is this punishment? For incestuous relations the punishment is *death.* The punishment that he unconsciously and imminently administers to himself, is conceived to be more awesome, inflated, and drastic when executed by God, who is really the surrogate for his father. Within the Temple area, there is the very stark apprehenseion that a slip of the tongue, a thought that might insinuate itself, some inner curse would bring down on his head a wrathful thunderbolt, an arbitrary and fierce punishment that his father used to administer without meaning or cause. Qohelet never knew the God of the Psalmist, the God of the heart, of mercy and compassion.

The portrayal of Qohelet is beginning to fill in with lines more firmly drawn: the depreciation of himself, his symbolizations as an *'adam,* a mere person of no worth, his identification with *kesil,* the dog, the misbirth, his respect for wealth, the antithetic fashion with which he formulates his doubts, the phobias that frighten him, his apprehensions what time will do to him in old age, and the compulsions that beset him and occupy this time, his ill luck—all serve to delineate the unhappy condition of this man. The portrait, however, is not yet finished. We have yet to deal with the more basic eternal verities that affected Qohelet's existence: his relationship with his father, with sexuality, with life and death.

Children are aliens and we treat them as such.
                                                    —Emerson

*The words a father speaks to his children in the privacy of the home
are not overheard at the time, but as in a whispering gallery, they will
be clearly heard at the end and by posterity.*
                                                    —Jean Paul Richer

IX

The Links Form a Chain

It is well established that the relationship between an inferior and
superior, or in the discussed instance of Qohelet, between himself and
his attitude toward God and His power, really follows through and is a
replica of the relationship between a man and his father. Now the word
"father" does not occur in Qohelet. However, the word "sun" occurs
some thirty times in grim and forbidding associations e.g., 2.11: "and
behold everything is futility and illusory; and there is nothing
worthwhile under the sun"; 4.1: "the evil under the sun"; and
especially in association with *ra'*, "evil," 5.12;6.1;10.5, very much like
La Rochefoucauld's idea that the sun is evil in his apothegm: "It is
impossible to look at death and the sun steadily."[53] By the common
consensus of Freud, Stekel, Rank, Jung, Reik, Jones and Roheim in their
investigations of dreams related by their patients, the sun is identified
as the substitute for the father.[54] It is quite probable that Qohelet's
father, for whatever period Qohelet knew him, was not the most genial
or kindly of men: stern, forbidding, vindictive, unforgiving (Qohelet
never uses the words "forgive," or "mercy," or "compassion," or
"kindness," either as verbal or nominal formations), and Qohelet never
forgot him. The terror and cruelty that Qohelet experienced as a child
carried through in his later experience in his attitude towards God.
Doubtless there were the malignant wishes that his father would die.
Qohelet could barely pray to God, and sacrifice (4.17) was to a
participating Qohelet much too close, uncomfortable, perilous. This
apprehension of retribution which he expects and dreads is central to
Qohelet's inner life.

The truth is that Qohelet never escapes *shemesh. The sun is always*

60

watching him even as his father did. The living father and the dead one—the eternal sun, the direct manifestation of God in the heavens and the old dead father—merge into a collage, into a never-ending continuity in time, a signal again of Qohelet's neurosis. The vanished father has more influence on him now than the living one had. This is the poignancy of 3.15: whatever is or was remains the same. But one thing is sure: God harasses me constantly. God-father-shemesh watch his every move (compare also the restored text at 5.19).[55]

Qohelet also has a different, secret frustration that focuses on to the inner core of his being. The passage in 9.13-16 recounts an experience which Qohelet himself considered in his own words "highly significant":

There was a small town with but few persons in it; a great king surrounded and besieged it; its doom was apparently settled. There happened to be a poor but wise man there and he rescued the city through his strategy, but, concludes Qohelet, "Nobody remembered that man [me]. Then said I [note again the change over from the third to the first person] I still maintain that brain is better than brawn; nevertheless, the intelligence of the poor man is held to be of no value, and his words are not heeded."

It is apparent that Qohelet at one time participated in a military experience of some sort. Observe that Qohelet in his little book makes use of military terms, weapons, and soldiery on a number of occasions. ("war" or "battle" 8.9;9.11; "weaponry" 9.18; "battle-ax" 10.10; "soldiers" (?) *ibid.*) and the present passage. Qohelet probably exaggerates the role he played. It does not seem likely that a "great king" would spend his time besieging a small town, a task he would relegate to lieutenants. However that may be, the episode purports to contrast the "great king" with a "poor wise man." Undoubtedly Qohelet, who was not in command, contributed some advice, intelligent enough to break the siege, but his suggestions did not receive the proper recognition or appreciation. Not all heroes get medals. Here again we perceive the frustration of Qohelet and how strongly he feels his disappointment. The marked emotion, "And no one remembered that man [me]!" he expresses with crestfallen wistfulness. All his life Qohelet worked, attended, served faithfully at the king's court, never advanced anywhere, and remained unesteemed and miserable. This, too, is to him a cardinal frustration.

It should be remarked incidentally that in such statements suffused with emotion and outburst, we find a true index, a revealing index of Qohelet's feeling, and not contrastedly when he endeavors to philosophize. Even so, his philosophizing masks the inner doubt and discord of the man. As Strindberg had occasion to say, behind every thought there slumbers an emotion. Thus in chapter one, where Qohelet reflects on the seeming futility of nature, that the sun rises and sets, and continues on its monotonous round, and the wind makes the rounds going back to its abode (see Commentary), and the river waters circulate to and fro—all these perpetual aimless motions are observations really not of nature's processes, so much as a reflection of Qohelet's confused state of mind. Moreover, the sun, wind, and water (and so Jung) are symbolically the great fructifying powers that have failed in him (*Symbols of Transformations*, p. 251). The cycle of the sun, wind, and rivers round and round are a demonstration of a certain cyclothemic tendency in Qohelet: he too is going around in circles: the winds that whirl around are his thoughts. The judgment that Stekel made on one of his patients would suit Qohelet very well:

"Life is a circle round which we get back to the beginning . . .He [the patient] is weary of life and would be glad to die. [But] he will have to wait till death. Death wishes with regard to his wife may have induced a sense of guilt which discloses itself as a suicidal impulse [no one kills himself without having wished to kill another] . . .There are always two ways of doing things, and he is subject to continual ups and downs . . ."

A number of key words are employed by Qohelet which again mirror his attitude toward the fundamental life verities of sexuality, life, and death; however, they articulate again his antipodean tendencies of doubt and tension.

Sexuality: Qohelet uses the *ra'ah,* "see," on frequent occasions and with different meanings. The term *ra'ah tobah,* "enjoy oneself," literally "see good," is characteristic of his mode of expression, the verb frequently signifying "enjoy" 4.8;5.17; with *tob* in 2.3.24; 3.12.13;6.12. What is the "good," and what is the "seeing/enjoying" that Qohelet recommends? Now the "eye" that patients report about in dreams turns out to be an organ of pleasure. Gutheil considers it to be feminine in character: it is receptive, and it has a vulvate quality. On the other hand, since symbols are bisexual too, and indeed all organs may be regarded as both masculine and feminine, the eye likewise possesses power and energy: one may challenge with the eye (compare the Hebrew *'oyen,* 1 Sam. 18.9); it may be reckoned as a masculine organ. Freud considered round eyes in dreams as symbolic of testicles.[56] Any part of the body that yielded pleasure (an erotogenic quality as he called it), even internal organs, may be a substitute equivalent for the genital. It may be the mouth as in thumb-sucking, or *it may be the eye as in the delight in seeing* (italics added).[57]

Qohelet advocates as the best life plan for a man "to eat, drink, and 'see' good." This would be the substitute satisfaction for sexual pleasure and experience, denied Qohelet. "See" in English slang means to "coit with a woman" and, collaterally, means to "enjoy" as in the expression to "see a breeze=enjoy the breeze (Partridge, *Dictionary, op.cit.*). "Eat" is likewise a symbol of sexual pleasure, as in Prov. 30.20 ("So it is the way of the adulterous woman: she ate and wiped her mouth and says 'I did not commit a sin!'". Compare similarly the symbolic action of Nora in Act I of Ibsen's *Doll's House*, where Nora eats the cookies. Conversely, hunger may symbolically represent desire.

Thus the conception that seeing=sexual fulfillment undoubtedly underlies the significance of the verse in 5.10: when prosperity increases, those who enjoy it increase too, but what advantage is there to those who consume it save in the beholding of it with one's eyes [58]. Ostensibly the latter part of the verse means that the rich man only enjoys his wealth through the sight of his wealth alone (Levy, *Das Buch Qoheleth*, p. 96). This, however, is palpably and empirically untrue. Anyone can see the rich man enjoying his wealth. For Qohelet, however, with his sexual neurosis and his yearning for happiness, inconsistent as usual and probably under the greater pressure and drive of his longing, considers wealth for the moment as of lesser consequence. The passage bears the signification: When prosperity increases, more persons may participate. But fundamentally, what good is it all if a man is deprived of sexual fulfillment?

The same idea is expressed basically at 10.19: for hilarity, people prepare a party; and wine stimulates to life's joy; but money supplies everything. It is well known that *kesef*, "money" is a sexual symbol. The homonymous *kasaf* as a verb means "yearn," "long for." Again, Qohelet unconsciously discloses the latent observation: one may attend parties, and wine is the elixir of living; but only sexual satisfaction and fulfillment, the fundamental expression of the life instinct, countervails all.

On other occasions, Qohelet employs "see" with an entirely different connotation, with special application to himself, i.e., "I saw," some eighteen times. Typical are: (3.16): "And moreover I saw under the sun, in the place of justice, wickedness was there; and in the place of righteousness, wickedness"; 4.4: "Again I saw that all labor and excelling of work was but a man's rivalry with his neighbor." This

persistent "seeing" on the part of Qohelet with the repetitive
scene-shifting ("And again I saw," etc.) are an index of the
retrospection which Qohelet shares with many other neurotics who
feel that their lives have been a failure, who are looking back as if in a
theater upon the drama of their lives. This of course illustrates the
melancholy regret with which Qohelet surveys his life gone by.
Pertinent in this connection is 4.1: "Again I saw all the exploitation
that is done under the sun, and behold the tears of the oppressed and
there is none to give them relief" (see Commentary); and "power is in
the hands of the oppressors, and there is none to give them surcease."
One notices first of all the aforementioned surcharged emotion in the
verse about the woeful condition of the poor and the exploited, not the
reflection of the rich man. This is obviously Qohelet again, and he is
identified manifestly with the 'ashuqqim, the downtrodden, with
whom he empathetically associates himself.

Death: All mortals to some degree fear death, hate death. To some it
is a frustration (H.G. Wells). Others console themselves that it is a law,
not a punishment. Qohelet likewise fears death but in a different
fashion, from a different perspective. Because Qohelet is torn by bipolar
tension and cannot resolve his doubts, his attitude towards death is
ambivalent: He fears death and at the same time welcomes it.

The sex instinct is the clearest manifestation of the will to live.
Suppression of the sexual instinct, or because it is denied him by law or
morality, e.g., because of a fixation either on his mother or sister, leads
to the rise of its opposite, the death-wish. Moreoever, the death-wishes
that Qohelet has for his wife and which in turn merits punishment by
death through *poena talionis* ("an eye for an eye, a tooth for a tooth")
not only makes him anticipate and fear death; he sees ghastly images of
his own death in repeated scenes as if they were heralding his own.
This decidedly makes him fearful. The chapter that sets forth his own
death scene is of course chapter twelve:

Before man goes to his grave,
And the mourners go about in the streets. . .
Before the dust returns to the earth as it once was
Before the spirit returns to God who gave it.

Qohelet is watching his own funeral, for something has already died
within him.

On the other hand, Qohelet welcomes death: "better is the day of
death than the day of birth" (7.1); "better to go to the house of
mourning than to go to the house of feasting" (*ibid.* v.2); "better the end
of a thing than its beginning" (V.8); "I praise the dead over the living"

(4.2). In a number of verses, nevertheless, and for the moment when hope springs eternal, and because of his pathologic tension, he regards life as a good: 9.4–6: "For he who has still a hold on life, there is hope, for a living dog is better than a dead lion. For the living know that they shall die, but the dead know nothing." And similarly in 8.17: "Why die before your time?"

While death is to be feared because of the eventual punition for his death wishes, why should he welcome death? The answer is to be found in c.12, unmistakably suggesting his impotence (p. 24). That which bids him to behold death with welcome is the *tedium vitae*, the loss of interest and motivation in living, his hopelessness about life, his frustration stemming from his sexual maladjustment and incompetence, his melancholia bound up with the unfortunate alliance with his wife, the loss of his beloved for whom he longs but is denied, the steady physical portentous deterioration (as Qohelet sees it), and sexual depletion. Death is nothing; he has already expired inside. He faces the horror of long vacant years *(horror vacui)*, of isolation, deprivation of being cared for, the lack of one to love and be loved, the finality of enjoyment and happiness, the contempt of superiors. He would be happy to die. This is the reason, as Stekel has argued, that there are certain individuals to whom death would signify happiness, and the dread word "death" finds association with happiness.

Qohelet's preoccupation with death and its terrors, and his apprehension over what old age would do to him unquestionably were conducive to additional dark thoughts. Anticipations of suicide and even procedures as to how to carry out an end to his existence, in common with other persons who have such dark premonitions and plans, undoubtedly were present in Qohelet too. "Better death than birth" (7.1). Suicide, the death wish, the denial of life, rises when the significant sexual object becomes impossible to attain. The compulsive starts to speculate about death, and considers at times on impulse, at times in lengthy deliberation, the whole idea and means of suicide. Self-punishment is a contributory factor in the fleeting speculation, as well as the sympathy he would gain from sorrowing relatives and acquaintances. Nevertheless, suicide never took place with Qohelet (compare Stekel, *Compulsion*, 290). Ideas of self-destruction become submerged in the larger confluence of obsessions and compulsions that preoccupy him. His doubt, the old old shadow, would inhibit his action. But there is another factor too that played its role: his creative impulse, or as Rank would put it in his *Art and the Artist*,—his desire to immortalize himself by writing. As we shall see, it was the writing and the composing of his book that served as a saving cathexis (p. 87).

Burial: It may be noted too that Qohelet mentions burial twice (8.10;6.3), the latter in a puzzling connection. The passage in 6.3 runs in effect: If a man beget a hundred children, and live many years, but did not have his fill of pleasure, *and moreoever he had no burial,* I say that an abortion would be better than he. Why is this question of burial set disjointedly in the context of this verse, and inserted anticlimactically as if a life of blessing (longevity and many children) would be completely at naught, and futilely lived if there is no burial at the end? Why is Qohelet so concerned with proper burial?

The solution to this question does not admit of one answer. Heidel[59] has pointed out that in Babylonia failure to bury the dead made it impossible for the spirit to gain admittance to the underworld and find its rest there. Failure to supply the dead with food for its journey would inflict on him pangs of hunger. Deprived of food, the spirit was compelled to roam around the world and feed on garbage thrown out in the street (compare the closing passage in the Gilgamesh Epic, Pritchard, *Ancient Near Eastern Texts,* p. 99) or eat clay, or drink dirty water in the subterranean realm of the dead (cf. Ishtar's descent into the underworld, pp. 108, 109). Were he not to be interred in the earth properly, he could not have any rest at the last. Elsewhere in folklore too "the dead without proper funeral rites cannot rest in the grave."

Undoubtedly some of these feelings affected Qohelet as well. Certainly at the grave, as we learn from Tobit,[61] food was set aside for the dead in the popular religion. At any rate, Qohelet would know that mourners would be gathered at his grave. In addition, since Qohelet took special care of his body (2.24;8.15;9.7.8;12.1) (according to the restored text: "be mindful of your health") he was quite apprehensive that his body might be desecrated by others (beasts, vultures, man) if unburied. But knowing Qohelet as we increasingly do, the answer in the main must be that one who is unburied will not be honored by a visit to the grave, will hardly be remembered or revered by the setting up of a monument, even though he may have had a hundred children. The ultimate and most grievous curse in the Bible is that one's name will not be remembered (Jer.11.19; Ps. 83.5; Job 24.20; etc.) and among other peoples as well, as in Sophocles' *Antigone:* "A corpse unburied, unhonored, and all unhallowed." *Qeburah* does not only imply burial but associatively the lament by the family, the eulogy by friends (8.10), threnody by the professional mourners[62] with a monument or tombstone and his name graven on it. Tombstones and monuments of course were known in biblical times (2 Kings 33.17; Jer. 31.20) with the purpose that the dead be remembered (Ez.39.15). It is therefore quite likely that Qohelet was haunted by both considerations: to have his honor and name memorialized at the end and to rest in peace in his grave (return to the womb).

Cursorily it might be assumed that Qohelet, with his skepticism, uncertainty, and doubt, and his tacit inner defiance was a heretic, an irreligious man. True as this is, it is not absolutely so. If he prayed, it was with two minds. The words issuing from his lips may have been fervent, but his mind was watching. He never suggests that one should pray to God for guidance or help, or pray for the salvation of the Jewish people. As a human being he must have articulated at some time some prayer, but it was never a wholehearted fervent one. His doubt blighted his fervor.

> *I looked to heaven and tried to pray*
> *But or ever a prayer had gusht*
> *A wicked whisper came and made*
> *My heart as dry as dust.*
> —*Rime of the Ancient Mariner*

While he has an abiding skeptical outlook and mood, it is only intermittently so. His skepticism simultaneously is modified by a pietistic alternate—a second thought emanating from his doubt (8.12 and elsewhere). So we see him observe the forms: he goes religiously to the House of the Lord (4.17), and he watches and listens to the ritualistic proceedings there; and he reads his Bible (5.3). Of course, on another level his exaggerated obedience is another example of self-punishment, perhaps over-defensiveness too (8.2–5).

Many actions that Qohelet would seek to perform were not carried through without a struggle in his inner psyche. At the start he would seek to be good, kind, charitable and just, well-disposed, and helpful—which might be termed an anagogic trend. We see this in his pronouncements in chapter seven, for example, where he avers it is better to listen to the rebuke of the wise than to listen to the praise of fools (v.5); or the heart of the wise man is in the house of mourning (v.4); or better to go to the house of mourning than a house of feasting (v.2). On the other hand, the doubts arising from bipolar tensions, and which impel him to carry through the more malign alternate, attract him to downward trends. His compulsions play their role too. All this is reported again and again in the analysis of neurotics: how guilt feelings inhibit strivings, how the need for punishment circumvents the development of personality, how their criminal aggressive tendencies defuse their defiance. Whatever urgings come from the environment, the worldly conventions for success or even a goal in life, the patterns that demand a cultural upbringing, the mores of the group that require achievement—all these are stymied by the sense of guilt which forbids and freezes.

Ill-health: Qohelet not only suffered from mental anxiety *(Angst)* but from physical ill health as well. In 2.23 he writes in effect: For all his (my) days are pains, vexation, and trouble *(='inyan)* and he *(=I)* does not rest at night; 5.16: for all his days he eats sparingly, and in much vexation, sickness and malaise; 8.16: for neither day nor night does he enjoy sleep. His mental agitation psychosomatically may also be seen from express passages where Qohelet has disturbing dreams (5.2.6) which do not let him sleep and which Qohelet in his good sense manfully tries to annul and devalue. We may reasonably surmise that Qohelet suffered, as many neurotics similarly complain, of insomnia, anxiety, irritability, indecisiveness, self-reproaches (the latter a sign of guilt feelings).

Because of Qohelet's compulsion to punish himself and yet overcontrolling himself, he deprives himself of food, enjoyment, luxury, and contentment so as to atone for his real or fancied misdeed. The key passage referred to previously is 4.8: the lone man, without relatives, and no end to his work or his desire for more wealth ("why do I labor and deprive myself of enjoyment?"). By implication 2.18: and I hated my work that I labored at, to leave it to a man who will come after me! The antisocial aggressions that he entertained forced Qohelet into ill health. Compulsive neurotics cannot assume in their minds that they have good health, and cannot live without some kind of symptoms. A typical oath formulated in their minds, and akin to the vows of children, might run: As long as I suffer from pain, I am saving or sparing my father (or my mother, or my beloved) from being stricken or dying. Qohelet might frame his formula: If I suffer pain, perhaps God will spare me further punishment and may prolong my life. This is the motif behind the fasting of most penitents. Still, Qohelet is not quite sure that he has fully atoned for his crime(s). Neurotics are never certain that they have carried through their atonement (compulsions) in full measure, and so they must perform their compulsions again and again.

According to Stekel, moreover, pain may be interpreted in other facets as well. Emerson put it succinctly: "There are people who have an appetite for grief; pleasure is not strong enough, and they crave pain.''

Thus pain may represent not only punishment for an old sin but it may be a reminder too of an old forbidden pleasure which Qohelet is desirous to atone for; or better yet, the pains are retained as a souvenir of memories which should be suppressed but are not, perhaps serving both as punishment and reminder, that is, both as a reproach and pleasure to conceal the desire of that very first experience. It would be quite safe to say in conclusion that Qohelet's ill health was perennial—that he could not tolerate a life without pains and compulsions.

There is another interesting passage in Qohelet which depicts another side to the neurotic pact that he formulated and adhered to. The book evinces no evidence that Qohelet proffered aid to anyone in distress, again a facet of a neurotic pact. In 7.16 he affirms: Don't be righteous overmuch, or be too wise; why be derided for your pains? (see Commentary). Be not evil overmuch and don't be foolish. Why die prematurely? First we note the antithetic statements, the quandary of bipolar tension. The suggested advice in verse 16 interpretatively is: Don't be too good, and don't be too smart. You will be the loser in the process. Now, what should be the reason for this? The answer seems to be that certain individuals refrain from doing good, or from aiding the unfortunate because they feel they will bring upon themselves misfortune—a neurotic pact. Qohelet might have well said: I will not do good to anyone; then harm will not come to me, i.e., have nothing to do with people who are unfortunate lest misfortune rub off on you by association (infection). The Midrash to Qohelet (Ḥoreb 95.7) remarks: ''This is what people say, 'Don't do favors for an evil person and harm will not befall you. If you have performed an action for an evil doer, you yourself have done evilly.' '' If you are saintly, you will suffer! Cleverness too might lead one into trouble, rather than the simple common sense in conduct, very much in the spirit of Pope's line: ''Be good, sweet maid, let those who will be clever.'' We understand now Qohelet's remark in the context: why die before your time?

Reference has been made to Qohelet's concern about his body. He also pays careful attention to his attire. In 9.8 we read: ''At all times let your clothes be white, and don't spare oil on your head.'' Wearing white clothes has a special significance for Qohelet. Note that this is a deviation from the well-known parallel in the Gilgamesh Epic:

Let thy garments be sparkling fresh,
Thy head be washed; bathe thou in water.

Pay heed to the little one that holds on to thy hand,
Let thy spouse delight in thy bosom!
For this is the burden of (mankind)!

It will be noted that Qohelet deviates from the Gilgamesh passage in three particulars. Mention has been made previously that in his culling of the Gilgamesh passage for his own purpose at 9.7f. he did not include—he annulled—the reference to the "little one" for the dislike and suspicion about his son. It is also clear that he wants his clothes to be white rather than "fresh," meaning clean. Moreover, instead of the head being washed, Qohelet advises that one should not spare oil on one's head. The differences at first glance seem not to be momentous but Qohelet strives for other objectives. As Stekel puts it,[64] "Resistance dreams betray as much as they desire to hide; they show us the central idea of the parapathy." It is well known that *beged* has a number of meaningful connotations. The word means "cloak," but in the verb the root signifies "play falsely, play treacherously" (cf. "to cloak one's actions"); *beged* also means "treachery" in the noun (Is. 24.16; Jer.12.1). Thus clothes may serve as a dissemblance for one's inner thoughts, and so Nietzsche: "An adornment is also a concealment." Clothes may serve as a sexual device to attract, as in the case of a woman in her sexual adornment, and equally, on the other hand, to serve as a protection against the world in the form of encompassing cowels, veils, or even sunglasses, etc. But as the nineteenth-century Samuel Butler affirmed, "Our minds want clothes as much as our bodies." For Qohelet, and so we would interpret our verse at 9.8, clothes should always be white to dissemble and conceal his black thoughts within. Brides wear white for virginal purity, and so similarly inner impulses may be covered up by dressing in decorous propriety. A parallel observation is made by L. Edel in his study of Hawthorne's symbolism in the analysis of Dimmesdale, the minister-paramour of Hester in *The Scarlet Letter*. While the cleric symbolizes all that is pure, and is a paragon of godliness, "The whole of Dimmesdale's robes is really a covering for blackness," and Edel adds, the name suggests the man.[65]

While the Gilgamesh Epic reads: "Thy head be washed," the biblical verse in 9.8d counsels that one should pour oil on one's head, i.e., on the hair to keep it down, so that the hair is not unruly or wild, which may give the impression that your thoughts are disorderly (and this Qohelet does not want others to know). More importantly, oil was employed to break the spell of evil spirits, and so oil was needed for

Qohelet's anointment every day.[66]

Qohelet would dearly love to talk, to converse freely and impulsively. Unfortunately, Qohelet found himself in an irremediable dilemma. As an official, mediately attending at the court, he had to be measured and diplomatic in what he had to respond to (with a good dose of doubletalk and doubtlethink) and not to blurt out what he had at the top of his head. With his obsessions and neuroses, moreover, he was in an intolerable situation. He may have even possessed a stammer; words in the mouth of the wise, he says, are with grace; the lips of the fool make him *swallow* his words. Stammering may have the semblance of swallowing. The *kesil* starts his discourse foolishly, and finishes with incoherence (10.12–13); the fool (i.e., Qohelet's counterego) talks volubly, and repeats himself constantly—all this a sign that it is a persistent trouble. Qohelet can not focus on the main point and idea without a good deal of verbiage, which he pours forth when required, and which he strives to correct while talking but can not do competently. As much as he desired to talk, he had to be restrained in the presence of his superior. This is the behest to watch the king's countenance (so the restored text by Ginsberg) in 8.2, and he who keeps the king's order won't get into trouble. Of course, these signs, too, of an excessive obedience on Qohelet's part is another bit of evidence of his self-punishment according to the well-known formula that an overzealous obedience is the repression of a rebellious attitude.

While we have remarked on the darker side of Qohelet's personality, his apprehension about death, his melancholia, the search for his lost love, his self-denial, the valuelessness of his work, the suppression of memory, annulment, oath clauses and vows, isolation, omnipotence of thoughts, concern about "time," compulsions, split in personality, self-denigration, we may be in a position now to assess in a trial balance another side of Qohelet's psyche and temperament. There is a certain sturdiness of character, a pragmatic levelheadedness, an objective appraisal of a complex circumstance, a certain keel while riding at anchor. This equilibrium paradoxically originated from his own doubt. *He is doubtful of his own doubt.* In the other strengths in his makeup, this doubt proved in a large measure his veritable salvation and life preserver.

Throughout the world, and particularly in Qohelet's country of Babylonia, dreams played a most significant role. The Greeks and Romans recognized dreams as prophecies, similarly the Bible as in Joseph's, Pharaoh's and Nebuchadnezzar's dreams, and most interestingly by Freud and his school. The great legal authorities 'Abayye and

Raba in Babylonia, resorted to soothsayers for interpretation of their dreams. We are surprised that Qohelet had scorn for dreams and combatted their significance. We should have expected that Qohelet would have been overwhelmed by them as having portentous, dark signification. At 5.6 in condemnation he conjoins "dreams" with *habalim*, "vain things, delusions." Similarly, he regarded magic, sorcery, incantations with disdain (5.6;6.11). In Babylonia, the air swarmed with demons, evil spirits, male and female, with a bewildering number of names, and people profoundly believed in their power (compare the pious author of Tobit and his belief in the potency of Asmodeus). Qohelet will have none of it: "Fear God alone" (5.6).

In another direction, we see the value that Qohelet places on intellectual endeavor in his latent thought. He may express consciously how he is skeptical of ḥokma, what value does it have, and indeed is it attainable at all, but we perceive nonetheless how, latently, he puts his trust in mind and reason. Thus he will say, I gave my mind to study and meditate (1.13); I gave my mind to know wisdom (1.17); my mind was calculating with wisdom (2.3); I tested with ḥokma (7.23.25); he taught the people and his disciples (12.9f.).

Similarly, the way he is revolted by injustice, perversion of law in the state, bribery, (3.17; 5.7), we learn of his faith in justice, honesty, and integrity in government. He believes in government and has respect for authority (10.16f.) En passant, we discern that he has courage in the face of adversity (7.13), he praises experience (6.9), and one should explore life to the full (9.10), and if people are alive, they have hope (9.4). Most interesting is the fact that he unconsciously believes in and yearns for love (9.6;7.28) and that rewards do come to a man *(sakar)*. Life therefore has some sweetness (11.7), and if tragic, nonetheless must be lived.

The earlier in life the first fright occurs, the more dangerous it is.
—Richter.

X
Psychograph of King Solomon

To understand Qohelet's strong identification with King Solomon, it will be necessary to review that monarch's life and activity, and to mark whatever elements in his biography fascinated Qohelet, and which he discovered to have counterparts in his own life. We may start our inquiry by asking a seemingly artless question: Why did the prophet Nathan seek to name the second newborn infant Yedidyah; "Beloved of God," but his parents King David and Bath Sheba set this name aside and called him Solomon (II Sam. 12.24-25)?

The answer to this question must take us back to David's first encounter with Bath Sheba (II Sam. 11.2). Every evening (note the definite article: *le 'et ha-'ereb*) David took an airing on the roof of the palace. One evening he saw a woman washing herself. Commentators use such language as "He sent for her, and completed his lust upon her." It is more likely however, that Bath Sheba seduced David. In the first place, how did it happen that she was taking a bath at a time that David was promenading on the roof and from which he could level his gaze at her? Then too, she enticed him in the most seductive way possible: she was washing herself. Shortly afterward she returned to her home,[67] and then deployed one of the oldest feminine wiles: she informed him that she was pregnant. It should not be forgotten that her husband Uriah was for some time at the war front; she was open to adventure; she may have had secret court ambitions.

It may be assumed that David, for his part, had had many sexual experiences: he had six wives, and nineteen sons, and a minimum of ten concubines which he left, as is reported, in Jerusalem when he fled from Absalom, to say nothing of the daughters which the biblical sources say that he had but which they do not name or enumerate.[67] While the Book of Samuel states that Bath Sheba was a very beautiful woman, which may be discounted for the moment as David could have had any maiden he wanted (I Kings, chapter one), Bath Sheba intrigued David on two counts: he watched her bathing with all the titillation of a

73

voyeur gazing at someone who was apparently unaware that she was being observed, and secondly, he knew that as the wife of one of his most prominent officers—Uriah the Hittite was one of the so-called *Thirty,* i.e., distinguished heroes (II Sam. 23.29)—she was a tabooed object, a forbidden married woman. David, in a quandary, sent for Uriah, slyly suggesting a furlough, but Uriah would not think of pleasuring himself while his comrades were in field. David then contrived to have Uriah killed in battle. When a son was born to Bath Sheba, David was much taken with him—the fruit of forbidden love. The prophet Nathan condemned the illicit union; the child was stricken and shortly died. Subsequently another child was born.

Nathan the prophet sent word that the second child should be called Yedidyah, "beloved of God," meaning that now all was clean and legal. The parents persisted however in calling the child Shelomoh (Solomon).

It is usual to explain the Hebrew name in a quasi-homiletical way as if it were based on the word *shalom* signifying "peace," and that Solomon as a king of peace had a peaceful reign. The name, however, can scarcely be associated with "peace." It was not known beforehand that Solomon was to be king, and then again his rule was troubled by three serious insurrections (I Kings 11.14.23.26f.)

The root *šlm* means "be whole, complete, fill in, fill out," and philologically cognate with the Aramaic and Syriac, may likewise bear the meaning of "fill in, fill out, follow, take the place of, substitute." Thus in Syriac, say, "follow me along this road," the root *šlm* is employed; the Ammonites succeeded the Moabites" again *šlm* (cf. Payne Smith, *Syriac Dictionary,* s.v.). And so *mashlamanutha,* "succession in the kingdom," *ibid* 307. So the word Shelomoh means "the follower, the substitue one." It is a designation, not a name.[68]

In ancient times, there was a pervasive belief that if a child died and another was born, the parents would not give the second child a name. There was the apprehension that the demon or evil spirit who snatched the first child might very well spirit away the second. This is the reason, for example, that when a Jewish child is dangerously ill, the parents will give him another name to supplement it, or add another name. When a child is not given a name, the demon is not able to find him.[69] This notion was extant and persisted in early Jewish tradition. Thus we have the names *Hilfai,* "the substitute one," varied with *Hilfa, Ilfa, Tahlifa;* for a girl *Tahlafta* (Dalman, *Grammatik* p. 179); Alphaeus in the New Testament (Matt. 10.3; Mark 2.14 and elsewhere) and so even earlier *'aḥer* (I Chron. 7.12) signifying "the other one, the one who came after." In the case of Solomon, the parents David and Bath Sheba, haunted as they were by the awesome sense of guilt for the first child's death as a consequence of their sin, did not want to be responsible for the death of another child.[70]

As Solomon grew up, he had a rough time at the royal court. He competed with eighteen brothers and half-brothers, nine older than he was according to the list (I Chron. 3.1-8) and nine rivals after him. He was in a cross fire, and enjoyed neither the prerogatives of the elders, nor the favoritism of the younger. Then again, his mother was a commoner. She did not have the aristocratic position of Michal, who, after all, belonged to the old royal dynasty of Saul, nor even to the status of Abigail who had been the wife of a wealthy landowner and herdsman—to say nothing of the aspersions bruited about Bath Sheba and how she shamelessly connived to come to court. There seems to have been an attempt at one time to give Bath Sheba an aristocratic pretension by changing her name slightly to *bath shu'a*, i.e., *bath sho'a*, "daughter of a nobleman," daughter of nobility" (I Chron.3.5), but the old name was never displaced but persisted, and with pejorative association.

We also know that of his sons, Absalom was beloved of David despite his act of treason; about Adonijah I Kings c.1 remarks that David never reprimanded him with "why did you do thus and so?" However, it is never mentioned that Solomon was a favorite of David. With Solomon's accession to the throne, it certainly would have been remarked upon in the sources that have nothing but adulatory comment about Solomon. It is quite likely that Solomon was never allowed to forget his inferior status. He was a nobody.

When Solomon came to power, in a plot engineered by Nathan and Zadok but carried through by Bath Sheba in a palace revolution, he got rid of his rivals and opponents summarily and ruthlessly. It is unquestionably true that political motives prompted his actions. It is equally true that Solomon could not tolerate the look in their eyes—the critical senior looking down on the young inferior—that condemned him as a base upstart who gained the throne by fraud, and had the lesser royal claim by every count: he was not the oldest, nor of aristrocatic descent, nor even a legitimate pretender. So he slew his brother Adonijah, executed the old army general Joab, removed Abiathar as High Priest, and put to death Shimei ben Gera—all on the flimsiest pretences (I Kings, c.2). In an understatement, I Kings 2.46 observes that Solomon's kingship was firmly established.

Solomon had seven hundred wives. The explanation usually offered is that he wished to stabilize his borders by marriages. Undoubtedly this consciously played a significant role in Solomon's political policy. But there was a much more fundamental reason. He married all these women to *legitimize* himself. This was an attempt to obscure an unarticulated question that was in everybody's mind: who is this fellow and where did he come from? In the plethora and hubub of the marriages,—in fifteen years, say, there would be about one every week which would keep everyone surprised, and gossipy tongues supplied with fuel—the question would be amply but obliquely refuted: Well, he is the husband of that queen and married to that princess.

Even these seven hundred marriages did not satisfy Solomon. He needed connections with an exalted royal line. The marriage that he negotiated with Pharaoh for his daughter's hand was a brilliant maneuver in Solomon's self-elevation and magnification. It will be remembered that only once before—some four centuries before Solomon[71]—did the Pharaoh deign to allow his daughter to be married to a foreigner. Solomon could now claim royal estate of high order: he was the husband of Pharaoh's daughter. As a mark of his respect, he built for her, rivaling his own (!) a separate palace (I King's 7.8). Correlatively, he was the son in-law of the most powerful man on earth—no, not a man, but a king-god.

Solomon also took to himself three hundred concubines. This shows his contempt for women. When as an adolescent Solomon at the court heard of the moral delinquency on the part of his mother, in the breakup and dissolution of a moral code that he idealized about woman's sweetness and devotion now turned spurious, most assuredly would have he with many an adolescent pronounced a most harsh and cutting judgment: "All women are faithless. They break the sacred vows of devotion and marriage. Without scruple they betray their husbands. They will wantonly give away their love and their virtue to the first man who comes along."[72] Stekel defines this as the "shattering of moral authority."

With regard to Solomon, his feelings of shame and stigma could have been considerably intensified. Did his mother not play the harlot who had betrayed her hero-husband Uriah; and his father David, for all that he was a king—was he not an adulterer as well? And was not David a murderer of an upright man, Uriah, as everybody knew? It is hardly possible that Solomon was not aware of the shameful record of the bastard birth of his brother now displaced on to him ("guilt by association"). He lived on, carrying an historical continuous burden of his brother's illegitimacy. I will not go into detail upon the blood-stained horrifying episode of the beautiful Tamar (II Sam.13.1) half-sister to Solomon, who was raped by her half-brother Amnon, and then shamefully set adrift into the streets. Then Absalom, another half-brother, contrived to have Amnon murdered. The young Solomon at court had to bear the infamy of the greatest crimes known to man: murder, incest, and adultery, a permanent scar in his ill-starred development.

That Solomon was always conscious of this shattering of moral authority is evidenced by a number of circumstances. First of all, the books of Samuel and Chronicles record in what obviously is an official list the name of the king, the wives, and his sons. Thus for Saul there is a list of his three sons and their names, two daughters and their names, and the name of his wife (I Sam. 14.49f.) Similarly David has an official list with the names of his six wives, his nineteen sons (although the daughters remain unnamed;I Sam. 3.2f.;I Chron. 3.1f.). In the case of Solomon, nothing. There is no official list. It is only known incidentally that he had children, one *Bosmat* and one *Tafat* [73] (I Kings 4.11.15) and of course *Rehab'am.* If Solomon were capable of having three children, he must have had more. Chapter five tells of the enormous expense of maintaining his menage: Solomon's provision for one day was thirty kors of fine flour, and sixty kors of meal, ten fat cattle, and twenty cattle fed at pasture, and a hundred sheep, besides harts and gazelles and roebucks, and fowls artificially fed (I Kings 5.2f).

There is no official list, however, even of the most important wives and children, because Solomon suppressed all the records. His steadfast intent was that there should be no more records of aristocratic or noble lineage that might reflect pointedly on Solomon's mean beginnings. Interesting in this connection is the fact that in the replacement of Abiathar as High Priest, Solomon appointed Zadok. Certainly one of the reasons would be that Abiathar had a priestly genealogy dating to before the monarchy, beyond Eli, and therefore was of an old and highborn family. Of Zadok there is no genealogy whatsoever. We merely know his father's name. Records of noble lineage should count for nothing so Solomon determined.

Secondly, we are informed that Solomon loved very many foreign women from Moab, Ammon, Edom, Zidon, and from among the Hittites. It may be questioned whether Solomon married a single Hebrew woman. Even *Rehab'am* his successor was the son of *Na'amah,* the Ammonitess. There would always be from the Hebrew wife of Solomon the smirking chortling remark: "At least my family is cleaner than his!" This Solomon could not tolerate. In the popular mind, and certainly in the mouth of Solomon's detractors, there would always be irreverent reflections and a scent of scandal about his whorish mother, his adulterous father, his bastard dead brother, his murdering half-brother, his raped half-sister. Among the foreign wives with their claim to priorities, with their thoughts of their genealogies and royal lines back home, and the jealous competetiveness with one another, the rights of their children, Solomon's inferior origin would be of little importance or concern. This was Solomon's aim and he calculatingly induced the confusion. He introduced a whole fashion of intermarriage, taken up by the new aristocracy in the boom times of his reign, and all the old records of pure descent counted for nothing. In the new order of things, no Hebrew family could boast of its eminent connections; it was tantamount to *lèse majesté*. The seven hundred wives therefore, with their conflicting claims of their own royal distinctions and their demands for royal favor, blanked out Solomon's family dishonor.

A third index of Solomon's denigration of himself is his attitude towards the royal descent. He deliberately bastardized the whole royal succession. Every king the world over is concerned with entrusting the rulership in proper hands, usually the eldest son. Now, with regard to intermarriage, the Hebrew texts presuppose a strong sentiment against it. Abraham wants a wife for his son Isaac from his own family and not from the daughters of Canaan. Rebecca remarks, that if Jacob were to marry one of the Hittite women, "Why should I go on living?" When Samson wished to marry a woman of the Philistines, his parents objected: Can't you marry a woman of your own people? Miriam and Aaron cast aspersions on Moses when he married a Cushite woman. Those women who come from another nation and marry Hebrews are always designated according to their country of origin: the Cannaanite woman, the Aramaean woman, the Moabite woman, and so on. Of the prohibition against intermarriage in Deuteromony, we shall deal with shortly. There can hardly be any question, however, that only the son of a proper wife could succeed to the throne. Thus the two sons of Rizpah, the concubine of Saul, Armoni and Mefiboshet (II Sam 21.8), are not mentioned in the official list (I Sam. 14.49) and therefore could not legitimately succeed to the throne. Similarly, to take a foreign wife as queen, as Solomon and Ahab did, is roundly condemned (I Kings 11.2;16.31), and their issue could not qualify (Deut. 17.15: you cannot appoint a king over you who is not of your kinsmen).

Now Solomon was suspicious that his son *Rehab'am* was not his own. The first reason for Solomon's suspicions were the thousand-women harem. It may be arithematically if crudely put. If Solomon were to visit with one woman every night—for which he would be famed in history as a *gibbor* rather than a *ḥakam*,—it would take him three years to come around to the first one again. What was she doing all this time with her desire for the love of a man? In the meantime, the 369th wife, say, told him she was pregnant. We can reasonably guess Solomon's reaction: Was it by me? Is this my child, or someone else's? Who knows what goes on in the harem of 1000 women? Not even Solomon and his secret police (I Kings 2.29.41) could know everything.

The second ground for thinking that Solomon had suspicions about Reḥab'am is found in Rehab'am's election by people. Solomon, who had more power than David, could have easily designated Reḥab'am as his successor, very much as David, who had less power, interceded to have Solomon selected as king. But the truth seems to be that Solomon did not care a whit; he did not care about his son: he considered that the boy could have very well been a bastard from among the seven hundred wives. Solomon's thinking ran in the groove of a well known formula: My mother was adulterous: who knows about Na'amah the Ammonitess, *his* mother? Moreover no one concerned himself about me in my debasement and mean status when I was young; why should I be concerned with aiding him? Let him gain his ends and his power himself.

This is essentially a neurotic pact. We may justly say that the evil men do lives after them neurotically. A man will transmit to his son the trauma of his experience, especially that of a sexual character.[74]

In the third place, Solomon's suspicions were prompted by the old fraudulent suspicious relationship between himself and his mother whom he regarded as perfidious and disloyal to her hero husband Uriah. As Solomon grew up at court, everyone supplied him with full information (except his mother) about his adulterously conceived brother, the treachery in the death of Uriah by David, and how his mother got herself pregnant to gain entry into court circles,—all the tidbits furnished by eager malicious brothers and sisters and their baiting, knowing mothers. Solomon was alone; he needed support, but there was none. As an adolescent he had to ponder some very fundamental questions in his mind: Is it absolutely certain that I am the son of David? My mother stayed at first only a few days at the palace and then returned home (*see* 2 Sam. 11.4). Could she have played David falsely too as she acted toward Uriah by making absolutely sure she was pregnant, *and by some one else?* Why could I not have retained the name of Yedidyah, "beloved of God," instead of the name Shelomoh "the substitute one," a *changeling?* Where do I find myself in my family with regard to my full brothers (I Chron.3.5), my step-brothers (2 Sam. 3.3; 1 Chron. 3.3), to the brothers, sons of the concubines, to my non-Hebrew brother (1 Chron. 3.2) to my mother, step-mothers, non-Hebrew step-mother, and all the sisters of high and low degree? If Nathan the prophet intervened to give me a name, and he liked me, why did David and Bath Sheba give the name Nathan, in honor of the prophet, to my other brother? Since all have the same father, where do I stand in all this confusion? *Who am I?* The uncertainty about himself, the question whether he was the son of David really or not—that suspicion is the start and origin of his doubt about Reḥabʿam.

All that Solomon did, the building of his palace (thirteen years) and the erection of the Temple seven years: a true reflection of his religiosity; (I Kings 6.38; 7.1) was only *ad maiorem gloriam Salomonis,* essentially to compensate for the poverty within himself. He thought to become famed for his building, Solomon's Temple, Solomon's Palace (ego building): "See my magnificence but don't look at me!"

Of related interest too is that Solomon had a craze for horses. I Kings 5.6 states that he had forty thousand stalls. Scholars emend to four thousand stalls, as the larger number seems incredible. Not at all. To overcompensate, the puny Solomon needed the outward symbols of power, panoply, control, dazzlement, flourish, spectacle. He also recruited twelve thousand horsemen, fourteen hundred chariots (*ibid* 10.26), the chariots costing six hundred pieces of silver each, and a horse of one hundred pieces of silver, and some five hundred shields made of pure gold (ibid 16-17) all from his Egyptian father-in-law! He made a great throne of ivory, and overlaid it with fine gold; the throne had six steps and the top of the throne was arched at the back; and there were hand rests on either side attached to the seat; and the two lions standing by the handrests; and twelve lions stood on the six steps, on the one side and the other (awesome magnificence, to inspire fear in one who approached the throne; to give courage and confidence to himself). At any rate, no other king had anything like that, as I Kings 10.20 remarks. With his military equipment, Solomon could impress the populace and control them (as the taxes on them were enormous [ibid 12.4] and at the same time indulge his fancy as a great military leader without going to war.

All the building, however, and the display of power, and the splendor did not satisfy an inner need of Solomon; in his urge to glorify himself, he directed his energies to another area of creativity.

Solomon had a sexual problem. In the thousand women that he had—these faces that came and went—he was looking for one woman really. However he could not find her because each woman reminded him, and evoked the distrust and old suspicion inherent in his primary relation and misgivings, about his mother. Solomon, however, resolved his sexual problem by sublimating it *and displacing it onto a literary activity.* In I Kings 5.9f we are informed that Solomon became wiser than all the legendary wise men of the East and Egypt. He composed three thousand *meshalim* and five thousand poems (so the Greek reading correctly). These *meshalim* were compositions, as I Kings 5.12 records, about trees, from the cedar in the Lebanon to the hyssop on the wall and of beasts, of birds, of reptiles and of fish.

The subject matter gives the clue what these *meshalim* were. Not proverbs, as the later tradition mistook the word, and so attributed to Solomon the Book of Proverbs. *Meshalim* here means parables, fables. In the manner of Aesop, Meir, the mishnic authority who composed three hundred fables about the fox, and La Fontaine, so did Solomon compose five thousand poems and, most interestingly, three thousand fables—altogether a fairly good output. The point about the composition of the fables is this: it permitted him to act out with animals and birds, in their relationships, what he could not personally establish with human beings. Since literary activity must have occupied a good deal of his time, it dawns upon us that Solomon wished to achieve fame as a *hakam,* a wise man, a sage. Verse 11 relates that he was far "wiser" than any man, than Ethan the Ezrahite, and Heman, and Kalkol, and Darda, the sons of Mahol. These sound very much like court wits and court poets who gathered at the court of the Sun King. Now the name of Solomon would rise from obscurity by means of his literary creations to the brilliant radiance of Solomon the Sage. We shall see how much this inner world of Solomon influenced Qohelet.

It may be noticed in conclusion that the Book of Deuteronomy warned about Solomon. In Deut. 17.14f. it is stated that if Israel should desire a king like the rest of the nations, a king may be selected with the following stipulations: his origin must be from among the kinsmen of the Hebrew people, i.e., he cannot be a *nocri,* one who is not of Israel (I Kings 8.41). He must not acquire numerous horses, nor import them from Egypt; nor shall he increase the number of his wives unduly, nor aggrandize his hoard of gold and silver, and he shall write a rescript of Deuteronomy, and read it all the days of his life so that his heart shall not be arrogant toward his "brothers." It is apparent that the

Deuteronomist had a certain king in mind with these particular provisions. Who could this king be that he was warning against? It seems to me that this king was Solomon. It was he who married that great number of women and acquired that great number of horses for forty thousand stalls, and so much gold and silver that siver became commonplace as stones, i.e., the bottom dropped out of the silver market (I Kings 10.27). The Deuteronomist also believed, I think, that Solomon introduced on a large scale a disturbing element into Hebrew life—intermarriage. Solomon, by virtue of his position, had introduced a fashionable practice of taking spouses with royal sanction other than Hebrews, giving a setback to Yahwism and the dilution of the ideals of the prophetic party. This is the reason that the Deuteronomist proscribes intermarriage with the "seven nations," and absolutely prohibits a Moabite and an Ammonite from admission into the Hebrew people (Deut. 23.4). He could not go so far with the regulation regarding the Egyptians and the Edomites (*ibid* 23.8.9). The Edomites after all were descendants of Esau the brother of Jacob. The descendants of the Egyptians were a marked segment of the tribes, since Ephraim and Manasseh, the sons of Joseph, had an Egyptian mother. Note also the name Pinḥas, meaning in Egyptian "negro," who served as priest, a grandson of Aaron (Num.25.7). After the third generation, one descended from an Egyptian or Edomite could enter the congregation of the Lord (Deut.23.9). There was the provision, however, that the king had to come from "your kinsmen" and not a foreigner—which points up *Reḥab'am* as a persona non grata, whose mother was an Ammonitess, and therefore not qualified to ascend the throne. Undoubtedly, what was unwritten law before now became codified in Deuteronomy.

A man does not look behind the door
unless he has stood there himself.
—Henri du Bois

Almost all absurdity of conduct
arises from the imitation of those
whom we cannot resemble.
—Dr. Johnson

XI
Qohelet's Identification with Solomon

It is evident that Qohelet read Solomon's biography in the Book of Kings very carefully. He quotes *mutatis mutandis* one verse from Solomon's prayer ". . .for there is no man who does not sin. . ." (I Kings 8.46); compare his version, "No man succeeds to do but good and not sin" (7.20, with a slight reconstruction of the text). His choice of the Kings text is revealing. A great solace was afforded him momentarily: even the wise Solomon affirmed that everyone sins and everyone is guilty. Therefore, he was not alone in the punishment he expected. Then again, he looked back to Solomon's era as a golden age where the common people seemed to be so gay and carefree, "eating and drinking and happy" (I Kings 4.20). The latter words provide the cue for his suggested goal in a man's life, "eat, drink and be merry," which Qohelet, as far as he was capable without too many reservations, affirmed. Qohelet also noticed that Solomon was admired by the Queen of Sheba in that he had "more wisdom and wealth" (this is the meaning of *ṭob*, cf. *ṭub* "wealth"; Latin "bona" goods, property; *ta agatha* "fortune, goods" I Kings 10.7) than even the reports coming to her. Qohelet used the phrase in 1.16.

With his feelings of inferiority, it was a tempting compensation for Qohelet to dream of himself at one with Solomon as the famed Grand Monarch who was, in the Hebraic tradition, the most celebrated legendary rich man of all time. In his fantasy, Qohelet readily assumed the Solomonic activities that he scrutinized in the Book of Kings but translated into his own epoch. He built mansions, parks, groves, canals (Babylonia); he acquired male and female slaves, home-born slaves, herds of cattle; amassed silver and gold, the exotic treasures of kings and faraway provinces; male and female singers, all the delights of men.

Qohelet cannot rise above his station. Unconsciously he has translated royal activities into his own times and on his own terms, and naively ascribes such activities to the king, really the actions of a rich man on a less pretentious scale, one who is climbing a social ladder, not a king at court.

Qohelet recognized, however, that such activities give but temporary satisfaction, following Solomon in this particular regard; he yearned for "wisdom." To the pursuit of *Hokma,* then, Qohelet dedicated himself for he knew he was not wealthy; just as Solomon would be famed as a *hakam,* so would Qohelet.

More proximate in his affinity to Solomon was Qohelet's identification with him in family relationships. Qohelet shrewdly suspected that Solomon was not happy with his wives. The ultimate source of this unhappiness stemmed from their mother/sisters. It is quite likely that Qohelet also suspected, with his sensitive antennae, that Solomon was suspicious that Rehab'am was not his son and had taciturnly spurned him for nomination as successor to the royal throne; similarly, Qohelet, more neurotic and more obsessive, discredited his son as his own. Likewise Qohelet identified himself with Solomon as a lad, except that Qohelet never succeeded in breaking away from his wretched status.

Qohelet was particularly fascinated, elated, and jubilant at his discovery that his name Kansha, more likely to be pronounced Kanosha, was identical with Solomon's.

Names play a very important role in the life of neurotics. Freud remarked on one occasion that an individual unconsciously lives up to his name. R. Eleazar ben Pedat maintained that a man's name influences his life (Ber.7b) *Nomen est omen* ("a name is an augury"). As other investigators have shown, the name of an individual is so significant that in many cultures concealment of one's name is part of one's conduct. The god Re concealed his name, but in extremity revealed his name, and was overthrown by Isis (Pritchard, *Ancient Near Eastern Texts,* p. 13). The angel who wrestled with Jacob, and the angel who appeared to Manoah, actually manifestations of Yahweh's many-faceted presence, would not disclose their names. Were they to do so, Jacob and Manoah would acquire power over them. Possession of the secret name of God, and its pronunciation among the Jews, as well as the employment of the name of Jesus among the Apostles, enable the possessor to perform miracles, heal the sick, cast out demons, etc. Rabbi Meir, the mishnic authority, would not have dealings with anyone who had an evil-sounding name.

Neurotics, and especially those who feel that their origins are obscure, will play with their *names*, changing and distorting them so as to give themselves another persona, another nature, another character. Without a rationale, many actors will change their names similarly. Those who are inferior or who think they are will endeavor to acquire names strongly suggestive of the well known or famous to intimate that they are tied by family to great national leaders, great authors, great scientists, etc. Name-dropping in modern society is a form of this phenomenon.

Qohelet, who undoubtedly believed with his contemporaries in the power of the name for good or evil, mentions *shem*, "name," as if it were tantamount to "existence."[75] He approved the misbirth in 6.4 because its existence would be covered by the grave. Then in 6.10, it is apparent that *shem* signifies "personality, character," and the sense of the passage is that a man's *shem* is irrevocably set with a permanent stamp. In 7.1 Qohelet apparently quotes a proverb that a "name," i.e., renown, fame, glory is better than perfume but he multilaterally *misconstrues* "shem ṭob" as meaning a good existence (!) and then gives his own dour reflection in contrast—not to exist; the day of death is better than the day of birth.

Qohelet, however, also understands "name" in the sense of prestige, and he sought to elevate himself and escape from his prosaic existence by connecting himself with the royal house of David and associating himself with Solomon. Reference may be had at this juncture to the chapter in this book where evidence is given in a conclusive fashion, as I believe that Qohelet was composed in Aramaic. Now the root *knash*, meaning "gather," is found in the Targums and the Peshitta as a translation of the Hebrew *qahal*, and therefore the equivalent of the Hebrew Qohelet represents an underlying Aramaic *kanshah* (the feminine participle). Unfortunately, in the rendering of the Aramaic into Hebrew, the translator *translated* the name instead of transliterating it, and so we have Qohelet instead of kanshah/kanosha just as Ecclesiastes, der Prediger, the Preacher are translations of Qohelet and not a transliteration.

Neurotics moreover scrutinize trifles to uncover matters that they assume to be of great moment, and contrariwise gloss over matters that are really of import and consequence.[76] Stekel, for example, reports of a patient who came to his office quite excited. He had received a streetcar transfer, and thereon printed in significant large numbers were the

digits of his birthday! Astonishing! What could that mean? Now
(Qohelet)–Kanosha in looking closely at the name of Solomon saw that
the letters of his name add up numerically to 375: Shin=300; Lamed=30;
Mem=40; He=5; total 375. His own name added up to the same sum:
K=20; Nun=50; Shin=300; He=5; total 375. Most interesting! Verily, he
could be another Solomon!

KNSH as found in the inscriptions is a good Canaanitish-Aramaic
name.[77] In origin, however, it is not a name but a designation of a man's
occupation. The verb is used for one who gleans or harvests in the
fields, also for sweeping the house (b. Mezia 85a, and Jastrow, 651 and
for the form of Ḥullin 68a, Jastrow, 648, Payne Smith, *Syriac English
Dictionary*, 219, Arabic *kanasa*, "sweep"). It is quite likely that
Kanosha, as his name suggests, was of quite humble origin who worked
in the fields, or inside a house as a sweeper of floors, or, as one name in
the inscriptions probably indicates, as "a gatherer of wood."
Qohelet–Kanosha was so able to advance himself, however, that at the
time of the composition of his book, in the fantasies about himself that
his name was identical with Solomon, he did not hesitate to add the
genealogical designation that he was the son of David. That this leap
was an invention on his part is shown by the fact that after the biblical
David, the latter's name was never used again for an individual for the
next 1600–1700 years as far as the records of the Bible, the Apocrypha
and Pseudepigrapha, and the talmudic records show. Only in the
geonic period did the name come to life again. He could feel that his
name did not signify that he was a simple sweeper but he was a
"reincarnation" of Solomon, if not greater than he. This is one of the
reasons be became a lecturer at the Academy.[78]

The scorn for women, the inferior origin of Solomon, his putative
changeling status, stemming from Bath Sheba's betrayal of her husband
Uriah and her seduction of David, Solomon's legendary reputation as a
framer of proverbs and name as a sage—all this had a marked
fascination for Qohelet–Kanosha. Qohelet, as one impotent, and of
enduring doubt, had ever recurring thoughts too about his wife's
fidelity. Does he not say that he could find a man of rectitude among a
thousand but a woman among all of these thousand (the thousand
women of Solomon symbolically) he could not find? Qohelet also never
mentions his son except indirectly, in a distant and detached way. Like
Solomon, too, he suppressed all the records. In early marriage he had a
son, true enough, but Qohelet became impotent, and on this and other
grounds already discussed suspected his wife's infidelity. The
identification with Solomon through his name Kanoshah, his

fantasying about the Sun King, with the fanciful living in the grand style, Kanoshah's thoughts about his mother/sister, wife and son completed this congruence. Qohelet too wanted to be a *hakam*, a sage greater than Solomon.

Qohelet–Kanosha desired and loved power, glory, fame, wealth, authority, but he never succeeded in attaining these goals. *Faute de mieux*, he became a teacher, a lecturer, and taught groups and classes, balanced couplets in aphoristic wisdom, testing them by experience but withal to countervail his lack of status and a distinguished name by attaining a reputation as a sage. He sought a way to salvation, to use a theological term, a self-fulfillment through creativity. Perhaps at one time happiness could have been achieved through a beloved. Man is born twice, says the proverb, once through his mother, again through his beloved. *Qohelet–Kanoshah achieved a victory for himself, like Solomon, in that he displaced his problems in sexuality onto a literary composition and cathected his neuroses and frustrations.* His propositions do not stem from sagacity or wisdom but from the unconscious, from whose depths of turmoil, cares, strivings, and defeats he speaks to us—and to another important man, his disciple and translator.

A man is not responsible for words spoken in his affliction.
—Baba Batra 16b

A word is not a crystal, transparent and unchanging, it is the skin of a living thought and may vary in color and content according to the circumstances and time in which it is used.
—O.W. Holmes, Jr.

XII
Qohelet's Vocabulary and Syntax

Words transmit different ideas, different images to the mind, to different individuals. A man with neurotic temperament will supercharge with meaning words that have a special signification for him. The dictionaries will give the ordinary meaning; the grammars the usual rules, the common usage. Qohelet seemingly violates these rules frequently.

The special vocabulary and syntax has been remarked upon by all investigators. A goodly number of his words and expressions, even through the diaphonous curtain of the Hebrew translation, seem to be off center. It is quite apparent that he says one thing and means another. In the light of his neurotic complex, however, it is possible to determine the origin of a number of peculiar words and their employment. The collocation of words, both in combination and contrast, will frequently provide a correct insight into his meaning.

For example, Qohelet never uses the term *'abodah,* "work." For him, it is *'amal,* "toil and trouble," for his ordinary work is charged with compulsion and worry. He would love to combine his work, if he only could, with some joy and verve, as if one could combine mysteriously (so Qohelet fondly imagines) work with pleasure (2.24;8.15). Then again *'amal* means "profit, benefit" (compare *le'utha* in the underlying Aramaic, the synonymous *yegi'a)* ascending actually to the Akkadian *nemelu* (C.H. Gordon). Note 4.6 where *'amal* is contrasted with *naḥat,* "satisfaction," meaning obviously "discontent." Then *'inyan,* "business, affair" carries for Qohelet the meaning of "affliction," associated with its verb *'innah,* "afflict, torture," which indeed he puns upon in two instances (1.13;3.10). It is clear that the employment of these words with their melancholy significance derives from both his self-drive and self-punishment; *'ani,* therefore, is not only the poor man but the suffering one as well. And similarly, *ka'as,* normally "anger" (7.3), in contrast to *sehoq,* "hilarity," means not only "agitation" (1.18;11.10; actually these may very well be a nuance that the translator failed to reproduce of the Aramaic *rugza, ritha* which have the meanings both of "anger" and "agitation," compare Jastrow, *Diction-ary* under the respective determinants, both noun and verb) but for Qohelet "sobriety," his inability to smile, to permit himself a momentary pleasure because as he says, "with a downcast face, the mind improves" (7.3). If he had for the moment a sense of joyousness, he would have guilty feelings in complete contrast and inversion of the rational healthy minded epigrammatist in Prov. 15.13, "A happy heart improves the countenance." Contrast Qohelet at 7.3 "With an evil countenance the heart improves." One is reminded here of the observation of Arieti[79] that the difference between the healthy-minded and the disturbed individual is that the latter confuses the subjects and predicates. Thus, one would normally deduce from the statements "All men are mortal" and "Socrates is a man" the correct inference that Socrates is mortal. Not so the ill-minded. If a woman, she may think, "The Virgin Mary is a virgin. I am a virgin. Therefore I am the Virgin Mary." This inversion of Qohelet, too, sponsors the thought in the verse at 7.3 which he may have formularized for himself: "If I am sad, no harm will befall me"—a forestalling neurotic pact.

Allusion has been made to *'et,* "time," fraught, however, with different connotations (see above, p. 44 f), not chronological time but a time that must be filled in with certain individual actions (compul-sions) or the refraining from these acts through fear. The word *'et* imports into its meaning the connotation of judgment and fate because Qohelet is quite apprehensive of judgment (punishment, including death) that will be decided against him, and so, unconsciously anticipating the oncoming calamity, he punishes himself. The meaning of *'et* originates from Qohelet's ambivalence: he has to waste time in pseudo-activities; time is a void which stretches out monotonously without limit; simultaneously he is despondent about the quick passage of time, because as chapter twelve shows, with its description of the old man fading away into death, the time is getting short.

Similarly, Qohelet uses the term *hokma* in a special denotation although it is difficult to pinpoint the meaning with any accuracy. *Hokma* does not only mean "wisdom, sagacity." In Qohelet's usage, it means a certain awareness and danger, the ability to circumvent it, the

capacity to solve a problem rationally, a solution to his frustration
(compare Prov. 14.16: "a wise man is fearful and turns aside from
evil"). A *ḥakam* has vigilance, circumspection, with his guard
mounted: a *kesil* is without brains ("leb"), asinine, vacant, a booby;
siklut, "unruly impulse." On the other hand, *ḥokma* is an aspiration to
the highest ideal (actually his lost beloved); and yet, it is knowledge
how to converse and persuade with grace and flourish as well (10.12f.)

Qohelet pairs off two words with interesting variegation: *tob* and
hote', the good man and the sinner. In the passages where the words are
extant, however, they apparently do not have that meaning. No moral
judgment is predicated as it turns out. A "good" man is one who is
mysteriously favored, lucky, and God imparts to him in addition
wisdom, knowledge, and enjoyment of life. On the other hand, the
hote' is ill favored, hapless (Qohelet himself see pp. 00ff.) and is
burdened with compulsion *('inyan)* to gather and amass (so in the text
at 2.26), and then with dramatic irony hands over his heaped-up wealth
to the one who is well favored.

Yitron, yoter means "addition, excess," hence "profit, advantage."[80]
Then it may mean "remainder, what is left over" (cf. Akkadian *wataru*
and 1.3). For Qohelet, moreoever, *yitron* in some instances means
"compensation, spiritual compensation, satisfaction, psychotic relief"
(1.3; 2.11; 3.9; 6.8). This elucidation is in line with the helpless
situation in which he finds himself. Normal persons find profit in their
work, either money interest, hope for prestige, or whatever. For
Qohelet this is a futility for he is compelled to repeat over and over
again the same action with only partial temporary relief. The word
yitron, therefore, at Qohelet's level signifies ease, release, satisfaction, a
carefree relief from tension.

In a number of instances, *dabar*, "word," is employed with a special
significance in Qohelet's outlook. Thus in 5.6 Qohelet employs the
word in the nexus of "dreams, phantasies, and words in which people
are led astray" (*see* Commentary on "astray"). It is apparent that
"words" here are not vague trailing off, expletives of some sort, but of
some consequence to Qohelet. The Aramaic *miltha*, "word," goes its
own way with a special usage: magical words, hence, magic, sorcery.
The word *miltha* is found in the later literature with this special
pejorative connotation. A *miltha bisha* is a "bad thing" used for
"pollution," *yoma d'abed miltha*, "the day that a man went to the
surgeon to be bled," *miltha dequsmin*, "words of sorcery"; and then
absolutely *'amra 'ihi miltha*, "she spoke a word in magic spell"
(Jastrow, s.v.) and Midr. to Qohelet, (Soncino, p. 29): "The *minim*

worked a *millah* on him," and the spell was broken by R. Joshua who poured oil on his nephew's head. In our verse, Qohelet, while unconsciously in a painful struggle against the power of the spoken word (5.1;6.11), musters courage for the moment to deride magic spells and dreams.

Quite intriguing is the usage of *hebel*, "breath, vapor, gas," which Qohelet employs, sometimes alone, sometimes in combination with *re'ut ruah*, "vain desire" *(but see below)*. *Hebel* obviously means something special to Qohelet. In a number of instances, he clearly implies "outrage," "without purpose" (2.15); "futility, frustration" 2.21; "bane, scourge." 2.23; "wasted effort," 2.26.

The synonym *ruah* (Is. 57.13) meaning "breath, spirit, psyche, animus," exhibits an interesting deployment in the Hebrew Bible. It has, first of all, fermentative, fertilizing power. The Ruah itself can produce, create, as for example Is. 57.16, "because the wind shall go forth from my face, and breathings I will make"; similarly the Vulgate; Ps. 33.6, "With the word of Yahweh the heavens were created, and with the breath of his mouth all their host"; Ps. 104.30, "Thou sendest forth their breath, and they are created." On the other hand, with its potency, breath may be a destroying force: Is. 11.4," with the breath of his lips he will slay the wicked"; and implicitly Ex. 15.10, "Thou blowest with thy breath, the sea covers them."

The idea that breath *(ruah)* wind can destroy is a concept that is found universally. Interesting is its usage as "wind" in the early Epic of Gilgamesh:

With a blazing flame, he [Marduk] filled his body.
He then made a net to enfold Tiamat therein.
The four winds he stationed that nothing of her might escape.
The South Wind, the North Wind, the East Wind, the West Wind.
Close to his side he held the net, the gift of his father Anu,
He brought forth Imhullu "the Evil Wind," the Whirlwind, the Hurricane,
The Fourfold Wind, the Sevenfold Wind, the Cyclone, the Matchless Wind,
Then he sent forth winds *that he brought forth* [emphasis added] the seven of them
To stir up the inside of Tiamat, they rose behind him.
Then the Lord raised up the flood-storm, his mighty weapon. . .

Then joined issue Tiamat and Marduk, wisest of the gods;
They swayed in combat, locked in battle.

The Lord spread out his net to enfold her,
The Evil Wind *which followed behind* [emphasis added], he let loose
in her face.
When Tiamat opened her mouth to consume him,
He drove in the Evil Wind that she close not her lips.[81]

Observe that aside from the four natural winds of the world, Marduk
has a special wind, a sevenfold wind *that he himself brought forth*
whose purpose was to enter Tiamat, distend her so as to pave the way
for the mortal thrust of Marduk's sword. And so it transpired. As
Marduk and Tiamat were locked in battle, the Evil Wind, which
followed behind, he let loose in her face. It was the wind actually that
rendered her helpless, and then Marduk released the weapon that tore
open her belly. It is the present writer's opinion that the slaying of
Tiamat by the sword is anticlimactic, and that the power that paralysed
her and was chiefly her undoing—this power proceeded from the body
of Marduk. The four winds of the world were but secondary. It is clear,
at any rate, through the tenor of the section and the space and
proportion allocated to the wind, that it was the primary potent
destructive force.

By association, the *Ruah* became the wind with the fertilizing power
which primitives associate with pregnancy. In classical times, for
example, Zephyrus or Flavonius begat Euphrosyne with Aurora; and
Ovid describes how Chloris (=the Roman Flora) was ravished by
Zephyr. Among the Mohammedans there is a tradition that reports how
a pre-Adamite race consisting of women conceived by the wind.[82] It
seems to me quite likely that the pregnancy of Mary, based upon this
primitive idea, was thought to be accomplished by the *ruah ha-qodesh*
(the Aramaic was *ruha dequdsha*), the wind coming from God. It is a
Hellenistic idea, using Hebrew or Aramaic terms.[83]

The question now to be considered is: where did *ruah*, "breath,"
acquire this fertilizing power, and since it comes from the body, what
part of the body did it come from? It must strike one as incongruous
that breath, being of such delicate and invisible effusion, should
possess the potency to ferilize and create, and then *per contra* to
destroy.

The outlet for vapor, gas, breath in the human body is not only
through the mouth, however. At the other end of the alimentary canal,
gas accumulated intestinally may be expelled through the anus. The
ancients (including the Romans) had a special god who supervised that
function.[84] In Hebrew the root *napah* is used for breathing life into man

(Gen. 2.7), used also for sniffing in contempt (Mal. 1.13), and in the postbiblical literature as expelled bodily gas (*nepaḥ, nippuaḥ, nepiḥa,* Ben Yehudah, *Dictionary,* 3716–20). The bodily gas, however, stems from an area denoted by Freud as an erogenous zone, an area around the genitals that has secondary erotic characteristics and sensations (cf. the term anal eroticism). In his studies of infantile sexuality, Ernest Jones was able to demonstrate that in childish fantasy, the father impregnated the mother with this gas,[85] and for this reason flatus has been identified as having this fertilizing power, and so indeed in analyses of neurotic patients. By transferring this power from below to above to suppress the unpleasant, the unmannerly and the unsocial—a familiar procedure just as the Madonna's conception of Jesus is considered to come from the ear as portrayed by some painters[86]—it is the breath coming from the mouth that acquires this power. Similarly, *hebel* used for breath has also the meaning of flatus as in modern Hebrew, as well as in other languages *ventus, ventositas,* "wind, flatulence"—"flatulence" itself from the Latin *flo=blow (German, Blähung).*

However, *hebel* would not only be used for a destroying force, but as in ancient and modern times as a supreme expression of contempt and disgust, as for example the Latin *oppedere,* "break wind, deride." The term *hebel* is employed by Qohelet in a number of instances with this same connotation. Thus in 8.14 the surface meaning suggests that God's providence in human affairs is a puzzle, a futility: There is a *hebel* carried through on earth: the good people receive the reward of the bad, and the bad get the reward of the good. This is *hebel,* says Qohelet, this is an outrage, a perversion of things as they ought to be, an indictment of God's justice. By this use of *hebel,* Qohelet shows his contempt, his defiance of God, and the ordering of human affairs only arouses his disgust. Side by side with *hebel,* of course, is the word *ruaḥ* signifying also "flatus," and so in Job 32.18 *ruaḥ biṭni,* "the wind in my stomach." Now conjoined with *hebel* is the phrase *re'ut ruaḥ* meaning on the surface "a futile desire." If we did not presume that Qohelet were a translation, the most obvious reading would be *re'ot ruaḥ,* "chasing after wind" (Hos. 12.2).

Our word, however, must come from the Aramaic *r'i,* "desire," that is to say, it cannot come from a geminate as the form *re'utha* cannot be found or formed among the geminates (compare Payne Smith *Syriac-English Dictionary)* nor can the targumic translation *tebirut ruḥa* implying *rey'uth* with Yod ("broken in spirit") be admissible. Note that *re'ut* varies with *ra'ayon* in 4.16 (and further at 1.17; 2.22) and the probability is that the Hebrew translator found in his Aramaic text *ra'ayonah* meaning both "desire" and "thought" (Jastrow, *Dictionary*, 1487; Payne Smith, *Dictionary* s.v.). Compare moreover Ps. 40.6 where the Hebrew reads "thought" and where printed editions and manuscripts vary with *ra'ayonah* and *re'ut*. We should therefore consider *re'ut ruah* as "idle thought." However, in conjuntion with *hebel*, the term *re'ut ruah* as usage for his style, and the reflection of his unconscious, is unique in Hebrew literature. There is an intimation and undertone to the words in some instances which do not apply. Thus in 2.26; 1.17 where Qohelet articulates his sense of despair and outrage, "empty desire" does not quite fill the requirements of *le mot propre* for Qohelet's indignation. Just as with hebel, he *implies* another word (*ra'aya, re'i*, "excrement"), which is Qohelet's defiance again, and an expression of contemptuous disgust, so that the expression *hebel ure'ut ruah* means flatus and excretory wind.

The neurotic chain leads to distortions in syntax, in the coherence of thoughts and appositeness of illustrations, in the dislocation of logic and especially in ellipses. In ellipsis, the most familiar form to us is the telling of a humorous story wherein the narrator leaves out an essential point which the listener quickly perceives and is thus provoked to laughter. Patients in relating their dreams frequently suppress an essential part of the dream which the therapist has to supply. A pertinent case is reported by Gutheil:

"I touch my husband's genital, and find it is bleeding." Undoubtedly touching by the woman caused the bleeding (a castration wish). This action, however, would be intolerable to her, and gives her a profound sense of guilt; so she suppresses the thought and relates that she found it bleeding (ellipsis).

Qohelet has a number of abrupt transitions where part of the thought is left out. This is not to be identified with or comparable to the prophetic style and form, where the thought as an omission in stich b is to be supplied from stich a, and is a characteristic feature of high poetic art.[87] With Qohelet the thought is disjointed, abrupt. Thus for example (5.12f.): a man hoards money for his misfortune. The wealth is lost in an unfortunate venture—and he begat a son (!)—and he has nothing left; just as he emerged from his mother's womb, so, stripped, does he return, taking nothing with him. The interruption—and he begat a son—which has nothing to do with the anterior or posterior thought is interpolated by Qohelet with the memory of the ill-starred business of being reminded of his son. The son is a bad "venture" too, and if he were lost. . . .but Qohelet does not wish to finish the thought.

In 6.8 the sense to be supplied is more obvious: what advantage (satisfaction, relief) has the rational over the impulsive man, and what does the unfortunate possess to struggle against life? The sense to be supplied is *vis-a-vis* Qohelet: (But even if one should be wise, rational) how can the distressed poor cope with the exigencies of life?

The next verse (6.9) likewise contains an ellipsis which must be supplied. The verse reads: "Better the enjoyment of the eyes than the death of desire. This too is a frustration and a will o' the wisp".

Both philologically and unconsciously, "go, depart," means "die." (Compare the Dictionaries s.v. *halak*). The meaning of our verse should be: Better sexual satisfaction (cf. p. 27) than the loss of desire altogether. Now the ellipsis; (But because I Qohelet am unhappy because of sexual frustration, and whatever substitute satisfactions I must work out in compulsions—eating, drinking, and other external pleasure) then this too is a futility and a vain aspiration.

Chapter 6.6 likewise gives evidence of this phenomenon. It reproduces in essence the preceding passage in v.3. The latter ends with: but he has not enjoyed himself, and also has not received proper burial then I say, better the misbirth than he! Verse 6 reproduces the same idea, but with an ellipsis: And if he were to live a thousand years twice over, and does not enjoy himself (ellipsis: And even if he were to be buried properly), still. . .does not everyone end up in the same place?

Other ellipsis may be shown in 4.2–3. After Qohelet noticed the oppressions under the sun, and the tears of the oppressed, and there is none to give them relief, and the oppressors have all the power (ellipsis: and with such oppression without let-up makes life endless and futile, and no point in living), I would praise the dead therefore who have expired already than the living who continue to exist.

Similarly, 3.22: Then I saw that a man should be happy in his activities for that is his lot (ellipsis: and about death and the future after that) who can bring him to see what will be after him?

The inclination to doubt himself impaired seriously Qohelet's composition of his book. Stekel has identified a symptomatic trait of some neurotics in what he called "the belief in a great historical mission" (*Compulsion and Doubt*, 97) The patient has fantasies about a great historical project that he wishes to execute. As Stekel describes his patient, he would found a new religion; he would write a new "Quest for the Historical Jesus" (like Schweitzer). The patient studied and took courses in theology. Indeed, he would write a great magnum opus. After writing a few chapters, however, the whole venture bogged down. An old enemy, pathologic doubt, commenced to assail him. Perhaps he is not the great thinker, the great teacher of theology, the great writer that he believed himself to be? The project was abandoned. Stekel reports identical projected undertakings on the part of those who would be great painters, musicians, conductors, who think they have genius, but actually are mediocre talents, who begin ambitious enterprises and "great works," and whose efforts dribble away in lackluster trivialities, as dubious suspicions about their capabilities assail them.

This illumines our understanding about Qohelet and the uneven character of his work. Qohelet, too, thought that he would immortalize himself by being famed as a legendary *ḥakam* like Solomon with whom he markedly identified (Freud more correctly uses the term assimilated) himself. He would formulate proverbs, bon mots, observations on life, epigrams of experience that would be hailed with universal accolades. This is certainly implied in 1.16: "I increased and added more wisdom than any one before me in Jerusalem." He would become the new Solomon. His book starts bravely enough: the first three chapters are the best organized, the most coherent. His doubts, however, intrude; *he repeats his doubts again and again owing to their pressures on him, and for which he cannot find a resolution:* why must be hand over his property to some one else (1.18;6.2)? Who can tell what will happen in the future (3.22;6.12;8.7;10.14)? What advantage is there to work (1.3;2.11;3.9)? Whatever was will recur again in the same monotonous way (1.9;3.15). Qohelet thought that he would write a great book but it is evident that he did not master the craft. The incohate thoughts reflect the disharmony of the psychic process. Beginning with chapter four, his work fragmentizes; the scene constantly shifts, the thought is not sustained, ideas are not developed, the sense is obscure in the flitting from one thought to another, the point of an observation is often blurred except where analysis enables one to recover the latent thought.[88] The first eight verses of chapter seven seem to be a collection of proverbs with a mere sequential miscellany of random thoughts. Chapter ten is quite dispersed and drifting. Chapter twelve represents a supreme effort wherein Qohelet summons all his powers in a final dirge on the decay of old age.

Nevertheless, Qohelet had one significant rule and method for his own composition, not indeed in accordance with our canons of Greek and Latin literature. In the Semitic languages, both the thought and grammar of a sentence is much more free, more elastic. In the case of Qohelet, to provide some sort of coherence which he himself recognized was requisite for the disorganization and incongruities of his writing, a rote system was devised. In the face of his disordered ideas, he contrived to formulate a mechanical sequence of sentences which he considered an appropriate coherence. Like pearls that are strung one after the other, Qohelet likewise arranged his sentences in the following way: *he used one word of the first sentence as a springboard to compose a second sentence for his thoughts; he repeated the word in the second sentence.* As far as the thought is concerned, the sentences may have nothing to do with each other, but for Qohelet the fact that the word is repeated serves as a pattern of unity for him. At times it is merely the root that is repeated, or simple demonstrative pronouns, and the like. At other times Qohelet will vary his routine by interlocking a number of words in the first sentence and repeating but part of the number in the second.

We see how this works out if we take chapter two as an example. Verses 1 and 2 have the identical word *simḥa,* "joy"; 3 and 4 *ya'asu-ma'asai;* 5 and 6 *'asiti li,* but note that he employed *nata'ti* twice in verses 4 and 5; in the "odd" sentences they provide an additional link in the chain; 7 and 8 *li gam* twice in that order; 9–10 *kol;* 11–12 *paniti 'ani;* 13–14 *ḥoshek;* 15–16 *kesil;* 17–18 *sane'ti;* 19–20 *'amal;* 21–22 *'adam;* 23–24 *gam zeh* (zoh); 25–26 *ki.* Observe, however, that 24–25 (the "odd" verses as here presented) have the interlocking *yokal. In over ninety percent of the verses in Qohelet the concatenation of one word in the first verse tied in with second holds good.* For a discussion of the rest of the verses in Qohelet and the seeming exceptions, the reader is referred to the chapter on Structure and Unity.

> *To translate means to serve*
> *two masters—something nobody can do.*
> —Franz Rosenzweig.
> BELINDA: "Ay, but you know we must return good for evil."
> LADY BRUTE: *"That may be a mistake in the translation."*
> —*The Provok'd Wife* by Sir John Vanbrugh.

XIII
Qohelet's Hebrew is a Translation from the Aramaic

In the ninteenth century, all the apocryphal and pseudepigraphical works of First Ezra, Tobit, Judith, Rest of the Chapters of the Book of Esther, the Wisdom of Solomon, Book of Baruch, Epistle of Jeremy, the Additions to the Book of Daniel, the Prayer of Manasses, I Maccabbees, the Book of Jubilees, the Martyrdom of Isaiah, I Enoch, the Testament of the 12 Patriarchs, II Baruch, IV Ezra were almost universally considered to have been originally written in Greek. Some of the most distinguished Semitologists such as T. Nöldeke argued that such a book as Tobit must have been written in Greek.

In the 20th century an almost complete reversal has taken place. It is agreed now on all hands that these books were written originally in Hebrew (or Aramaic). The present writer himself took a hand in the analysis of these books and was able to add proofs in numerous elucidation of texts that Tobit, Judith, the Wisdom of Solomon, the Books of Baruch severally, the Additions to the Book of Daniel (Bel and the Dragon, the Story of Susanna, Story of the Three Guardsmen), I Enoch (both Hebrew and Aramaic interspersed in a block-like fashion) and the Fourth Ezra (Hebrew and Aramaic) were translations and not written Greek as previously thought.[89] It caught my attention, too, that the Hebrew of Daniel (c.8-12, but not 9.4-20) was a translation from Aramaic as well as certain parts of Chronicles.

Scholars who have been convinced of the Hebrew/Aramaic origin of these writings have found their own rule and method in the problems and solutions by the texts themselves. An examination of the two volumes of the *Apocrypha and Pseudepigrapha of the Old Testament* edited by R.H. Charles will exhibit the lines of inquiry and procedure that scholars have pursued in affirming their conclusions:

1. The unaccountable presence of many Semitic words in the text.

2. Idioms that are peculiar in the extant text (whether Greek, Syriac, Ethiopic, Armenian, Latin) become natural and recognizable when retroverted in Hebrew or Aramaic.

3. The abrupt tense sequences become understandable and easy-flowing when retranslated to Semitic.

4. Dittographs in the text become understandable when they are retranslated, as the words retranslated are quite similar to one another.

5. A strange syntax in one language becomes understandable when retranslated to the original language.

6. Word plays appear in the recovered retroversion(Charles II, 287, *passim*).

7. When the translator is not sure of himself, or thinks that a word can have two meanings in a context, he will straddle the issue. He will translate a word according to the first meaning and then according to the second. Examples of this are found in the doublets in the Greek translation of the Hebrew Bible or in the Revised Version with the marginal or footnote readings.

8. The translator may fail to grasp the sense of the text in front of him, or fail to catch the proper nuance, or the subtle significance of the phrase, or may make use of a meaning most familiar and customary to him, and as a consequence mistranslates. This is one of the most important factors in the proof of translation.

These guides are the principal signposts in traversing the road. There are bypaths just as significant. All add up to a sure result. If investigators have employed these methods to arrive at their conclusions and are almost universally affirmed, then the legitimate use of these procedures will produce equally authentic results. The documentation adds up to a proof. The same documentation exists for Qohelet as I will attempt to show, and has the same validity as in the apocryphal and pseudepigraphical studies.

In the book of Qohelet there are many Aramaic words. A substantial number of these words have not been assimilated into Hebrew and are mere reproductions of the Aramaic text the translator had before him; it is an easy way of translating to employ the same word common to Hebrew and Aramaic. The translator, however, does not realize that both the Hebrew and Aramaic go their own way and the Aramaic word that he has incorporated into the Hebrew makes for a peculiar context. The translator also thinks that if he runs into difficulty, it will be of small importance as he looks at both the Hebrew and Aramaic text, and has both in his mind. He fails to understand that the Hebrew text will eventually stand by itself without the Aramaic, and will invoke other associations in the mind of the reader.

A.　*The presence of Aramaic words embodied in the Hebrew.*

For the large number of Aramaic words in the Hebrew text, in itself a striking phenomenon calling for notice, reference may be made to the list compiled by F. Delitszch, *Das Buch Koheleth* (1875), for fairly complete list of "Aramaisms," words, idioms, and constructions, running to nine pages. By *large* is meant a greater proportion of "Aramaisms" to the Hebrew text than any other book in the Hebrew Bible. Delitszch, however, did not surmise translation and therefore his list should be amplified and qualified by the following observations.

1. *Kebar,* "already," is found eight times in Qohelet. In two instances, however, it merely registers the Aramaic *kebar,* meaning "perhaps." Thus in 9.7 it would be presumptuous on the part of Qohelet (or anyone else) to say that you should enjoy life because "God *already* has been pleased with your actions." The correct interpretation undoubtedly is: Enjoy life anyway; *perhaps* God favors your actions. And then again in 1.10: one will say, this is new. *Perhaps* it was of (belonged to: cf. Brown, Driver, Briggs, Lexicon, p. 512b) life-times before us. (*see* Commentary.) Again, this explanation of *kebar* is more apposite with the psyche and character of Qohelet's impulsion to doubt.

2. *Tur* means "spy out, explore" as in the usage of "spy out the land" (Num. 14.34 and frequently). To employ the word with "heart," as for example in 2.3, is meaningless (and so Ehrlich). The root is *tar,* med. Alef, sometimes Waw (Brockelmann, *Lexicon Syriacum*[2], 814a) and means "notice, meditate" (Payne Smith, *Dictionary,* 603). This is what is required for all usage in Qohelet: 1.13 "to seek and meditate with wisdom"; 7.25 "to know, to meditate (*tur*) and seek wisdom."

3. *Hu',* "this, that," is a demonstrative particle preceding the noun in Aramaic (so Dan. 2.32: "this image"; likewise Ezr. 7.6: *hu'Ezra,* "This Ezra," and similarly in translation Hebrew elsewhere with a personal name; 2 Chron. 28.22: "*That* king Ahaz"; 2 Chron. 33.23: "For *this* king) Amon sinned exceedingly," the *hu'* scarcely translatable). A sign of the Aramaic locution, *hu' 'inyan ra'* is found at 1.13 (contrast 4.8;6.2) anacoluthically. . . to meditate on everything that happens under the heavens—that evil business that God gave man to be afflicted with.

4. *Re'ut* means on the surface "desire," found seven times in Qohelet,

nowhere else in the Hebrew of the Bible, in Aramaic at Ezr. 5.17;7.18. Combined with *ruaḥ*, supposedly "desire of wind, windy desire." It varies with *ra'ayon ruaḥ*, 1.17;4.16 and signifies, however, "thought," as in 2.22: *ra'ayon libbo*" (so Ehrlich). *Ra'ayonah* (or *ra'ayana*) in the underlying Aramaic has either the meaning of "thought" or "desire" Jastrow, 1487 and Targ. Ps. 90.6 ms. ed. *re'utak* MT *maḥshabot*, and Job 17.11 *zimmotai* (thoughts), and like the Syriac *ra'ayon* "a way of thinking." The usual translation "idle striving" if kept punningly combines both senses of "striving," mental and physical. For the undertone of the root meaning "excrement" combined with *hebel* "flatus" see the remarks on p. 94.

5. *Ḥefeẓ*, "matter" especially at 5.7;8.6, is the Hebrew translation of the Aramaic *ẓebu*, "thing, matter," but the translator, knowing that *ẓbi* signifies "desire" or "be pleased with," spuriously etymologized by rendering with the Hebrew lexical equivalent. Through translated Hebrew in Qohelet, (cf. further 3.1.17) the word is found elsewhere: Is. 58.13; Prov. 31.13.

6. *Siklut*, "stupidity," is a form found seven times in Qohelet, but not elsewhere in the Hebrew Bible, the form taken from the underlying Aramaic document. Miswritten for *Siklut* (with Sin) at 10.1, "intelligence."

7. *'Asah . . . tob* (3.12;6.12), not *eu prattein* in Greek but as the Aramaic *'abad*, "spend the time," e.g., *'abad shinta*=passed the year, *'abad qalil zabna*=he stayed a while. Parallel to Hebrew *'asah*, "spend time". At 7.14 the expression *hayah beṭob* is a precise reproduction of the Aramaic phrase *hawa beṭab*, "enjoy oneself" (as in Tob. 7.11 Peshitta.).

8. *Dibra*, *'al dibrat* reproduces the underlying Aramaic. In 7.14 *'al dibrat she* is a Hebrew copy of Dan. 2.30 *'al dibrat di*. In 8.2 *'al dibrat* means "with regard to" again exactly like the Aramaic *'al dibra* found in the Elephantine papyri (Cowley, *Aramaic Papyri of the Fifth Century*, B.C., VI, 5.8). The passage at 3.18 is the culmination of the inverted order of verses 20,19,18 and is to be translated: I said in my heart, 'With regard to the sons of men. . . .' In the Hebrew Bible, *dibra* has other connotations. In Job 5.8 *dibrati* signifies "my cause." Ps. 110.4 *'al dibrati* means "according to the usage of Malki-zedek, " where *debar* is a different Aramaic root meaning "lead, take, have a *custom* or usage." (Cf. Jastrow.)

9. *Ra 'al*, "distasteful," not "evil upon;" in 2.17 a reproduction of *be'esh 'alai*. (cf. Dan. 6.15).

10. *Yitron*, Aramaic *yutran*, "advantage," "what remains over,"

"plus" (Ginsberg), is found ten times only in Qohelet in this form. The form *yoter* (anomolous) reflects in one verse the Aramaic *yattir*, as an adverb meaning "especially." Thus 7.11: *weyoter lero'ei hashemesh* adds up to: "Wisdom is good with an inheritance *especially* those who enjoy life."

11. *Tob . . . hote'*, "luckless and ill-favored." *Hote'* is an inadequate retroversion of *serah* meaning "be in bad odor, ill favored, or sin". "It is the latter meaning that the Hebrew translator seized upon erroneously (so in 2.26; 7.26).

12. *Lebad* (7.29) without the preposition *b* is anomalous at the head of a sentence. It reproduces mechanically the Aramaic *lehad (lehod)*. The Hebrew should have been rendered much more idiomatical by *raq* (Gen. 6.5;14.24 and elsewhere), but *lehad* with the initial *Lamed* suggests *Lebad*.

13. *Mishlahat* (8.8) does not signify "message, embassy" but represents the Aramaic *meshalahta* most probably (fem. part. passive) "a stripping, an undressing, a casting off," and the verb with *zaina* means "cast off armor" (Payne Smith, *Syriac-English Dictionary s.v. shelah*. Cf. *'arom*, "without weapons," Amos 2.16).

14. *ma'aseh*, with the verb Nif. *na'asah*, not "the action that was done" but "the event that happened" (Cf. Aramaic *'abid*=happened, *'obada*=happening, event, and so: "I saw all the events that have taken place under the sun" (1.14); "So I hated life because of all the events that occurred under the sun were foul to me" *ra'*=*bish*, "distasteful" Dan. 6.15); "Whatever happened before will happen again" (1.9).

15. *'abadehem* 9.1, "their activities" instead of the usual *ma'asehem*. The translator was cued by the two preceding words of his text, *zaddikayya, hakkimayya*, easily translated *hebraice*, and so *'abadehem* was rendered mechanically without regard to translation.

16. *gumaz* "pit," Aramaic word although the translator knew the Hebrew *bor* at 12.6.

17. *'asah lehem* in Hebrew means "make bread." In 10.19 it can only signify "make a feast," an idiom characteristic of Aramaic *'abad lehém*, Dan. 5.1.

18. *Beshel 'asher* (8.17) is recognized as peculiar Hebrew but is an exact replica of the Aramaic *bedil de*. While the Hebrew is supposed to mean "because though" (Jewish Version), "however much" (Revised Version), "forasmuch" (Odeberg) and similarly others, all are unsubstantiated and doubtful. *Bedil de* "for the sake of which," should have been translated as *ba'abur, lema'an* in the Hebrew as the latter targumic equivalents show. Likewise 5.15 *kol'ummat she* is simply a

duplicate of *kol qobel de; de=she* 5.14; 12.7; and 9.4 where the translator took his Aramaic *bedil* and separated it into two words *bedi+ l, ki-lekeleb* (see Commentary).

19. *Yehu'* in 11.3 is a monstrum; it is simply a prototype of the Aramaic: it is *yeheweh* "[there] it will be".

20. *Lahag* (12.12), usually translated "study" from Arabic *lahag*, "devote oneself," is rather to be derived from Aramaic *lahaga*, "steam, vapor," and should have been rendered *hebel* with the idea that much vaporing i.e., useless talk, as in English, is a weariness of flesh.

21. *Sof dabar*, 12.13, is Hebrew for *sofa di miltha* in Aramaic (as in Dan. 7.28).

22. *sefod . . . . reqod* at 3.4 both go back to the Aramaic root *rqd* which has, with different vocalization, two meanings. "mourn" and "dance" (cf. H.L. Ginsberg a.l. and the Peshitta) forming in the Aramaic a characteristic Aramaic wordplay.

23. The phrase in 4.1 *umiyyad 'oshqeihem koah* is difficult. The translation of the phrase must be: "and from the hand of their oppressors there is power." The Hebrew, however, merely reproduces the antecedent Aramaic *min yad*, "on the side of" (see Payne Smith, 280b for examples).

24. At 5.8 we have the peculiar expression "But the profit of a land in every way is a king that is servant to a field" (JPS), where the translation, however should run: "But the advantage of a field lies in this: a king is subject to agriculture," where *ne'ebad*, the *Nif'al of 'abad*, strange in itself, is the counterpart of *mishta'abad* meaning "subject to."

25. In quite a number of instances, the retroversion in Aramaic exhibits the substrate word play: e.g., 5.10 contains a wordplay with *ṭuba*, "goodness," and *tuba*, "much, very"; 11.5, "way of the spirit, animus," *'orah* and *ruah*; 10.10, where *holala*, Hebrew *garzen*, Levy: *Chaldäisches Wörterbuch*, 261 played upon and mistranslated in Aramaic *wehailin mehayyal*: "It may enfeeble, dismay soldiers," (see Commentary); *lehod . . .uhranin . . . . .yehdon . . .;rqd*, as in 22.

The presence of these Aramaic locutions in the text is not the result of happenstance or of how the author thought in Aramaic. The fact is that the Aramaic, because it is proximate to the Hebrew, provides a strong unconscious suggestibility to the translator. If a word shares a common root in Hebrew and Aramaic, the translator will rewrite the word in his text, for he did not have to labor in finding another word in his rendering, even though elsewhere, when he is more alert and consciously aware of differences in the semantic deployment of the word, or he is not hurried, he will translate differently, e.g., no. 16; contrast no. 14. He will duplicate Aramaic forms that have no parallel in Hebrew (no. 17, no. 19, no. 20.) Other times he will strive to translate, and not copy the Aramaic, and give a more Hebrew turn to his translation, but then fall into error, as in no. 11 and Commentary on 5.5. In still others the exigency of the Aramaic will give a bizarre Hebrew, as in no. 3. This will compel him, whether deliberately or no, to invent new words, as in no. 1. He will miss nuances naturally. The first clue, then, that Qohelet is a translated document is the presence of Aramaic words, phrases, and locutions imbedded in the Hebrew text, rarely used even after his time and never before his time in some instances.

B. *The inexact status of nouns in Qohelet.*

Hebrew follows a fairly definite rule about the use of the definite article. A word that appears in a narrative for the first time will not have, as in English, a definite article. Thereafter the article is prefixed, as an invariable rule. It is the same in Hebrew. Thus the books of Samuel and Job open with *'ish 'ehad,* "a man," and thereafter the article precedes. This is not the case in Aramaic. In the Samuel and Job texts we are confronted with the following: the common prints in the pseudo–Jonathan translation to Samuel reads *gabra* (definitized) *had;* Sperber's edition reads *gabra had;* the Peshitta *gabra had.* In Job however, the common text reads *gebar had* (indeterminate); the Peshitta, however, *gebra had* (*gebra* definitized); Syrohexaplar indefinitely *'enash.* Actually, however, the coalescing of the determinate states ascends quite early. In the Elephantine Papyri (ed. Cowley) the regular rule expectedly is followed at 10.10;14.4. However, cf. in Ahiqar, 11.111,116,117, or contrast *kaspa* 30.12 and the duplicate in 31.11, *kesaf.* Abstracts are likewise employed with or without the article (Cowley, 11,166, 188 and elsewhere). In Daniel the emphatic state is similarly employed when the absolute is required: Dan. 3.5 *qol qarna:* 5.1 *hamra;* v.7 *hamnuka.* We have *'alam* 4.31, 7.27, but *'alma* 2.20; seven times *'almin* but *'almayya* in 2.44. The Palestine Jewish Aramaic exhibits the same tendencies though less markedly. For example in Dalman's *Dialektproben,*[2] pp. 18-19, note *'anaka, 'isba,* p. 19 *shuqa, sandala,* with the emphatic state, although the meaning is indefinite. In the Eastern Aramaic branch, the later Syriac and Babylonian Aramaic, the breakdown in these distinct states proceeded so much apace that many nouns in Syriac are known only in their determinate state. In the case of the translator who has to handle the text before him, the difficulty is heavily compounded. He has the problems of usage of the author and his manner of thought; he has his own habit and pattern and there is the exegesis of the particular verse and its syntax. For example, *'abda* "slave," with its first mention in a narrative, e.g., in Dalman, op. cit. p. 18, par. 2, is it a slave, the slave, or a word already stereotyped in the emphatic state? The difference may be important.

In Qohelet's Hebrew, concordant with Aramaic usage and at loggerheads with the regimen of Hebrew grammar, no satisfactory rule can be presented for his usage of the definite article. It is employed when not required in 3.17 (*hefez* shows that *ha-ma'aseh* should be undertermined); 5.18: "Also every man to whom God has given . . ." where the definite article in *ha-adam* is otiose; 10.5: ". . . like an error that proceeds from a ruler," not *ha-shalit*.

On the other hand, the article is wanting where it is required: 4.4, *'amal* should have the definite article, note *ha-ra'*; 9.3, "This is the evil"; commentators emend with the definite article; 9.9, "Enjoy life with *the* wife whom thou lovest." Similarly, in 8.9;10.20;12.1;12.14 not only does the meaning require it but observe the *nota accusativi*; 12.12, "the end of *the* matter"; Dan.7.28 *sofa di miltha*.

Then again, and even more striking, is the circumstance that in nouns that follow in a series, one noun mysteriously has the article, another not: 2.18, "the treasure of kings and *the* provinces"; Ezr. 4.15, *malkin umedinan* is the identical phrase *without* the article; 7.25: The wickedness of folly and *ha-siklut holelut*, where *siklut* impossibly has the article; observe again the fluctuating omission and appearance of the article in 4.9-12; in 8.1 *kehehakam* (emendation uncalled for: the Aramaic was the stereotyped *hakkima,* and *'adam;* in 11.3 *geshem* but 12.2 *ha-geshem;* 12.4 *delatayim,* but one expects the definite article, compare the other three nouns in the verse. In 12.6 *kad,* but we should have *ha-kad;* compare *ha-bor, ha-galgal, hebel ha-kesef, gullat ha-zahab.* Sometimes a whole verse appears without the article and then at the end it peculiarly comes in sight again (10.19).

Finally, certain words integral to Qohelet's theme, and which are repeated again and again, manifest themselves strangely with, and then without, the article: 5.17 *tobah,* 6.6 *tobah* but 6.3 *ha-tobah.* The word *shemesh* occurs some thirty times in the book and always with the definite article, but in 6.5 no article.

There are hundreds of nouns in Qohelet and it would not be surprising that a number of errors should be made. How is one to account for this vacillating employment of the definite article? It cannot originate in the mannerism or style of the writer for such an eccentricity would be unprecedented; nor could the fluctuation come about from corruptions, for such an hypothesis could scarcely be conceivable. The only possible explanation to this phenomenon is to assume a translator who, not continually alert in his rendition of the determinate and indeterminate, fell into error. The hypothesis does double service: it explains on the one hand the lack of the article, although expected, *and* on the other hand the uncalled for, redundant qualification of the noun.

    C.   The translator's confusion with hu' (hw') and hawa' (hw').

It is instructive how the translator confused *hu'* and *hawa'* in his Aramaic document. In the unvocalized texts, *hu'* and *hawa'* are precisely the same, He, Waw, Aleph consonantly. Yet it is surprising that the translator misapprehended and confused the two words almost half the time, i.e., six out of some thirteen times, where the root *hayah* occurs in the Hebrew. First, he incorporated the word *yeheweh* in 11.3, strictly an Aramaic form, which the Masora had difficulty with, and uncertainly vocalized as *yehu'*, a grammatical anomaly. Then again, at 3.15 he confused the copulas *hu'* and *hawa'* fore and aft. The verse reads: *ma shehaya kebar hu' wa'asher lihyot kebar hayah we'elohim yebaqqesh 'et nirdaf*. To make sense we are obliged to take the first *hayah* in the present tense although the form is perfect, then *hu'* in the preterit although it implies a present, and despite the complicating *kebar* indicating clearly the past tense. The translation "Whatever was already is" adds up to an absurdity; similarly, the erroneous rendering of the Authorised Version, "That which hath been is now." Observe that *kebar hayah* is in the very same verse. If, now, the sense of *hu'* and *hawa'* were interchanged, the whole phrase becomes immediately understandable. When one retroverts to the Aramaic, the source of the confusion becomes clear. In the first instance, the translator mistook *hu'* for *hawa'*; in the second, *hawa'* for *hu'*. His confusion in the unpointed texts becomes comprehensible. We now have a logical consistent sequence in the new translation:

    Whatever is, has been for a long time;

    And whatever will be has been for a long time.

(For the remaining part of the verse and its connection with the preceding, see Commentary.)

Another interesting example where *hu'* and *hawa'* were mistaken one for the other is found at 4.16 and when the retroversion is secured in Aramaic the verse receives a natural unforced explanation. The preceding verse, however, needs some analysis. The text runs: *ra'iti 'et kol ha-hayyim hamehalkim tahat ha-shemesh, 'im ha-yeled ha-sheni 'asher ya'amod tahtaw.* The usual translation would be: "I have seen all the living walking under the sun with the second child who will stand in his place." Apparently what the author is describing is either a coronation scene, or an important state announcement to the effect that the king is stepping down, and the new prince is to take his place (pp. 146.) But who is *ha-yeled ha-sheni,* "the second child?" Many critics would delete *ha-sheni* as a gloss or error. It would appear that the translator, as was his wont, rendered word for word, which seemed intelligent enough for him but obviously lacks the more comprehensible interpretation via the Aramaic. *Tinyana* means "viceroy" (Payne Smith, p. 616b). The phrase probably read: *talya d'tinyana,* or *talya tinyana,* the *de* being redundant as it frequently was and should be translated: "the youth who was the viceroy", or "the youth, the viceroy" being in apposition. The verse now carries the signification: Qohelet saw the endless throng to witness the king and the boy prince who was to succeed him.

The next verse (4.16) reads: *'en qez lekol ha -'am lekol 'asher hayah(!) lifneihem . . .* which may be translated as "There is no end to all the people, to all that was (?) before them" which makes no sense. Translators perforce are periphrastic: ". . . even of all of them whom did lead," which with difficulty squares with the Hebrew. The Aramaic reads: *la 'ithai sof lekol 'amma lekol di* (de) *hu 'qodomeihon,* which means "there is no end to the people before whom *he* is standing"—precisely what is needed. But the translator mistook *hu'* for *hawa'.*

Similarly 6.10: *ma shehaya kebar niqra' shemoh.* We cannot translate as per convention, "Whatsoever cometh into being, the name was given long ago." The phrase obviously means: "whatever is *now* was given its name long ago." Again the Aramaic retroversion gives the correct interpretation: *ma shehu',* "Whatever is " was mistranslated *ma shehawa',*"whatever was."

In 7.10 the same mistake manifests itself: *'al tomar meh haya shehayamim harishonim hayu tobim me'eleh.* The contrast is clear: How *is* it (not: how *was* it) that the former days were better than these days are (i.e., *hawa'* for *hu').*

There are two other instances requiring more analysis but which may be alluded to in this category in the mistake identity of *hu'* and *hawa'.* The first passage reads (7.24): *rahoq mah shehaya, we'amoq 'amoq mi yimza'ennu.* The Jewish version, for example, is obliged to translate,

"That which is far off, and exceeding deep; who can find it out?" The copula, however, is in the perfect, but as the translation implies, the present tense is required. The retroverted Aramaic again provides the solution: *hu'* and *hawa'* were muddled again. The translation shapes up as: "it is far from that which is, " where "from" *min/man*, is the original reading. (For the complete exposition, see Commentary.)

Similarly, in the addition made by the epilogist at 12.9 the same error occurs: *weyoter shehaya Qohelet hakam 'od limmed da 'at 'et ha-'am*. It is quite wooden to render: and besides, Qohelet *was wise*, he also taught the people. As seems probable, a mixup of *hu'* and *hawa'* occurred: *weyattir dehu' Qohelet ḥakam* (verb) where *hu' Qohelet=hu' Ezra, hu 'ẓalma* (ut supra pp. 100 f.)

Noticeable too is the translator's misunderstanding of the copula in another direction. In Aramaic, *hawa'* combines with the participle to express the preterit and which should be rendered in English by the past tense. (Compare Nöldeke, *Syriac Grammar*, 277; Burney, *The Aramaic Origin of the Fourth Gospel*, 92). In 1.12, "I Qohelet was king over Israel," a source of temporal difficulty to commentators, and the foundation for the Midrash that Solomon after he *was* king wandered as a beggar in the world, is simply a word-for-word translation of *hawet malek* (participle), whereas the translator should have rendered simply *malakti*: "I ruled." Occasionally, *hawa'* simply bears the temporal signification of, "is", e.g., *haweitun*="you are" (Payne Smith s.v. hawa), not "you were." (This is reflected lamely in Qohelet's Hebrew, but as a translation it is understandable.) Perhaps too, *malek* was misread as *melek*. Too we must translate therefore in 7.19: "Wisdom strengthens the wise man more than ten rulers who are in a province." not "were." H.L.Ginsberg has found a similar misapprehension of *hu'* for *hawa'* at 9.15.

In one instance, (3.14), the translator misunderstood the participle as *futurum instans* which occurs with great frequency (cf. Dan 4.22: *tardin*, "they shall drive you") but which he should have rendered by the past tense: "I know whatever God has *done* shall be forever . . ." not "whatever God will do" or "does." Note *'asah fine* corroboratingly, and so perforce the Greek *epoisen* and the Latin *fecit*, for *ya'aseh*.

D. *Mistranslations*

The way of the translator is not easy. To translate, as a familiar Italian adage has it is to betray, and it may be added: not only to betray the author but the translator himself. With his translation, the weaknesses, the ignorance, the knowledge of the second language as well as the first, the miscomprehension of the context all become apparent. The ancient translators of the Hebrew Bible, notably the Greek translators, give clear examples how frequently they ill conceived their task.

In 1.8 the passage reads: *kol ha-debarim yege 'im*, which is usually translated "All things toil" or "all words toil," with emendations as *meyagg'im*, "cause weariness"; others add *le'adam* (compare *Biblia Hebraica*) but hardly to any avail or improvement. The Hebrew translator misvocalized his text, which read *kol millayya le'an*, meaning "what is the purpose of all this?" For the expression compare Yer. Yeb. XII, 12 d *ha-hu saba le'an leik*, "of what use is this old man to you?" The continuation of our biblical verse is quite appropriate: a man could not finish (*see* Commentary) talking about it, etc. The Hebrew translator, however, interpreted or read the word *le'an s la'in*.

In 1.16 the text runs: *hinneh higdalti wehosafti hokma 'al kol 'asher haya lefanai 'al yerushalaim*. The translations gloss over the difficulty: "I have gotten great wisdom." *Hagdil hokma* signifies "I magnified wisdom"; cf. Is.42.21. What is required is: "I increased wisdom," cf. the synonym *hosafti and* the phrase *marbeh hokma* (Abot, 2.7), not *higdalti*.

The passage at 2.20, *wesabboti 'ani leya'esh 'et libbi*, is usually translated "I turned about to turn my heart to despair," recognized as awkward and peculiar. We should expect *weshabti 'ani wa'er'eh*," I returned and considered," i.e., "I considered" again (4.17; 9.11), the language that is customarily employed. The Aramaic gives the much more natural turn to the expression: *hadret*, in our example, more idiomatically "I changed my mind," as in the locution *hadar 'amar*="he later changed his mind and said" (cf. Levy, *Dictionary* s.v.) The correct translation should have been *wehazarti 'ani; wesabboti* is a mistranslation.

The terms *tob* and *hote'* in 2.26;7.26 and perhaps even at 9.2 have evoked speculation. It does not seem likely that they are to be taken in the usual sense of "good man" and "wicked man" but seem to bear the connotation of "fortunate one" and "unfortunate one" (Ginsberg). Undoubtedly the Aramaic is the source of the unusual term *hote'* in *disrah* rt. *serah*, meaning, "one who sins," which indeed the translator followed. The other meaning of *serah*, "ill-favored one," would be the better rendition. There is the equal possibility that the elusive *ba'esh* in Aramaic signifying "be bad, wicked" and "malodorous, illfavored" was the source of the mistranslation.

An instructive example of the quandary in which the translator found himself, and indirectly for the proof of translation is extant at

3.21, "Who knows whether the spirit of man goes upward, or the spirit of the beast goes downward to the earth?" In the balance of stichs, "to the earth" is redundant. The translation hypothesis supplies the key to what transpired. The translator saw in his Aramaic text *l'ar'a* about which he was puzzled whether to render "to the earth" or "downwards." So he did that which many translators do as in the Septuagint with their doublets and the Revised Version with the alternate renderings in the margin or at the bottom of the page; he straddled the issue, by putting down a double rendering: both *lematta* and *la'arez* represent Aramaic *l'ar'a*.

There seem to be two instances where the translator failed to distinguish a Sin and a Shin (a diacritical point would not have been extant), and thus was led into a translation error. The first verse reads (5.6): "For through the multitude of dreams, and vanities, and sorceries [*see* Commentary] . . . . .but fear thou God" The first part of the verse makes no sense without a verb, and emendations are proposed. The translator saw in his text *shagayin*|(rt. *shgi*) which he mistakenly took as *saggin*, "be much," the Hebrew *harbeh*. The verse should have read more sensibly: "because in the multitude of dreams, vanities, sorceries persons go astray; as for yourself fear God (and you will be saved)." With all his weakness, Qohelet manfully combats the dread of magic and sorcery.

The same error is found at another passage at 7.29: "Behold this only have I found that God made man upright but they have sought out may inventions." What are these many inventions (or calculations)? The Aramaic read *hushbanin shagayin*, "They have sought out erring schemes," not "many." "Erring" is the proper antithesis to "upright" in the verse.

We have an unusual expression in 5.12 (also verse 15) where the passage reads, "There is a grievous evil which I have seen under the sun . . ." *Ra'ah holah*, "grievous evil," might be regarded at first glance as a locution reflective of the style and idiosyncrasy of the translator were it not for the fact that the same expression is inverted at 6.2 *holi ra'*. Now, it is characteristic of Aramaic to repeat a word for the sake of emphasis, e.g., *had had*, "each single one", *batar batar*, "one after the other," *medem medem*, "anything all " *tab tab*, "very good," and *bish bish*, "very bad." (Compare J. A. Montgomery, *Origin of the Gospel According to St. John*, p. 14) Our translator was not aware of this usage and missed his cue at this phrase. Believing that the repetition was pointless, he bethought himself of the usage of *bish* as meaning "illness." (Compare the lexica.) Accordingly he rendered the phrase *bisha bisha* with *ra'ah hola, ra 'ah* for the first bisha and *hola* for the second, thinking that bisha was feminine (!) The last he should have rendered, as he did in 6.2, but it would have even been more appropriate if his translation would have conveyed the sense of "a very great evil." Compare 6.1.

Incidentally, the phrase in 6.2 *holi ra'* may be perfectly normal despite what Barton, *Ecclesiastes*, a.l. avers. (Compare *mera' bish* in the Aramaic as well as the phrase *holi ra'* in rabbinic Hebrew. Compare Berakot 17a.) I incline nevertheless to the sense of "a very great evil" in the Qohelet passage.

10.17 describes the good fortune of a country whose king is of his own mind, and whose officers have the proper responsibility for the conduct of governmental affairs. They eat at the proper time, and the verse continues "with strength and not in debauchery." *"Strength"* juts peculiarly at this juncture in the verse. We should expect something like "in moderation" and the like. The Aramaic original actually suggests this apposite alternative. The Eastern Aramaic has an expression *behusana* rt. hs, med. Waw, meaning "with moderation," "sparingly," which would fit the context very well. The translator failed to recognize the word as such, and associated it with *hasna* rt. hsn, "Strength" (the letters being the same consonantly), hence his *bigbura*.

The familiar verse of 11.1, "Cast thy bread upon the waters for thou shalt find it after many days," has been worn by usage and it would seem sacrilegious to find fault with its meaning. The truth is, however that the verse as it stands makes for no clearcut meaning. Moses Mendelssohn, Morris Jastrow, Ehrlich and others interpret the verse as a bit of shrewd advice to assume ventures in business, which will show a return eventually, provided one does not concentrate one's risks all in one venture. Levy, (*Das Buch Kohelet*, a.l) is right in supposing that *lahmeka* must mean "capital," "fortune," because that is the one interpretation that fits the context. The only difficulty is that no support is given for this meaning. *Lehem* as "bread" makes for little sense even figuratively. Moreover, the use of *shalah*, "send forth," with *lehem* is very unusual. It is clear that *lehem* must contain some reference other that to bread.

The Aramaic underlying text has an interesting, enlightening suggestion. The root *peras* I in the Aramaic as in Hebrew means "spread, spread out" used for scrolls, curtains, hangings, and the like. Note especially its use for the sails of a vessel, Ez. 27.7 *mifraseik*, and the Targum *parseik*.

The   root *peras* II has the meaning of "break," and some nominal formations are found in the meaning of "bread" as in Syraic *perista*, Hebrew *perusa* (Jastrow, Dictionary, s.v.). What the precise form may have been in the Aramaic text need not be determined for the moment, but it is clear that the roots *peras* I and *peras* II were confused with each other and misapplied by our translator to our verse. The verse should have carried the meaning: "Set your sail upon the waters for after many days you will retrieve it." The next verse then forms excellent continuity: "make seven or eight ventures for you know not what disaster will befall the *land*" (in contrast to the waters).

Moreover, in the expression *mah yihyeh ra'ah 'al ha-'arez̤*, the masculine verb and the feminine noun are to be explained as momentary lapses on the part of the translator, who confounded the determinate masculine form *bisha'* and the indeterminate absolute feminine but identical form *bisha'*, rendering *ra 'ah* instead of *ra'*.

12.1: "And remember your Creator in the days of your youth." As is well known, a host of commentators have regarded *bor'aka*, "your Creator," as very strange inasmuch as the sequence has nothing of a religious exhortation, but is rather a portrayal of the infirmities of old age. Some commentators have contended (Ed. Chr. Schmidt, Graetz, Ehrlich) that *bor'aka* must in some way be connected with *bari'*, meaning "healthy." The form in Hebrew is left undetermined by the commentators, a form *beru'im* or *bore'* not being found.

The underlying Aramaic explains the matter quite simply. The translator misread *boryak*, "your health" (Targum Ex. 21.19), as *baryak*, "your Creator" (the letters are the same). Translate: "Be mindful of your health in the days of your youth before the days of illness come by. . ."

A difficult phrase in 12.13 becomes quite understandable when we seek the solution via the Aramaic retroversion. The passage reads: "The end of the matter: all having been heard: fear God and keep his commandments, for this is the whole man."

"The end of the matter" represents the Aramaic *sofa' di (de) miltha'* mentioned previously. "All having been heard," is inadequate and incorrect. It is not true to say, and certainly for Qohelet that everything *was* heard. The Aramaic participle, in a sentence where all the verbs are preterit, may intrude at any point and may involute all actions to the present and/or future. (Compare M.L. Margolis, *Aramaic Language*, par. 80). Thus, our text at this point should have been translated: "all things will be understood." The translator here failed to understand the temporal relation. Moreover, the final phrase,

"This is the whole man," make no sense as it stands, but it is clear what took place. For *zeh*, "this," the Aramaic had *Dalet Yod Nun*, which the translator read as *den*. He should have read the participle *dayen*, the Aramaic participle from *dyn*, "judge." Probably at the end of the verse there was the untranslatable *hawa'*=is or *hu'*, although for an exact parallel compare Ps. 75.8. The full force of the correct interpretation is brought out in the sequel of the next verse: "for God will bring every action into *judgment*." The continuity now informs a rational flow of ideas.

The poetic flight in chapter twelve forms stichs of three beats each, as a rule. It was pointed out previously that verse 5 is restored likewise to three beats by the reading of *hat hattim*, "he shall be afraid of snares/pitfalls." Verse 2 similarly requires some restoration as will readily be evident:

"Before the sun, and the light[?] and the moon, and the stars
          are darkened,
And the clouds return after the rain."

It is clear that the first part of the verse is overloaded; the word *'or*, "light," appears redundant. To explain "sun" and "light" as hendiadys is improbable as the combination is not found anywhere, the usual being "sun, moon, and stars" in the Bible (Deut. 4.19 and elsewhere). The translator saw in his Aramaic text *wenagah*, "and it shall be darkened."

The root *negah* is like *'urta* in Aramaic, ambivalent in character. *'Urta*, for example, may mean "light" or "darkness," depending on the locality, e.g., Pesachim 3a *mar ki'atreh umar ki'atreh: 'urta* may mean "light" or "darkness," each legal authority according to his locality. The same applies to *negah:* it may mean "to dawn" and "wait all night," hence *nagah*, with the participle used as substantive, signifies "dawn" or "twilight" (Payne Smith, *Dictionary* 327. Compare further C.C. Torrey, *Four Gospels*, 1947, 297). The original Aramaic probably ran:

'ad dela' yehshak shimsha'
wenagah yarha wekokabayya'
"*Before the sun is obscured,*
And the moon and the stars are darkened."

Wenagah participle at the beginning of the verse may be singular, quite according to Semitic, i.e., Hebrew and Aramaic usage. "Darkened" makes for the appropriate sense.

It is the contention of one scholar that translation from one document cannot be proved unless there be verses and connected passages, shown to have been rendered from the matric document, instead of sporadic words that may have been mistranslated. While this is a stern criterion, and mistranslations cannot be called for on demand or in bulk, and only come through the familiarity and ability of the investigator's linguistic knowledge of the primary and secondary document, it is fortunate that in Qohelet such evidence is manifest in some amplitude.

A section of the opening verses (1.5–6) runs as follows:
The sun rises and the sun goes down
And to his place he pants where he shines.
The wind goes to the south
And turns about to the north
Round and round the wind goes,
And on its circuits the wind returns.

1. It is very peculiar to say that the sun "pants," even though maintained by Brown, Driver, Briggs, in the Oxford Lexicon under the figure of a racer.

2. If the sun goes down, and goes to its place where it is invisible, what is meant therefore by the phrase "where he shines?"

3. The word *sham*, "there," in the Hebrew is strange.

4. The wind may go north and south, but does it have "circuits"?

When we retrovert to Aramaic, we secure a proper understanding and reconstruction of the whole passage.

The translator saw in front of him *t'b*, which he read as *ta'eb*, Aramaic participle *t'b* "pant," "desire." He should have read *ta'eb* (same consonants, same vocables) participle of *tab* (med. waw), "return." This is quite in agreement now with the idea of the winds and the streams, described as *returning* to their places: *shab* (verse 6); *shabim* (verse 7).

In addition the translator mistook his Aramaic *dnh*, which he interpreted to mean *danah*, "shine," in the participle. He was mistaken again. He should have read *d + nah* "where he rests."

The wind likewise returns to its place, and not on its circuits. The translator read *dara'*, "circuit," "circle," for *dira'/dara'/dura'*; the forms vary (cf. Brockelmann, Jastrow in their dictionaries) meaning "abode," for "habitation." There is an abode or chamber for the winds. This corresponds to the abode of the sun where it too rests for the night. Compare the Targum to the verse. The verses now assume a much more meaningful cast and focus:

The sun rises and the sun sets
And he returns to his place
Therein where he rests. . . . .
Round and round the wind goes,
And to its abode the wind returns.

Observe too the phrase "round and round," Aramaic *hazor hazor*, or
sehor sehor, doubling in Aramaic translation. *Sabib* is found some
three hundred times in the Bible with the almost invariable *sehor sehor*
whereas the Hebrew would use *sabib* but once. (Compare the invariable
usage in the Targums and the Peshitta at Gen. 23.17; Ex. 19.12; 27.17 *et
passim*.) Where the Hebrew repeats *sabib* twice as II Chron. 4.3, and
Ezechiel 8.10;37.2;40.5, the Aramaic made its impression on the later
Hebrew. In Qohelet, it's translation. It is our conviction that the
restoration of this passage with the triad of sun, wind, and streams that
return again and again to their starting points provides enough
evidence for an affirmative verdict of translation in Qohelet.

A connected passage which shows proof again of translation from
Hebrew into Aramaic is extant at 2.3:

*Tarti belibbi limshok bayyayin 'et besari, welibbi noheg
bahokma* . . . The literal translation would be: "I spied in my heart to
attract [lit. to pull] my heart with wine, now my heart was conducting
itself with wisdom."

Tar means "spy (out)"; with "heart," *undeutbar* (Ehrlich). No less
puzzling is *limshok*, "pull." This word is usually emended. *Noheg* as a
participle "conducting" not quite apposite in the context. The solution
offered by the Aramaic is enlightening: *tar*(variably as *t'r* in Chr.
Palestinian Aramaic, Samaritan *twr*, *t'r intellexit*; the nominal
formation is employed *syriace* for "contemplation", Brockelmann,
Lexicon Syriacum², *814a*) merely reproduces the underlying Aramaic
which the translator copied, but he assigned to *tar* a far different
meaning than the original writer ever thought of. One should translate:
"I meditated." *Limshok* is a mechanical rendition of the underlying
Aramaic *gerar*, meaning "pull," but also having the idiomatic Aramaic
usage "to stimulate with wine." Compare *Berakot* 35b; And did not
Rabba drink wine every Passover eve so that he might stimulate his
appetite to eat more unleavened bread? (Answer) "Much wine
stimulates *(garer)*, a little satisfies." *Noheg* represents a misunderstanding on the part of the translator of a grammatical form, i.e., *medabber*
and *middabber*, the *Pa'el* and the *Itpa'el/'al*. The translator should have
rendered with *mitnaheg*. However, it is quite possible that *middabba/-
er* carries along with it the idea of "planning, ruling, advising," cf.

madbaranutha/tahbulot Prov. 1.5;12.5;24.6 in the "Targum," and therefore the translation should have conveyed something like "my heart, however, was deliberating wisely."

5.5 contains a series of words which in analysing the original Aramaic document brings out the more pointed meaning: Do not allow your mouth to bring your flesh into guilt *(lahti')* and say not before the messenger *(mal'ak)* that it was an error *(shegagah);* why should God be angry at your voice and destroy the work of your hands?

It is the nuances in the verse that the translator failed to perceive, and he followed through in his rendering with the usual stock translations. A standard equivalent of *hata'* is *hab* in Aramaic. The Aramaic read *lehayyaba'* which the translator should have retained in the Hebraic *lehayyeb*, which would bring out the full vigor of the thought: "Do not allow your mouth to condemn your body."

Mal'ak cannot mean "angel" (!), so Authorised Version, and Revised Version, but "messenger" as Rashi correctly saw (hence JV "messenger)". Actually *mal'ak* is a mistranslation of *sheliha*, the messenger from the sanctuary whose function was to collect monies vowed to the sanctuary service. In the Mishna, the term used is *gabah* "collect."

Shegagah, "error," is misplaced here. A man never says that he gave something in error. He will apologize by saying that he forgot about it. The Aramaic *shelutha* means "error" and "forgetfullness," and the translator awkwardly chose the first meaning.

In 10.15 the translator misconstrued the whole verse, and the restoration of the Aramaic resolves in a striking fashion all the difficulties and makes for a new and original sense. The passage runs: *'amal ha-kesilim teyagg'ennu 'asher lo yoda' laleket 'el 'ir.* The translation would run: "the labor of fools wearies them for he does not know how to go to a city."

In the Hebrew the grammatical difficulties astonish: *'amal* is masculine, but the verb takes a feminine form. *Ha-kesilim* is obviously plural but the suffix of the verb is singular. Then, complicatedly, "know" in the second half is singular. Then again, what is the meaning of the thought that he does not know how to go to a city?

We retrovert to the Aramaic: *le'utha deshatya teshalhinneh de-la' yada' lemezal lemethe'.*

1. The translator employed the masculine *'amal* correctly as a rendering of *le'utha*. However, when he came to translating the verb two words later, he forgot that he rendered a feminine noun with a masculine one, and merely copied the feminine form of the word in front of him, not remembering the masculine *'amal* at the beginning of

the verse.

2. He misread *shaṭya* the singular as a plural *shaṭayya*. The consonants would be the same.

3. He misread *lemethe'*, "to come," as *lematha'*, "to a /the city." The second half of the verse bears the signification; he does not know whether he's coming or going: he does not know what he is about (going or coming, literally). For the parallel idea and the use of the phrase cf. Targum to Isaiah 24.20.

Our whole verse now may be translated: "the toil of the fool wears him out for he does not know what he is about." The asyndeton *lemezel lemethe'* would be idiomatic Aramaic.

An interesting example where the Hebrew is meaningless but makes for excellent sense upon restoration *aramaice* is found at 7.12: *ki beẓel ha-ḥokma beẓel ha-kesef weyitron da'at ha-ḥokma teḥayyeh be'aleha.* The translation would be: for to be in the shadow of wisdom is to be in the shadow of money. But the superiority of knowledge is that wisdom preserves the life of the one who possesses it. All students of the text are puzzled by the association of "shadow" with silver and wisdom, and therefore resort to emendation reading *keẓel* twice but this is scarcely a decided improvement. The Aramaic gives the correct solution which read: *debaṭlah ḥukmetha baṭel kaspa.* The Hebrew translator, when he looked at the verse, associated both verbs with *b'ṭulla* "in the shadow of," and hence rendered doubly with *beẓel.* He failed to recognize the participles.

The restoration advanced here, "Where there is no intelligence, there is no money," makes for excellent continuity with the preceding passage of verse 11. Intelligence, the author avers, combined with an inheritance is good; and especially (the Hebrew *yoter* here represents actually the Aramaic *yattir* "especially") for those who see the sun. Where intelligence fails, the money will be useless.

The rest of the verse with its peculiar *da'at ha-ḥokma* rests on a misapprehension of the particle *de* or *di*, which the translator mistook as a genetival relation instead of a subordinating conjunction. The Aramaic probably ran: *weyutran manda' deḥukmetha teqayyem lemarah.* The whole should have been translated with the meaning: "But knowledge is an advantage *because* wisdom sustains its possessor." To the translator the words *yutran manda'* were constructs, as seems evidenced by *deḥukmetha;* and so he rendered with the strange *da'at ha-ḥokma.*

A translator who has not fully mastered a second language, and we have now observed this as a characteristic of our translator, has the most difficulty with the small elusive particles that make up the idiosyncratic fabric of the language. In English it is the small but significant particles "in," "with" "to;" in German *ab, zu, mit,* that come at the end of the sentence that confuse an alien to the language. In Qohelet the translator is at sea in quite a number of cases: in 2.15, "Why did I become wiser then the more?" where *'az* is a mistranslation of *beken,* "accordingly." The translator did not know this and followed through with meanings he knew of *beken,* "then"=*'az,* misplaced and incongruous in the Hebrew.

The Aramaic particle *leḥod (leḥad),* as well as *beram,* have in the peculiarity of the language double significations "also" and "but." (Compare Brederek, *Konkordanz zum Targum Onkeleos.*) Thus *lehod* is employed for *'ak* Num. 22.20 and similarly *beram* Gen. 9.4, and conversely *beram* is employed for *gam* in Ge. 20.12. In a number of times in Qohelet's Hebrew, it is clear that the Aramaic particles were confounded. Thus in 6.7: "All the labor of a man is for his mouth, and yet *(Wegam)* his desire is not filled," the Aramaic most likely read *lehod.* In the same fashion the following verses should be translated with "but, however" even though the Hebrew reads *gam:*

3.11 *But* as for the people of the world (*see* Commentary).

4.16 *However* the ones who come after will not rejoice in him.

6.3 *But* he did not have burial.

Note that the translator does not know the restrictive *'ak* or *rak,* which he never employs.

An additional particle that the translator missed is the particle *man* in Aramaic, which if vocalized with *pataḥ* means "who" and should be translated by the Hebrew *mi;* and *man,* if vocalized with *qamez,* should be translated by *ma,* "what." Thus at Ex. 16.15 the manna is called *man* because the Hebrews did not know *ma hu',* "what it was," and evidence is forwarded for *man=*"what" by Böhl (cited in Gesenius-Buhl, *Hebr. u. aram. Handwörterbuch* p. 433a, from the Amarna letters). Confusion reigns but the distinction between *măn* and *mān* are preserved and traceable. Compare for example such passages as *kol man dehaweina 'abed ken:* "Every time I used to do so" (Yer. Berakot, Krot. ed. 7c and pseud Jon. Gen. 33.9. G. Dalman preserves the distinction in his *Aramäisches-neuhebräisches Wörterbuch,* p. 229 and see his *Grammatik*², 120 for a discussion.) One may also cite Ezr 5.4 and translate: "what [not who] are the names of the men," where *mān* was mispointed as *măn.*

The Hebrew translator of Qohelet confused the two in 2.12 where the translation should run: "Who is the man (Heb. *mi ha-'ish*) that may come after the king," not "what is the man."

He made the same error again in 6.8: *ma le 'ani yodea' lahalok neged ha-ḥayyim*, where the usual rendering is: "or what advantage has the poor man who has understanding in walking before the living?" Similarly the Jewish version, but the Hebrew is obviously awkward. The word *man* was misinterpreted: it should have been read as "who" not "what" which made for the strange construction. We should read in the Hebrew *yodi'a/yode'a*. The verse now reads sensibly, "Who can tell the poor man how to struggle with life?"

On the other hand, the translator misread *min*, "from," as *man*, "what," in 7.24 (for which see Commentary).

The Aramaic translation hypothesis does excellent service in elucidating the cryptic name of Qohelet. Everyone recognizes that the name is most peculiar; it is a feminine participle: in some way it is Solomonic, clearly the name of a man, as the son of David implies. It is usual to explain that Qohelet means as the root *qahal* is supposed to imply, a collector of sentences, although it could be objected that the root is always used of living things, e.g., Ps. 26.5; Prov. 5.14 *et passim.* The term "preacher" is based upon Greek *ekklesiastes,* Jerome *concionator* but thus is theologically conditioned. The form is supposed to be identified with Arabic formations as *caliphate,* like excellency, majesty and so on. Such identity with Qohelet, i.e., the office of speaking, or preaching, hence the Speaker himself becomes incongruous in the mouth and first person of Qohelet himself; compare 1.12 (I the Speaker (?). I the Preacher (?)). Comparisons are likewise made with *soferet* Ezr. 2.55 (Neh.7.57) and 2.57 (=Neh. 7.59), i.e., persons without identifiable names as such but persons who belong to an office of *soferet,* "cutting the hair (sic!), barbering," or *pokeret ha-ẓebayyim,* "trapping deer/gazelles [not "binding"]" (compare Prov. 5.22 and the Targum) inasmuch as the Chronicler did not care to mention their names as they were merely the Nethinim and the "servants of Solomon." All the evidence seems to point to the function and office, with regard to Qohelet, rather to a name or to the man himself. However, it remains astonishing that Qohelet in form is never used for "preacher" before his day or since, that the root is never employed for composing or compiling sentences or proverbs, and that the nominal formation with the suffix...-*et* with the connotation of "office of..." is virtually non-existent in Hebrew. (For other objections, compare H.L. Ginsberg, *Qohelet* [in Hebrew], p. 35f.)

E. Renan was the first to suspect that Qohelet was a cryptogram concealing in some way the name of Solomon, in a sort of artificial device of substituting one Hebrew letter for another: Alef for Taw (Atbash). He admitted, however, that a solution was not yet found (compare Graetz, *Kohelet*, 17.). P. Cassel and E. König argued that Qohelet adds up, in numerals for letters, to 535 while Shelomoh ben David ha-melek add up to 536 (cited by Wildeboer, *Kohelet*, 122). The intuition of these scholars was heading in the right direction but it remains, as I think, for the Aramaic translation hypothesis to provide the correct solution.

The difficulties inherent in the word Qohelet are as follows:

1. As previously noted, not only is the feminine form strange, but the name is not found anywhere else, even with the root.

2. In one passage the word Qohelet is treated as a feminine with a feminine verb(7.27).

3. Elsewhere, however, it is treated as masculine (1.12;12.9.10).

4. The passage at 7.27 is corrected to read ha-Qohelet as is found at 12.8.

5. But ha-Qohelet at 12.8 is a monstrum itself, as you cannot add a definite article to a name.

This confusion of Qohelet as masculine and as feminine, with the article and without the article, must lead one to the conclusion that *this is not a name at all*.

The almost universal equivalent of Qahal in Aramaic would be *kenash*, as evidenced throughout the Targums and the Peshitta. The feminine Qohelet reflects the feminine participle *kansha,* or pointed more correctly *kanosha* since the translator did not vocalize his Aramaic text properly. In not performing his task properly, he moreover *translated* the name instead of transliterating it, a procedure which translators persistently but erroneously indulge in. The book of Qohelet itself is transmitted and known as Ecclesiastes, der Prediger, the Preacher and so on. In the Targums, too, Ararat is translated by Kardu (?) Gen. 8.4; Hazezon Tamar by En Gedi Gen. 14.7; Kaftor by Qaputqa (?); Cappadocia(?) Gen. 10.14; Kittim by Roma'e (Romans) Num. 24.24.

The explanation of the difficulties involved in Qohelet may be suggested as follows. The translator was at sea as to how he should render the word Qohelet and its syntax, and so he carried through his task in much the same way that many biblical translators have resolved their problems: he straddled the issue. An illustration of this would be in the marginal alternatives in the Authorized and Revised Versions of the Bible on any other verse or in the oldest Greek translation, where you have doublets inserted in the verse side by side with each other.

(Compare M.L. Margolis, *The Story of Bible Translations*). So in 7.27 the translator thought that with the *He* at the end of *kansha* perhaps the word should be construed as feminine and therefore he should translate with a feminine verb as he so did: *'amrah*. On the other hand, he thought that the *He* was an orthographical mark of the masculine, which is quite possible, even frequent in Aramaic, e.g., *baithah* Ezr. 5.12; 6.15; *dahabah* 5.14;6.5;7.18; *dinah* 7.26; *dikronah* 6.2; *yeqarah* Dan. 5.20; and even *malkah* king (!) 2.11; *naharah* some fourteen times in Ezra; *'ammah* 5.12. Observe that these very same words are also written with *Alef* in the biblical Aramaic sections as well. (Compare H.H. Powell, *The Supposed Hebraisms in the Biblical Aramaic*, p. 10.) So he treated *kanshah* syntactically as masculine at 1.12; 12.9.10. In 12.8 he considered the form as determinate, and then rendered astoundingly *ha-Qohelet*, "the Qohelet"—an impossibility. And with all this he did not recognize what was probably the original form, *kanosha*.

The word *kanosha* is a *fa'ola* form, i.e., a denomination of one who has a functional or professional character and means either one who gleans in the fields (compare the name Garner) or one who sweeps (floors) (compare Jastrow, *Dictionary* s.v.; Payne Smith, *Dictionary*, 219); and is an actual name found about a half-dozen times in Carthaginian (Phoenician) Inscriptions. (*See* p. 136.) The name did not originate therefore with Kanosha-Qohelet. Kanosha, himself of humble origin, and more notably one who completely downgraded himself as a creature of no worth, was lifted to the heights when he realized that his name, through magical numerology, added up to the same letters computatively as Solomon: K=20, N=50; S=300, H=5, total 375. S=300, L=30, M=40, H=5, total 375.[91] The name Kanosha adds up precisely and mathematically to Shelomoh, and as one scholar put it, after examining this computation, this cannot have been an accident. (Compare C.C. Torrey, *Jewish Quarterly Review*, vol. 39, pp. 151–60.) For Qohelet, with his aspirations to be another and even greater Solomon, this corroboration through his name was an intoxication and a sense of glory.

Enough has been shown, it may now be concluded, that the Hebrew of Qohelet is a translation from an underlying Aramaic. One scholar argued in a review of a preliminary draft of this evidence presented in the Jewish Quarterly Review, 1945, 17–45 that it was an overdemonstration of the case. If so, I do not know what that means. It is only with the accumulation of evidence and example do we arrive at conclusions and conviction, and there are over seventy-five examples of evidence of translation presented in these pages aside from the contributions of H.L. Ginsberg and C.C. Torrey. "The value of a principle," Emerson asserted, "is the number of things all pointing like arrows in the same direction." Or, as Thoreau his contemporary had occasion once to observe wryly: "Circumstantial evidence can be very strong, like the trout in the milk."

Babylon, the glory of kingdoms,
the splendor and pride of the Chaldeans.
—Isaiah 13.19.

XIV
Locale and Date

It is clear that Qohelet lived in an urbanized, sophisticated society, not a rural one. The setting "at Jerusalem," the building of houses, of parks and of vineyards with the artificially constructed canals, the exotic luxuries, the recitals of male and female singers (2.4–6), the throngs that come to see either the coronation or the introduction of the heir apparent to the populace (4.15–16), the corruption of city officials (5.7), the vicissitudes of politics in which the slaves have power and noblemen are humiliated, the debauchery of government officials (10.6.16)—all betoken the many-faceted human relationships, the web and mesh of city life.

The city, moreover, is a capital city where the king's seat and royal residence was, and where the royal court lay. Qohelet in his capacity as an attendant at the court, whether in high position or low, was at close enough range to see the shallowness of court life, the shout of the ruler against his stupid underlings (9.17), as well as the mistakes that rulers make (10.5). Qohelet carefully watched the king to observe his moods, and to carry out scrupulously what the king commanded (8.3). We must try now to determine who this king was, and which capital city Qohelet lived in.

It cannot be a Judean king because from the time of Ezra until Alexander Yannai (103–76 B.C.E.) no Jewish king ruled. That is to say, the rulership of Johanan Hyrcanus was, strictly speaking, that of priestly principate, not of a king, as he himself issued coinage with the legend of *yohanan ha-kohen ha-gadol* (Cooke, *North Semitic Inscriptions*, p. 353) although there can be no doubt that he exercised the powers of a secular prince. He was, however, essentially high priest. Likewise the rule of Judah Aristobulus of one year may be discounted. The "king" in Qohelet's thoughts and observations could only be Alexander Yannai, but the general consensus of scholars is that the composition of the book in the first century would be very unlikely (cf.

123

O. Eissfeldt, *The Old Testament*, trans. by Peter R. Ackroyd, 1965, 497).
The third century B.C.E. is the date most favored by scholars (cf. R.
Pfeiffer, *Introduction to the Old Testament*,[2] p. 731). It follows that the
capital city where Qohelet served at court was not Jerusalem, and the
king was not a Jewish king. The two capital cities which had the most
bearing and influence on Jewish life in the Hellenistic period could
have only belonged to the Ptolemaic or Seleucid empires.

Alexandria at first would seem to be a natural choice. There the
Septuaginta was conceived and written and where Philo later
flourished. Nevertheless a number of circumstances militate against
this view. The book of Qohelet refers to certain geographical
characteristics, climate, atmospheric conditions that would be alien
and peculiar to Egypt. In 11.3 for example the verse contains the
thought that if the clouds fill up, they will inundate the earth with
water; in 12.2 the clouds come back after the rain. This description is
out of character for Egypt, which is practically rainless. Or as 11.3
states, if a tree fall to the north or south, there it will lie (immovable).
Trees in Egypt are on the rare side, and the Ptolemies of Egypt strictly
regulated the cutting of older trees, of the branches and of the handling
of fallen trees (compare M. Rostovtzeff, *The Social and Economic
History of the Hellenistic World*,[2] I, 298). 11.1 implies that to operate a
fleet of vessels, or to divide one's equity in seven or eight different
ventures and send them forth on the water would be a customary and
ordinary business transaction, where the sea would be observable from
many vantage points and present in one's speculation. In Ptolemaic
Egypt, "the Nile, the lakes, and the marshes were parts of the king's
property" (Rostovtzeff op. cit. I, 296) and transportation, both on water
and land, was a key royal preoccupation and concern. As another
example, iron (10.10) was scanty in Pharaonaic Egypt (Rostovtzeff, I,
362), though considerably relieved by the Ptolemies, nevertheless had
to be imported. Forests were practically unknown (cf. art. Egypt,
Encyclopedia Biblica, 1208) and irrigation (2.6) would seem to belong
to another country. Egypt would not seem to be favored for the locale of
Qohelet.

The only alternative would seem to be Syria, neighboring to
Palestine in the north. Several considerations would seem to favor this
judgment. In the first place, the climatic conditions of Syria would be
reflected in Qohelet. The clouds that bring the rainfall, the trees, the
ports implied in 11.2 would be more suitable to that country.
Moreoever the trimetalism of the Ptolemies—the gold, silver, and
bronze (and they had a practical monopoly on gold)—is not evidenced

in Qohelet. The Seleucid empire, denied gold, based itself mainly on silver. Qohelet mentions silver and gold at 2.8, but silver is placed first, and gold as coin never mentioned thereafter, *kesef* (silver) being the ordinary term for money (5.9;7.12;10.19). In 12.6 the "silver cord" is placed ahead of the "crown of gold."

Syria, moreover, is old Aramaean country where the local population, in small hamlets, spoke Aramaic from a millennium and more, and had temples to Haddad, Astarte, Aglibol. In general, Aramaic was the *lingua franca* although ceding some ground to Greek in the Hellenistic period. The Mishna evidences much in accord with what we know from Josephus and the Gospels that commercial traffic and intellectual exchange with Syria was transacted on a much greater scale and more sweeping activity than with Egypt. Paul's activity was always directed to the north. The Mishna will deal with Egyptian sundries, Egyptian beer, Egyptian beans, etc., but the larger questions of Halaka relate severely to Syria.[92] If Qohelet were written in Aramaic, which I hope has been substantially demonstrated, then Syria would be the natural climate where the book would be composed.

Moreover, the locale is confirmed by the language. The dialect in which the book was written may be identified with some accuracy, that of Eastern Aramaic, a prototype of what might be Syriac today. Thus, for example, in 1.5 where the translator mistook *de + nah/danah*, the particle *de/di* of Western Aramaic reflects the Eastern provenance. In 3.4b–4c where the verb RQD is played upon with different vocalization (cf. Peshitta, Ginsberg a.l.), the language undoubtedly indicates the regional origin. In six cases out of thirteen, moreover (see chapter on mistranslation), the translator confused *hu'* and *hawa'* with *Aleph* instead of *He*, i.e., the predominantly Eastern Aramic form. The repetitious expression *bish bish*, characteristic of Syriac (*see* Commentary at 5.12) lends further confirmation. Note, moreover, the terms *husana*, "moderation" at 10.17 confused with *husana*, "strength," 1.13, *tur*, "meditate," *gerar*, "stimulate" (Babylonian Talmudic). In 4.1, "And *from* the hand of their oppressors there is power," meaning "*in* the hand," the expression is Eastern Aramaic. Seemingly then the internal clues from the book and the language and its grammatical formations point to Syria as the birthplace of the book's composition. Josephus (*War*, 7.2.3) implies that Syria had more Jews than any other country.

We may refine our investigation further. If Syria is the country, and Qohelet is a member of the court's retinue close to the king in whatever capacity, then the royal seat was at Antioch. This capital city as a place for Qohelet's composition has much to commend it. Antioch in the Hellenistic period became the third largest city in the world after Rome and Alexandria,[93] and one-third of its population was Jewish,[94] the total population being about 500,000 according to Strabo and Pliny, as cited by Rostovtzeff I, 498; II, 1140. It was here that Paul came fetched by Barnabas, and the term Christianity was coined. On another occasion, I have argued that Tobit in the second century B.C.E. and the Book of Wisdom in the first century B.C.E. were likewise composed there in Aramaic.[95]

There is another factor, however, that must be considered in determining the locale of the book's composition because there was a "co-capital" in Seleucid Syria—Seleucia on the Tigris, which shared the rulership of Syria with Antioch on the Orontes.

After Alexander the Great, the capital of the Seleucid empire was located first at this Seleucia on the Tigris. At the founding of Antioch on the Orontes, however, the main seat of government passed to the latter city. In 292 B.C.E., Seleucus I Nicator, recognizing that he could not govern the East from Antioch, assigned his son Antiochus the prerogative of being joint-king and governor of the East—a pattern of Seleucid delegation of authority to the heir apparent. Interestingly, Seleucia became the "Royal City" where Seleucus had transferred many Babylonians—Babylon having been partially ruined by Antigonus I—because Seleucia was more convenient and favorably situated than Babylon for the convergence of Asiatic trade. In addition, the city on the Tigris became important for military affairs both for expeditions to the East and for activities of the navy on the Persian Gulf. For a while Seleucia and Babylon flourished side by side, but under Antiochus I a large section of the population of Babylon was forcibly transferred to Seleucia where the Greeks and Macedonians, descendants of Alexander's men as well as new immigrants, held sway with a council of three hundred, a gerousia, magistrates, etc., in the Greek *polis*. Underneath, however, although the political power waned, the old forms in Babylon remained. Seleucians were still occasionally called Babylonians (*Cambridge Ancient History*, VII, 93). The old temples of E-sagila and E-zida were supported by the Seleucids; the old Babylonian banks continued with their business; documents in cuneiform with double names in Greek and Babylonian (interestingly the Greeks take on Babylonian names) are extant in good number; the old language survives and is used side by side with the Greek. As V. Tcherikover remarked (*Hellenistic Civilization and the Jews*, 35), the old hyphenated Greek and Semitic names of cities soon lost their Greek components and the Semitic name resurged to the present day.

The Jews constituted a goodly number in Seleucia, the exact number being hard to estimate. Philo and Josephus testify that the Jews were quite numerous in Mesopotamia and Babylonia, and in Ant. XV 39 the Jewish population of Babylonia is estimated as "not a few tens of thousands" (Tcherikover, p. 503, n.73). As mentioned, Strabo (for his day) assumed that the population of Antioch was smaller than Seleucia, and in Pliny's day the latter was estimated to have a population of 600,000 (Rostovtzeff, p. 1140). All in all, the area was a flourishing Jewish center and it is instructive that Josephus states that he had written his first draft of the *War* in "Hebrew," i.e., Aramaic for the use of his brothers in the East, and Vespasian and Titus encouraged him to prepare a Greek version for Hellenistic readers. By all the signs then, the many Jews in the Eastern part of the Seleucid empire might use Greek to talk to the Greek authorities and Macedonian minority, use Aramaic to converse with the Syrians (of whom there was a large number), and just as easily employ Babylonian as occasion would require, Aramaic and Akkadian sharing the largest number of cognates with one another. (*See* H.H. Powell, *The Supposed Hebraisms in the Grammar of the Biblical Aramaic,* p. 7 for the idea that "Assyrian [is] an older local variety of Aramaic.") For the Jews, Aramaic was the language of converse and study. Hillel the Babylonian (b. ca. 60 B.C.E.) would use both Hebrew and Aramaic, and letters to the Diaspora by Rabban Gamaliel (Dalman, *Dialektproben*[2], p. 3) to Babylon, Media, Yavan, were written in Aramaic. S. Zeitlin in his *The Rise and Fall of the Judean State* (p. 61) points out:

The Babylonian Judeans were religiously closer to the Judeans of Jerusalem than were the Judeans of Egypt. The Judeans of Jerusalem felt a deeper bond to their Babylonian brothers also because they spoke Aramaic, which was similar to the tongue of the Judeans of Jerusalem. The Judeans of Alexander however spoke Greek, a language foreign to the Jerusalemites. . . .

If the book's composition be laid in Syria, as its language was Aramaic, and Syria had two capitals in reality Antioch and Seleucia, it follows that Qohelet may have been written in either of the two cities, and while a choice is difficult to make, I favor on balance the view that the book was written in the East, in Babylonia.

The materials are scanty for the Jews in Babylonia in the Hellenistic period. We know that the Judahites who were exiled to Babylonia were the most important political and cultural forces the nation possessed, the king, the royal family, the nobility, the high-born families, the priests (Ezr. 2.36), i.e., the learned and cultured class,—Ezra the *sofer* (=bookman, man of books) was a priest—members of the urban and national government (Ezr. 2.1f.), the *dallat ha-'arez* being left on the land (2 Kings 25.12; Jer. 40.7). The Jews who did not come back with the Return became a dense population in Babylonia, so much so that Antiochus III transferred two thousand families from Babylonia to Asia Minor. Another stray item about Jews in Babylonian history tells that under Tiberius Caesar two brothers Ḥasinai and Ḥanilai sought to establish an independent territory under Jewish jurisdiction (*Ant.* XVIII, 310f.) The attempt failed. This aroused the hatred of the Babylonians and many Jews fled from Babylon to Seleucia on the Tigris. In the latter city, in the struggle for power, pogroms broke out and Josephus says that fifty thousand Jews lost their lives. This is about all that we know about Babylonian Jews in Greek cities.

Schools and academies undoubtedly flourished, however. It is only once in a while that a scholar surfaces and gives an inkling of what progress and expansion of learning and culture had developed. Hillel the Babylonian emerged as the leading authority and scholar of his day and displaced the Benei Bethira in Palestine, becoming the head of the Sanhedrin in Jerusalem, although a Babylonian. The episode indeed is questioned (compare W. Bacher, art. Hillel, *Jewish Encyclopedia*) but *bien trouvé* for Hillel as indeed by all the sources must have been truly brilliant if jealous scholars could admit his scholarship and greatness. For a moment *multum in parvo* a Babylonian luminary lighted the sky reflecting a cultured intellectual environment. Two hundred years later the Babylonian Talmud, intricate, sophisticated, of a long tradition had already taken root and was growing. Before Hillel, some 150 years *ante*, Qohelet was writing his book.

Aside from the fact that the milieu is Babylonian, it is altogether in context that Qohelet read and made use of Akkadian literature, notably the Gilgamesh Epic. In one instance it would seem where Qohelet may have had in mind the words *lu-ub-bu-bu zu-ba-tu-ka*, "let your garments be sparkling fresh," probably rendered *yeḥawwrun ma'nai-kak* meaning "let your garments be white," just as the Hebrew translator rendered *ḥawwar* by the more familiar "white" (=*lebanim*). He was also a peruser of Akkadian proverbs and precepts, one of which confirms the passage at 10.20: "Even in your *thought* do not curse the king," which he may have known as a precept (cf. ANET, 427:) "The words of your inner self do not speak when alone." In one instance, he probably made use of a locution found only in the Sumerian antecedent of the epic of Gilgamesh (ANET, 49): "The three ply cloth will not be cut. . . ." When cut, it was a symbolical act of mourning. Qohelet employed it for his own use in 4.12: the threefold cord will not be snapped. In one instance, 12.11, Qohelet borrowed a figure *ro'eh eḥad* which he symbolically employed for Moses. It is true that the Hebrew Scriptures use *ro'eh* for Yahweh, and for Moses par excellence as the real, and simultaneously the symbolical shepherd of his people, but the concept that as *ro'eh* Moses the *fons et origo* of all the written and unwritten tradition should be denominated as the shepherd is peculiar. Students are perplexed by the expression. Undoubtedly, Qohelet was influenced by the usage of *re'u* having the combined meaning of shepherd and overseer, as for example in the self-praise of Hammu-rabi who repeatedly refers to himself in his Code as "I Hammu-rabi the shepherd . . . the shepherd of the people" (Driver and Miles, *The Babylonian Laws* II, 400) who was "to make justice appear in the land, destroy the evil, to rise like Shammash over the dark-haired folk to give light to the land. . . the favorite of the most high. . . the prince pure in heart. . . the manly [king] amongst kings. . . the profoundly wise who bears the charge of government. . . who has attained the source of wisdom. . . [etc., etc.] I set forth truth and justice throughout the land and prospered the people" (Prologue, Driver and Miles, p.13). Unconsciously, the Jewish glossator with his strong traditional feeling made use of the term *ro'eh* for Moses as the legislator for justice and law to his people, in contrast to Hammu-rabi.

Of interest is the circumstance, and as a sign of the Mesopotamian setting, that one may detect Akkadian words and phrases in the writing of his book. Thus in 5.10 Qohelet writes: "When prosperity increases, many are those who [lit.:] eat it." Undoubtedly the phrase is modeled upon the Akkadian *akalu tabtu*=eat good food". The basic meaning of the verse is : With the increase of good food, there increase many who eat it. Similarly in 10.18b: "With the lowering of hands, the house leaks." The term *shiflut yadaim*, not found elsewhere in the Bible, undoubtedly has its inception from *qata nadu*=let down the hand, signifying not to do any work (compare Driver and Miles, II 170). Then quite striking is the passage in 7.24 with reference to wisdom, that it is *'amoq 'amoq mi yimza'ennu*, literally deep, deep who can attain to it, where the repetition of *'amoq* is unusual. In Akkadian *'emqu*, "wise," *nimequ*, "wisdom," *Assyrian Dictionary* (Chicago, 151), whether the Hebrew translator misunderstood the phrase or not, was either present or intended in the passage so that the verse should be translated: "and *wisdom* is deep, who can attain to it?" In the mystifying language at

4.8, there is one and not a second *(sheni)*, perhaps in the back of the Aramaic *tinyan(a)* was the usage of *sanum* philologically=other man which may stand alone in Akkadian (Driver II, 216.) Probably the Hebrew should have been *w'en aẖer*, "there is no other" (meaning his wife). The word *'amal* in Qohelet is utilized in a seemingly unusual way to mean "profit, benefit," founded in the Aramaic *'amla*, as one undoubtedly finds its cognate in *nemelu* in Akadian (and too with the special sense of "profit"; H.L. Ginsberg, *Qohelet*, 14–15).

From the language of the book originally in Aramaic, the Babylonian milieu that seems reflected in the book, the familiarity with certain excerpts of Akkadian literature, and the percolating of Akkadian words and phrases that come through will lead naturally to the surmise that ʄQohelet was a Babylonian Jew who knew Aramaic and Akkadian and who served at the court of the Seleucid monarch.ʆWhich king was this? On balance, it would seem to be the royal court of Antiochus III when at first he was governing Babylonia for his brother (cf. the *Cambridge Ancient History*, VII, 723) and who then, as an inexperienced youth of eighteen, came officially to the throne. From Antioch on the Orontes, Antiochus III appointed a non-Seleucid to be governor in the other capital at Seleucia, but the Governor-General proved to be false and disloyal, and for some time matters were touch-and-go in the Far East. Perhaps this is alluded to in 10.16-17, where Qohelet mourns the dissolute conditions where the king is an immature lad, and the nobles live a life of debauchery and unbridled licentiousness. Commendable, on the other hand, is the fortunate situation of the land where the king knows his own mind and the nobles act responsibly. The circumstances would jibe, too, with the introduction of the crown prince to the people (4.15f.), when the king "introduced" him to the populace.

Any later date is precluded by the fact that Ben Sira (ca. 190 B.C.E.) knew and made use of Qohelet's book (following Barton, *Ecclesiastes*, pp. 54f). Furthermore the *terminus ad quem* seems to be about 100 B.C.E., as evidenced by the Book of Wisdom having been composed, as I have argued for, in Aramaic at Antioch on the Orontes,[96] and is a conscious direct polemic against the doctrines of Qohelet. (Compare the connected passage at 2.1f. in Wisdom and note the similarities to verses in Qohelet.) It would be quite appropriate that the Wisdom author, who most likely knew the Aramaic text of Qohelet, should answer and attack him in the same language. The translation of Joseph Reider in his edition of the Book of Wisdom has been followed with italicized departures, where the Greek translator of Wisdom misunderstood his Aramaic.[97]

"For they said within themselves, reasoning not aright, 'Short and sorrowful is our life and there is no healing [l. *prolongation of life]* at the end of man; and none was ever known that returned from Hades [compare Qoh. 2.23;5.18]. For by mere chance were we begotten, and hereafter we shall be as though we had never been, for smoke is the breath of our nostrils, and reason is a spark in the beating of our hearts [3.19]; which being extinguished the body shall turn into ashes, and the spirit be dispersed as thin air [3.21;12.7]; and our name shall be forgotten in time, and none shall remember our works, and our life shall pass away as the traces of a cloud, and as mist shall it be dispersed, chased by the sun's rays, and weighed down [l. *dissipated]* by the heat thereof [12.7;1.11]. For our life is the passing of a shadow, and there is no retreat from our end, for it has been sealed and none reverses it [1.11;2.16;9.5;2.11;6.12;8.8]. Come therefore and let us enjoy the good things that are, and earnestly make use of *creation* as in *youth* [2.24]. Let us fill ourselves with costly wine and perfumes [l. *sweets]*, and let not a flower [l. *splendor]* of the spring pass us by [2.24;9.7]. Let us crown ourselves with rosebuds ere they wither(and let no meadow be uncoursed by our debauch); let none of us go without his share of overweening revelry; let us leave everywhere tokens of our mirth, for this is our portion and such is our lot [3.22; 5.18; 9.6]". The passage in Wisdom indicates that the ideas of Qohelet had gained considerable currency and were analogous to Epicurus whose philosophy of the attainment of pleasure and the avoidance of pain spawned a host of sensualist and hedonistic followers, so that Qohelet too generated certain circles of pleasure seekers that the author of Wisdom sought to combat.

In summary, it may be maintained that Qohelet was written in the last quarter of the third century during the reign of Antiochus III, most probably at Seleucia with the admitted but less likely probability at Antioch, but at any rate at either of these capital cities where Qohelet "saw the face of the king."

A man's style is his mind's voice.
—Emerson

XV
Structure and Unity

The opening verse, "The words of Qohelet son of David king in Jerusalem" were written by the author. It is true that the verse may be an introductory statement made by an editor. It is equally true, however, that many introductions are written by the authors themselves. Some authors are modest; others do not wish to hide their talents either! In quite a number of instances a book is introduced by its author. And so, like the introductory declaration of the Aramaic Ahiqar to his book, to Ezechiel, to Tobit, to Haggai. Qohelet even more deliberately intended to ally himself with the great names of royalty, both David and Solomon.

The unity of the book was achieved by mechanically having one sentence follow another wherein a word or phrase of the first sentence was repeated in the second regardless of whether the thought was allied, consistent, complementary, or the very opposite. Most interestingly, in this rote of stringing the beads, the sequence is disrupted when Qohelet is borrowing from the outside. Thus in 9.7f., "Go, eat with joy your bread," etc., where he is following the Gilgamesh Epic and he is not his creative self, the thread breaks. Similarly, in 10.20 where again he seems to be following an outside source ("Also in thought do not curse the king," etc., an imitation of a Sumerian–Akkadian proverb) again the thread breaks with the preceding verse, and indeed with verse 18, another proverb apparently.

The first part of chapter twelve, with its poetic flight, is nevertheless Qohelet's up to and including verse 8. His admiring biographer, akin to him in thought and psyche, added two verses about his master's activity as a lecturer, his message and style. The name "Qohelet" is repeated in verses 9 and 10. The master's literary device may have been known to his disciple; or in the nature of the circumstances, the name had to be repeated. Verse 11 introduces the objections of a firm, rigorous traditionalist, a clear interpolation, and not only because of

132

the antipodal ideas of an orthodox censor, but again the thread is broken in the two verses of 10–11. On the other hand, verses 13–14 as a postscript belong to Qohelet, not only because of the idea that a) a man will be summoned to a court of judgment, and Qohelet is very apprehensive about this, and b) and be held accountable for every *hidden* (unknown) sin, but the thread of similar wording is resumed *(ki)*.

It should be stressed, too, that the few breaks in the chain may have occurred in the Hebrew through the circumstance that our Hebrew is in translation, assumed in these pages, *and the links, while connective in Aramaic, were lost in the rendering.* Following are the chapters in which the verses *in situ* are indicated, with the interrelated words as strung together by Qohelet: Observe that in the interlocking of the verses through a–b, c–d, there are secondary overlapping connective words in b–c marked with an *asterisk:* the forms are cited lexically, stripped of accretions:

Chapter 1
Vv. 1–2 Qohelet–Qohelet, *kol; (bis, and so acc. to the restored text) 2–3kol–kol; 4–5 ba'ba'; 6–7 shab shab; 7–8 kol–kol; 9–10 hadash–hadash *haya; 11–12 haya–haya 13–14 'asah–'asah. v. 15 hiatus, a proverb apparently; 16–17 hokma–hokma, *da'at; 17–18 da'at–da'at.

Chapter 2
Vv. 1–2 simha–simha; 3–4 'asah–'asah, 'nata'ti; 'asiti li–'asiti li, nata'ti; 7–8 li gam–li gam; 9–10 kol–kol; 11–12 paniti 'ani–paniti 'ani; 13–14 hoshek–hoshek; 15–16 kesil–kesil; 17–18 san'eti–san'eti 19–20 'amal–'amal; 21–22 'adam–'adam; 23–24 gam zeh–gam zoh, *'akal; 25–26 ki–ki, 'akal.

Chapter 3
Vv. 1–8 'et–'et; 9–10 'asher–'asher; 11–12 'asah–'asah; 13–14 'elohim–'elohim, *haya; 15 haya; vv. 20–19 kol–kol,*behemah, so the seq. *see* Comm.; 18–17 rasha'–rasha', behemah, *zadaq; 16 zadaq; 21–22 'adam–'adam.

Chapter 4
1–2 'ani–'ani; 3–4 'asah–'asah; 5–6 yad–caf (synonym, due to translation?); hebel–hebel; 9–10 'ehad–'ehad; 11–12 'ehad–'ehad; 13–14 mal'ak–mal'ak; 15–16 kol–kol; 17–1 (c.5) 'elohim–'elohim, *dabar

Chapter 5
V.2 dabar; 3–4 nadar–nadar; 5–6 'elohim–'elohim; 7–8 medinah (synonym for 'erez, cf. 2 Chron. 9.5 Peshitta medinah/'erez)–'erez; 9–10 hamon–tobah, both in the meaning of "muchness, affluence" conceivably synonymous, though lost

in the Hebrew, Aramaic ṭuba, ṭab "very, much". *'akal; v.11 'akal, *'asher; 12–13 ra'–ra', 'asher, *yad; v.14 yad; 15–16 ḥalah–ḥalah, *'akal; v.17 'elohim–'elohim, 'akal (*akal), *'amal, *'amal, *'elohim; v.18 'elohim, 'amal, 'akal, *simḥa (*'elohim); v.19 'elohim, simḥa.

Chapter 6

Vv. 1–2 ra'–ra', *'adam; v.2 'ish (synonym) *nefesh, ('*ish); v.3 'ish, nefesh; v.4 hiatus. 5–6 lo ra'ah–lo ra'ah, *halak. V.7 hiatus (a proverb, an interpolation?) note that *halak is carried through to the *next* verse; 8–9 halak–halak; v.10 hiatus; 11–12 'adam–'adam.

Chapter 7

Vv. 1–2 tob–tob, *tob, *leb; 3–4 tob, leb; 5–6 kesil–kesil, *ki; 7–8 ki; 8–9 ruaḥ–ruaḥ; 10–11 ḥakam–ḥakam; 12–13 ki–ki; 14–15 ra'–ra', *zadaq; 16–17 lamah–lamah, zadaq; 18–19 'asher–'asher; 20 'asher; 21–22 leb–leb; 23–24 raḥoq–raḥoq; 25–26 leb–leb; 27–28 maza'–maza', *'adam, *maza'; v.29 'adam, maza';

Chapter 8

Vv. 1–2 panim–panim (so the restored text); 3–4 'asah–'asah; 5–6 mishpat–mishpat; 7–8 'en–'en; 9–10 ra'ah–ra'ah; 11–12 ra'–ra' *tob; 13 tob; 14–15 'asher–'asher; 16–17 'asher na'asah–'asher na'asah.

Chapter 9

1–2 kol–kol *miqreh; 3–4 hay–hay, miqreh, *met, *hay; 5–6 'en 'od lahem–'en lahem'od, hay, met; 7–10 hiatus (an adaptation of Gilgamesh epic)' 11–12 'et–'et; 13–14 'el–'el, *'ir; 15–16 misken–misken, 'ir; 17–18 hakam–hakam.

Chapter 10

Vv. 1–2 hakam–hakam, *sakal; 2–3 leb–leb, sakal; 4–5 moshel–shalit (synonym, variant due to Hebrew translation?); 6–7 rabbim–sarim (variant due to the Hebrew translator? Perhaps the Aramaic root *rbb* was employed in the two verses); 8–9 hiatus (proverb; 10–11 yitron–yitron; 12–13 peh–peh *siklut; 14–15 yada'–yada', sakal; 16–17 melek–melek, *sar; 18–20 (proverbs; v. 20 is a Sumerian–Akkadian proverb, *see* p. 128).

Chapter 11

Vv. 1–2 ki–ki, *'erez; 3 'erez; 4–5 ruaḥ–ruaḥ; 6–7 tob–tob; 8–9 samaḥ–samaḥ, *yaldut; 10 yaldut.

Chapter 12

1–2 'ad 'asher–'ad 'asher, *hashak; v.3 hashak; 4–5 shuq–shuq; 6–7 razaz–razaz, shab–shab. The writer apparently departs from the usual linkage; 8–10 Qohelet (ter); 11–12 hiatus (interpolation! from the traditionalist glossator); 'elohim–'elohim (a postscript from Qohelet, or one of his school).

Over ninety per cent of the verses are concatenate, a mark of the book's unity, which, however, we discerned by a different route— i.e. Qohelet's personality. Where a hiatus occurs, it is likely that an extraneous source has been looked at, either a proverb, or the Gilgamesh Epic; undoubtedly the Aramaic original would exhibit greater cohesiveness. Note c.7 where ṭob, a sign of the Heptad is yet seemingly original with Qohelet as he concatenates the verses with other words. (For the Heptad, compare R. Gordis, "The Heptad as an Element of Biblical and Rabbinic Style," in JBL, no. 62, 1943.)

Commentary

1.1 These are the words: An introduction to the book with the author's signature with the high pretension that he is connected with the most famous name in Hebrew history, implying that he Kanosha, is Solomon. Kanosha: The Hebrew reads Qohelet. Since the assumption in these pages is that there was an underlying document in Aramaic, it follows that the original Aramaic of the feminine participle Qohelet was the feminine participle *Kanshah* in Aramaic. The Hebrew translator mistook the Aramaic *Kanshah* on two counts. He translated the word instead of transliterating it, a familiar procedure as for example Ecclesiastes/Qohelet. Secondly, he actually mistranslated the word; *Kanshah* is masculine though with a *He* orthographical mark, quite usual in Daniel and Ezra where masculine nouns are ended with He and Alef fluctuatingly as in the cases (cf. H.H. Powell, *The Supposed Hebraisms in the Grammar of the Biblical Aramaic*, 1906) marked with an asterisk *naharah* Ezr. 5.3 x 12 times; * *'ammah* Ez.5.12, *telata* 3.24 + 5 times *baithah* Ez. 5.12;6.15; *dinah* Ez.7.26; *yeqarah 5.20;* *dahbah;* Ez.5.14;6.5;7.18; *ketabah* Ez.5.7.15 even *malkah* "king" (!) Dan.2.11. Alternatively the word might be vocalized as *kanoshah,* a *fa'ola* form signifying a function or profession. Either *Kanoshah* or *Kanshah* is a good Canaanitish-Aramaic-Punic name. (Compare H. Donner-W. Röllig *Kanaanäische und Aramäische Inschriften*, 1964, II, 80 and 148. Note the Aramaic form KNS' 'N reading as if with masoretic pointing the whole name as *Kenesh/Kanesh ben Kanesh, 'a'in* "wood gatherer", ibid. I, no. 159.1.) *The name in its functional character, Kanosha*(h), is found in Babylonian Aramaic. (Compare Kohut, *'Aruk,* s.v. 264 and the various verbal forms and *kanasa* "sweep" in Arabic; Jastrow, 651.) The Aramaic author of Qohelet, neurotically inclined, fantasied himself as the great Solomonic *hakam* of the age. He was overwhelmed with the discovery that his name *kanshah* added up computatively in letters for numerals to 375, i.e., *Kanshah* = *Shelomoh.* He did not hesitate to ascribe to himself regal connection as the son of David, as discussed in the Solomonic psychograph. For a suggestion about the meaning of this expression, see note at 1.12: all things are futile, everything is futile. At the summation in 12.8 there is only one *habel habalim,* and in the present passage, the presence of the expression twice is suspect. The translation assumes the emendation *ha-kol habalim.* The passage in 2B totalizes the particular and the universal; all things individually are futile, the whole is futile, the universal scheme is futile. *Hebel* signifies a number or meanings for Qohelet: outrage, futility, injustice, breath, with an implication of defiance and disgust.

1.3 *yitron,* Aramaic *yutrana* from the root *yatar,* Akkadian *wataru* signifies advantage, profit, what is left over. The verse means then: "What is left over for a man after he works?" Sun: *Shemesh* plays a very significant role in Qohelet's life as it is mentioned over thirty times in the book. "Sun" means *father* who is always watching him. (Compare p. 00f.)

NATURE'S MEANINGLESS ACTIVITY

1.4 Dies . . . is born lit. comes . . .goes. Cosmos: lit. the world continues forever. The phrase forecasts for the next verse how the world does not change: the sun rises and sets, etc.

1.5 There is something wrong with the sense of the verse as it is in Hebrew: the sun cannot "pant" (*sho'ef*) to its place; it does not "shine" (*zoreah*) when it arrives at its place "there" (*sham*). The Aramaic ran:

ודנח שמשא ועל שמשא ולאתרה תאב, דנח הוא תמן

Because the letters *DNH* occur twice in the verse, the Hebrew translator regarded them as identical roots. The second word, however, should be of two components: the particle *de* + *nah,* "rest," the stich now bearing the meaning "Where he [the sun] rests." (For the idea of the sun's resting, compare the Targum to the verse.) The problematic "there" complements the stich properly. Secondly, the Hebrew translator mistook *ta'eb* as the verb for "desire"; he should have read it as *ta'eb,* the Aramaic participle of *tab,* "return." We now have a triad of natural phenomena that go round and round repetitively without purpose: the sun (v.5), the wind (v.6), the rivers (v.7).

1.6: Round and round; The repetition of *sobeb sobeb,* questioned by *Biblia Hebraica,* is simply a reflection of Aramaic idiomatic reduplication of *sehor sehor* though the translator decided to employ a verbal form. To its abode the wind returns: The Hebrew *sebibotaw,* "its rounds," "circuits," is problematical; the wind would hardly have circuits on which it would turn again and again. The Aramaic probably had *drhy* which the Hebrew translator considered to be "his rounds," hence his *sebibotaw,* reading the Aramaic as *darohi.* He should have read *dirohi,* "his abode," "his chambers," a good parallel to the sun and his "place." (For the idea that the wind has a "chamber," compare Job 37.9. For the root *dur,* "go round," compare Payne Smith, 87.)

1.8 What is the purpose of all this?: The Hebrew is difficult: all things are weary? The English translation presupposes the Aramaic text כל מליא לאן which the Hebrew translator translated or read as *la'ain* rt. *la'y* "tire," "be weary." (Cf. Dalman, *Grammatik,*[2] 350) He should have understood *le'an,* "[to] where?" with its special meaning of: what is the use of all this? as for example in the Aramaic expression Yer. Yeb. XII, 12d: "Of what use is this old man to thee?" as cited by Jastrow, *Dictionary* p.80. For the Hebrew *yukal,* one should read *yekalleh* (Galling), "finish," and so in concord with "be satisfied," "be surfeited."

1.9 Happened: The Hebrew *na'aseh,* "been made," "been done," is an error in nuance on the part of the Hebrew translator. The Aramaic equivalent *'abid* means lexically "happen." Qohelet's point is that what has happened in history will happen again. Hence there is nothing new.

1.10: A statement is sometimes made: The Hebrew should be read as a

Nif'al: *sheye'amer.* The Hebrew represents an Aramaic locution *'amar miltha,* in its simplest form an idiom for "he made a statement." (Jastrow s.v. *miltha.)* Perhaps: not the *kebar* Hebrew meaning "already" but Aramaic "perhaps," because Qohelet with his propensity to doubt everything never makes a statement with complete assurance (*see* p. 42). *Haya* 1 =belongs (Cf. BDB, *Lexicon,* p. 512b.)

1.11: Latter: lit. those that come after, not the last. (Compare Gen. 33.2).

1.12: Kanosha: *(see note to 1.1).* Was king: the implication of the copula—*was* king—gave rise to the well-known legend that after Solomon's deposal from his throne, he was compelled to wander as a beggar over the face of the earth. Most likely *hayiti melek* reproduces wrongly *hawet malek* (the participle–"I ruled)," with the possibility the *malek* was misread as "*melek.*" Over Israel in Jerusalem: Difficult. Some commentators strike out "in Jerusalem" as one would not say that a king is ruler over his empire in his capital city. In Qohelet's case the situation may be a bit different. The Seleucids had two capital cities, essentially Antioch on the Orontes and Seleucia on the Tigris, and it was at the latter the co-regent, usually the king's son, held sway in the East while the emperor ruled from Antioch. Qohelet in his thinking modeled himself on that dichotomous situation while pretending to be Solomon, projected Seleucia, as "Jerusalem."

1.13: Meditate: *tur,* meaning "spy," "spy out," is not acceptable in the Hebrew context. In Eastern Aramaic, *tar* means "meditate," quite apposite here. (Compare Payne Smith, *Syriac Dictionary,* 603a) The root may be med. Alef/med. Waw, Brockelmann, *Lexicon Syriacum*[2] 814. (See especially Driver and Miles, *The Babylonian Laws,* II, 297 and note.) Transpired: Heb. *na'aseh,* so to be pointed in the Hebrew because the translator misunderstood *'abid,* which as the Aramaic passive may be ambiguously present or perfect temporally. That evil business: *hu'* is the demonstrative particle in Aramaic reproduced in the Hebrew text as a copulative. Note the word-play *'inyan* and *la'anot* conveying the overtones of mental distress, from *'anay='*"be afflicted".

1.14: Are being done: The Aramaic participle *'abidin* should have been rendered as present, not a perfect passive.

1.15: Qohelet is talking of the basic defects in the human personality, his own. "From the crooked wood of which man is made nothing quite straight can be built. Only an approximation to this goal is expected of us by nature"—Kant quoted by Otto Rank, *Will Therapy & Truth and Reality* p. xxii. (English trans.). And a minus cannot be made a plus: lit. that which is wanting cannot be counted in. The terms are business terms, *hesron* i.e., what is lacking in the account cannot be "numbered," added in. The stich again bears on Qohelet's psychic makeup. He feels that his failings and the defects in his constitution can never be made up or compensated for, very much like the remark of La Rochefoucauld (maxim no. 130). "Weakness is the only failing that we cannot put aright."

1.16: I have greatly augmented a store of wisdom: lit. I have magnified, and have added wisdom. The phrase of the Hebrew *higdalti. . .hokma* is peculiar; one may say *hirbeti hokma* (Abot 2.7) and this is what is required of the verse. Is.42.21 is different, cf. *ya'adir.* Most likely the Aramaic text ran *rabbet hokma.* In 2.9 he straddled but again mistranslated the phrase. (*See* note ibid.) Experienced: lit. saw. The word "saw" is characteristically Qohelet's, and the term is employed because he is looking back on the "theater" of his life. (See pp. 63, 139.)

1.18: anguish: *ka'as* in the Hebrew means "anger" but as a reproduction of the Aramaic *rugza* or *ritha*, both standard equivalents in the Targums; it is essentially a mistranslation of the Aramaic expression of "agitation" 2 Sam. 19.1; Hab. 3.2

Chapter 2

2.1: Read with Ehrlich *'elkah na*. For *'anasska*, read *'anasseh "I will try."*

2.3 Planned: the Aramaic *tar*, lit. meditated. (See note at 1.13.) Stimulate: *limshok* is impossible in the context. The underlying Aramaic read *lemegar*, rt. *grr* which the translator considered to mean "draw." With wine, however, the verb means "stimulate." Compare Berakot 35b: "And did not Rabba drink wine every Passover eve so as to eat a large amount of unleavened bread, so as to stimulate (*grr*) his appetite? Answer: much stimulates, (*grr*), a little satisfies. **Calculated:** parenthetical and psychological: the I that looks at the me. *Noheg*, in the Hebrew "conducted," and with "heart," "mind," is strange and atypical (with the participle). The Aramaic ran *middaber*, "conduct" (either *hithpa'-el/'al*) but with a special nuance, "calculate," "devise" "plan." Cf. *madbaranu-tha/tahbulah* "Targum" to Proverbs 1.5;20.18;24.6. Intelligence: or wisdom. The verse ends here.

Until I should reach a conclusion . . . .their lives: belongs to the following verse. The meaning of the verse is that while Qohelet was making up his mind what the summum bonum was, and the best activity for man to expend his time at, he busied himself with all sorts of activities. The staccato and the abrupt march of the verses 4-8 impresses with the business that prevents Qohelet from thinking. These activities at construction are compulsions. Compare 3.3d in the list of compulsions and see pp. 9 f., 45, 48.

2.4: The verse begins at "I kept busy with activities." (*See* the preceding note.) Kept busy: lit. increased. The Hebrew means "made great," but the text clearly implies "I increased"; the Hebrew translator misunderstood his text either *'asget/'arbet 'obadai* and which he should have rendered as *hirbeti ma'asai*, "I increased my activities." Note the sequence.

2.5: Parks: *Pardesim* in Hebrew with the masculine ending represents the Aramaic masculine ending. (Ginsberg).

2.7: Slaves home-born: Children born to slaves Qohelet had bought.

2.8: Exotic treasure: Aramaic *probably segullta*, Assyrian *segullu*, pl. *sugullati*, "herds." (Compare Gesenius-Buhl s.v. 536.) Note the Aramaic parallel in Ezra 4.15 *malkin umedinan*. Divans and couches: the Hebrew most puzzling is *shiddah weshiddot*; the Ancient Versions are completely at variance with one another (cf. Biblia Hebraica); and it is difficult to disclose what the Aramaic may have been. I have followed Rashi in interpreting the phrase as "divans," "couches"; if so, Qohelet is indulging his fancy in describing the sedans, palanquins, sedan chairs, divans, baldachins and all the divers royal conveyances in which he was carried about to impress the populace. Another possibility that might be suggested is *shiddah, shiddot conceals* the Aramaic root *shedi* meaning "to fly," used mainly of birds.

(Compare Deut. 28.49; Hab. 1.8; Is.6.6; Ps.91.5 Levy, *Chaldäisches Wörterbuch,
s.v.)* This interpretation would be in accord with Qohelet's identification with
Solomon, who brought from other countries (I Kings 10.22) ivory, apes and
peacocks (so the Targums, Rashi, and Qimhi although modern interpretations
differ.) *Accordingly shidda weshiddot* are the varied exotic birds that the
pseudo-Solomon collected. I doubt whether *shiddah* may mean "woman's
breast" and therefore love-making because Qohelet was not interested in
women. Interesting is *shada, ashday,* in Arabic "sing sweetly," Hava,
357,//"singers" in the verse.

2.9:   **Accumulated:** with "amassed," one must read "accumulated." The
Hebrew translator misread his text *rebet* instead of *rabet,* "accumulate." He
also misunderstood the phrase in Aramaic *wehukmethi qamat li,* "I kept
possession of my wisdom" (compare Gen. 23.17.20 MT and Targum) but which
he translated mechanically as *'amdah,* "stood".

2.11:   **A vain delusion and a fruitless endeavor:** *re'ut* is problematic. As
"desire," the word does not fit very well into the context. In this commentary,
re'ut ruah must mean something in the character of "frustration," an offshoot of
thought, (compare 2.22 *ra'ayon libbo* "thought," but not "desire" as in the
Hebrew *re'ut.)* The Aramaic *ra'ayana* and *tar'itha, r'eiy* as the root is associated
with *re'ut,* bear the meaning of "thought" and "desire" and either *ra'ayana* or
tar'itha was in the underlying Aramaic text, but the Hebrew translator chose
"desire," a little inappropriate. It is to be noted that in mss. *ra'ayo/ana*
interchanges with *libba* and *re'utha* (Jastrow, 1487). *ra'ayona* is employed for
mahshabah Targ. Ps. 40.6; /*zimmah* Job 17.11 and *tar'itha/'ezah* Prov. 27.9 and
ibid 1.4/*mezimmah. yitron*=meaningful activity.

2.12:   **Who is the man:** the Hebrew translator confused măn "who" with
mān "what." (Compare Gesenius-Buhl, *Wörterbuch,* [17] 432.) The Hebrew *'et*
was a misunderstanding of the particle *l,* meaning "to", not the *nota
accusativi.* The last word, *'asuhu,* is an error for *'asahu'=asah hu'.* The
contraction *'asahu* would be in line with frequent rabbinic writing (compare
Jastrow, 336a, for examples, as well as the fluctuating orthography in the Dead
Sea Scrolls.) The text bears the significance: who is the man who can follow in
the footsteps of the king to that objective that the king has attained? Answer: no
one. Qohelet had fulfilled his heart's desire. [Interchange 12a and 12b (Galling,
Ginsberg).]

2.14:   **Fate:** i.e., death. *Meqreh*=Aramaic *'ir'a,* "happening," a euphemism
for death ("If anything happens to you…"). Qohelet is afraid of death; by count,
he employs *mot* in verbal and nominal forms some fourteen times when he is
distantly regarding death for others, some nine times where he feels, directly or
implicity, involved. Two: Compare Ginsberg, *Qohelet* ad loc.

2.15:   **Then:** The Hebrew *'az* is a mistranslation of Aramaic *beken*
meaning "then," but also "accordingly" the required sense here. (Compare MT
and Targum to Gen. 4.26;12.6;13.7 and elsewhere.)

2.16:   **Future:** Qohelet uses *'olam* for future and past as elsewhere in the
Bible, Gen. 6.3; Ps.41.14;106.48. The time sequence in the Hebrew is out of
kilter; because already (!), the days that are to come (!) all is forgotten (has been
forgotten [?]). In Aramaic, the participle can be temporally past, present or
future, and the change, moreover, to bring out more vividness may be
interjected abruptly in the middle of a sentence. (Compare M.L.Margolis,

Manual of the Aramaic Language of the Babylonian Talmud, par. 58) The Hebrew translator misconstrued the whole time element here: Because already days *have passed,* and everything *was forgotten.* (Compare 1.11). *Beshekbar* merely represents the Aramaic *bedi + kebar,* "because already." In Aramaic, *bedi* is regularly joined to the following word. (Compare Dalman, *Grammatik,* ² par 50). The Hebrew formation is without parallel. And so: the Hebrew translator misconstrued his Aramaic again as he wandered completely off the path from his immediate previous rendering of the verse. The Aramaic had the word *heikden* which has the meaning (1) "how," and this the translator seized upon, and (2) "and so!," an exclamation, which should have been the translation here.

2.17: Most foul: The Hebrew renders too literally *ba'esh 'alai 'obada=* the matter was most displeasing to me. (Compare Dan.6.5)

2.19: Perfected: The conjunction of the Hebrew "that I toiled at and that I was wise at" is strange. Probably the translator saw *wesiklet* (with Sin) whereas he should have read *weshaklelet.* Having nothing but wisdom on his mind, he rendered *sheḥakamti.* In Aramaic, *siklet* and *shaklelet* would be identical except the translator read one *l* instead of two *ll's.*

2.20: *Wesabboti=*the Aramaic *we-hadret,* "I reversed myself" or "I changed my mind."

2.22: Moreover: With Qohelet, as in much neurotic thinking, "because" represents "and," a simultaneity, an addition. (Compare F.J.Hoffman, *Freudianism and the Literary Mind,* Grove Press reprint, p. 145 who, citing Freud, remarks about James Joyce:" Since the unconscious is not aware of either space or time, Joyce is able to employ simultaneity as a substitute for the usual orderly sequence of events.")

2.23: And: *see* note on "because" in verse 22. Agitation: the Hebrew *ka'as* is not apposite here as "anger" but represents *rigza/rithal,* "agitation" the nuance of which the Hebrew translator failed to perceive. For *'inyano* we should read *we'inyan* with a rearrangement of the letters. The word belongs to Qohelet's neurotic vocabulary meaning "compulsion" without the performance of which anxiety arises. (*See* p. 88f.) At rest: the Aramaic probably read *la naḥ libbeh* and the translator, going out of his way this time to translate consciously and not copy his Aramaic text, rendered with the lame *shakab.* The emendation *shakak,* "relax," "subside," however, is attractive (S. Mandelkern).

2.24: Than: the translation presupposes a correction *misheyokal.* Sate: *Her'ah* in a number of instances in the biblical literature=*hirwah,* "satiate." (Compare Is. 53.11;Ps.60.5;91.15;Job 10.15 [Qimḥi, Mandelkern] and so in Qohelet [Ginsberg].) For the compensation: the Beth pretii, Gesenius' *Hebrew Grammar,* 119 p. cf. *nimelu* "wealth," *'umlat,* "money" (Akkadian; Arabic). Yet: *gam* is a mistranslation of Aramaic *leḥod* or *beram* which have two meanings: "also" and "yet, but, however."

2.25: The verse seems curtailed, and what seems to be omitted is "who can drink." If this is inserted, the verse would now contain three members that would correspond to the three segments of the previous verse: eat, drink, sate with pleasure, and so our verse should run: eat, (drink) and enjoy.

2.26: Well favored; *ṭob* as opposed to *ḥote'* in the character of the verse means not "good man" and "sinner" respectively but "well favored," one to whom God is partial and "the ill favored" or "luckless one" (Ginsberg), who unfortunately has the compulsion to accumulate wealth and then hand it over to the Favorite. Perhaps *seraḥ*, meaning. "Be in ill favor" and "sin" were confused by the Hebrew translator.

Chapter 3

3.1: The introductory verse, with its flat assertion of Qohelet's need to fill the moments and hours with some activity, bespeaks his compulsions and the need to cathect his pressures that reflect the problems that beset him.

3.2: A time to be born and a time to die: This is the arching "life plan" (Ibn Ezra: *rei'shit ha-'adam wesofo* "Man's beginning and end"; Alfred Adler emphasized "life plan/life style"), the essence here of Qohelet's whole existence which Qohelet follows with illustrations and examples of what he must do. (*See* pp. 9, 46 for exposition and general elucidation of this section.) *Laledet:* a time to be born. In Arabic, the infinitive may bear an active or passive signification. (compare B. Halper, *The Participial Formations of the Geminate Verbs*, ZAW, 1910,42-57,99-126,201-228)

3.3: Time to murder: These are the death wishes that Qohelet harbors in his mind, primarily against his wife, earlier against his father (*see* pp. 29, 60, 152), which as intended violations of basic morality and law overwhelm Qohelet with an awesome sense of guilt. Time to refrain: the Aramaic read *lemirpe'*, "to desist," meaning that one should stop thinking about such horrendous aggressive thoughts. "Desist" is in keeping with the other refraining acts in the section as in verse 5 "refrain from sex play," verse 7, "refrain from talking," and implicit in verse 6, "time to guard," i.e., not to throw away. The Hebrew translator took *refe* as "heal", an incongruous contrast to murder.

3.4: Mourn–dance: *rqd* in Eastern Aramaic bears two significations merely by a change of vowels: *lemarqadu* (mourn) and *lamraqadu* (dance), Payne Smith, *Dictionary*, 549, and undoubtedly was a wordplay in the original Aramaic. Similarly Ginsberg.

3.5: A time to throw stones: stones are thrown at a woman convicted of adultery, and Qohelet thought his wife faithless. (*See* pp. 10, 45.) Embrace: preliminary sex play, (compare Prov. 5.20) The Targum too considers the verse an allusion to sexual congress.

3.6: Search–give up as lost: there is a time to search for one's beloved, and there is a time to renounce the search for her. The Peshitta should be corrected: *lementar* is to be substituted for *lemeqtar*, and *lemeshre* to be emended to *lemeshde* which by this slight correction concords with the Hebrew text.

3.7: Sew: an indication of Qohelet's latent homosexuality.

3.8: A time of war: This verse comes from another hand. Note the change from the infinitive to the noun, to the largeness of point of view, from the personal to the universal perspective, of period concerns of mankind as a whole, of epochal war and peace.

3.9: This verse is a conclusion to the preceding. What, therefore, is the purpose or profit to perform all these compulsive acts? The activities lead to nothing.

3.10: **Scheme of things:** Heb. *'inyan*, the business of life with the anguish that goes along with it. *la'anot* conveys the overtones of affliction as the meaning of the word suggests a play on *'inyan*, most likely in the Aramaic as well.

3.11: **But as for the people of the world itself:** The Hebrew *gam* is a mistranslation again of the underlying *lehod/bram* not *also* but *however;* *'et* should have been rendered as *l* as the dative of reference, not the Aramaic accusative. *'Olam* means people of the world, *tout le monde,* or as street=people of the street. The double negative, strange in the usage here may be the result of a variant reading in the Aramaic copy: *dela'/midela'*. Order: The underlying *sam* (/natan) was slightly miscued as "give," whereas it should have been translated by the Hebrew translator as "appointed," "instilled." *Sim/natan* Lev.19.14. *Shawi* could equally serve, Jastrow s.v. If *sam*, there are overtones to the meaning of the verb from Akkadian *samu, simu* "allot" "destine," which Qohelet seems to employ as e.g. in 3.18 and for the idea 3.14. Qohelet sounds existentialist. The world seems well ordered but man himself cannot find the reason for his existence or its meaning. What passes for existentialism, however, may at bottom be a neurosis. (Compare the well-known neurotic temperaments of existentialists Baudelaire, Dostoievsky, Kierkegaard, Strindberg, Ibsen, Kafka.)

3.13: **And yet:** Qohelet expresses the reservation that enjoyment is God's boon. *wegam'* however, a mistranslation of *lehod* (1) "also" (2)"but, however." *ha'adam:* the definite article in the Hebrew was added wrongly as a mistranslation of *'enasha'* which should be indefinite.

3.14: Deals with his compulsion. Qohelet will never be free of them. You cannot avoid or diminish them and one cannot change them ("one cannot add or substract from it"). God made them. If you attempt to escape them, (self) punishment follows. Does: The Hebrew reads *ya'aseh* "will do." Apparently, the Aramaic participle which may be rendered by the *pasta* present, or future (p. 108, 140, 149) was misinterpreted by the Hebrew translator as the exigency the verse shows. The participle *'abed* = does.

3.15: **Whatever exists now was in existence long ago:** the Hebrew translator failed to distinguish properly *hu'* and *hawa',* the letters being identical The verse should read: *ma dehu' kebar hawa'* :"whatever is now, already was." The sequence follows very appropriately. The guilt-ridden: *'et nirdaf/lirdifa'* in Aramaic, a probable slip on the part of the translator for *'et ha-nirdaf*. The connection between the first part of the verse and the second is easily perceived. Qohelet knows that his past will be the same as his future: his anxieties, neuroses, and compulsions in the past will extend monotonously in the future void without letup. One thing remains the same: God hounds him without cessation. The *redif'* is Qohelet. *Redif*=persecuted; *bqs*=Aramaic *tb'* which has the nuance of "seek out" in a pejorative sense, Jastrow 1645 (for a sinful act). Compare the sinister *tabi'atun* which as a genie follows and shadows a man wherever he goes. Cf. Lane, *Arabic-English Lexicon* s.v. p. 296a. Syriac tab'a' = a female demon that strangles women and children; *tab'eta/neqama* "poena;" Brockelmann, *814b.*

3.18-20: The order of the verses 18,19.20 has been disturbed. Most likely because the copyist saw *'amarti 'ani belibbi* of verse 17 and unconsciously repeated it in verse 18. Actually the phrase"I said in my heart" is a summing-up rather than an introductory phrase. (Cf. its position in verse 17) The verses in proper order run: 20,19,18 and have been so translated. Proceeding in inverse order:

v.20:   **dust:** Qohelet's denigration of self. (*See* 12.7.)

v.19:   **so:** lit. "and," like the Arabic *fa* having the signification of "consequently." Breath: the original meaning of *hebel* comes to the fore with the suggestion of "futility"; actually a wordplay, denominated by the Arabic stylists as *tawriyyat*, (cf. David Yellin, *ḥiqre miqra'* I, 17.) As in verse 18, see presently, *lahem/laham*, collective for beasts as in Ethiopic. The text is not quite in order and should run: *ki miqreh (MT miqre) benei ha'adam umiqreh ha-behemah umiqreh ha-laham 'ehad.* (Compare the translation. *Laham*=beast. See n.v.18.)

v.18:   **Are depraved:** the translation assumes an underlying Aramaic *bwr* (cf. *bor/bur* "uncultured person, ruffian," Targ. Jer. 10.14 [*nib'ar*], Payne Smith, *Syriac Dictionary*, 38). The Aramaic had the infinitive *lemebar* or another conjugational form which the Hebrew translator assumed to be *brr*, "sift." The interpretation advanced here is dictated by the sequence. **As beasts:** The beasts: the translation is based on the assumption that *lahem* is pausal for *laham* meaning *bos (taurus, vacca)* A. Dillmann, *Chrestomathia Aethiopica*, 1866, p. 163, i.e., in general "beast." The word is found in Hebrew as a verbal form Prov. 18.8; 26.22 and explained by Halévy from the Ethiopic (see Mandelkern, *Concordance*, s.v. and Zimmermann, *American Journ. of Sem. Lang.*, 1941, 99f.) Qohelet implies that at judgment time, man (i.e., including Qohelet himself, pp. 53 f., 144, 150) will be shown what he really is, a worthless bestial being. Syntactically we have a good parallel in the phrases: they are as animals, they are as beasts.

3.21:   **downward** (to the earth): it is clear that *downward* corresponds as a single word to *upward*, and therefore *to the earth* is superfluous. The double reading, however, came about through the Aramaic *l'ra* meaning both "downward" and "to the earth."

3.22:   Qohelet regards the ability to do what he wants, without inner compulsions, as a precious blessing. Qohelet suffers in that his actions are preordained, he is driven to perform them, and as drives from inner turmoil, can find no pleasure in them. If in respites he can find some pleasure, let a man enjoy it without self-reproach and discontent for that is the "lot" or allotment of pleasure prescribed for him.

Chapter 4

4.1:   **Respite—relief:** The vocalization of the Hebrew does not seem correct. The punctuator was apparently misled by the "tears" which entail a natural sequence of "consolation." Consoling words are given to one in mourning; for exploitation the proper word would be "give respite" or "relieve." We should therefore read *meiniḥam/menaḥem*. The emendation brings out more forcibly the sense in stich b where the power is in the hands of the oppressors, and there is no surcease. On the side: *min yad*, "on the side," probably was extant in the Aramic text but was lamely and literally reproduced in the Hebrew.

4.2:   We should read *umeshabeaḥ*, the *Mem* being omitted, because the scribe thought that he had already written the *Mem* (of the preceding word).

4.3: **Is the one who has not come:** the construction *'et 'asher* in the nominative is peculiar. Recourse is had to usage in the Mishna, centuries later. The suggestion may be offered, however, ex hypothesi and via the Aramaic, that the Hebrew translator misunderstood *ledi* as an accusatival Lamed instead of the familiar construction *ṭab l.*

4.5: **The fool folds his hands:** The surface meaning is that the fool by not working is but consuming his own flesh. Among the ancient Hebrews, fleshiness was a sign of good health (Deut. 32.15). The latent meaning is that this is a masturbatory fancy wherein the fool makes his flesh lean by sexual excess. (Compare *Merchant of Venice* II, 5.73–75: "How like a prodigal [ship] doth she return, with over weather'd ribs, and ragged sails, lean, rent, and beggar'd by the strumpet wind.") In ancient times, the sexual act was regarded as a depletion of one's powers. (*See* p. 27, 178, n.25 for the discussion.) The next passage likewise bears on this interpretation.

4.6: The verse contrasts with the preceding. Both, with the implied auto-eroticism of verse 5, reflect dour experiences of Qohelet about himself. This passage bears the meaning: Better one conjugal act with sexual fulfillment than repeated masturbatory acts of frustration and unsatisfied longing.

4.8: **A man:** *'eḥad* represents the Aramaic *ḥad* = a man which *aramaice* may start a story "There was a man..." for example, whereas the Hebrew would say *'ish 'eḥad.* Compare Dalman, *Dialektproben* pp. 16, 18, 19. **wife:** Heb., *sheni*, means "second"; in Eastern Aramaic, *tanyan* has the connotation of "mate," or "cell mate", (Payne Smith, *Syriac Dictionary*, 616f.), from which we have a ready association of "wife" (and so Ibn Ezra). The verse gives evidence of Qohelet's isolating tendency characteristic of neurotics and the desire to protect himself, (compare Stekel, *Compulsion and Doubt*, 444 citing Freud). Qohelet feels that his wife, son, brother are so far and alien to him as if they are not in his world. He has annulled their existence. (For the discussion of this characteristic of Qohelet, *see* pp. 52, 145.) Although Qohelet tried to objectify himself as if he were talking about another (p. 52), he passionately bursts out in the first person. On the one hand, his compulsions drive him to toil, and on the other hand, his self-punishment forbids his enjoying the fruits of his labor.

4.9: **Mutual benefit:** Aramaic *'agar* the lexical equivalent of the Hebrew *sakar*, means "hire," then "reward," then "compensation" in its double sense both materially and metaphorically.

4.10: The verb *nafal* is employed in the sense of "fall ill," elliptically for *nafal lemishkab* (cf. II Sam. 1.10; Jer. 25.27, as partial parallels). *Yaqim* is a misvocalization of the Aramaic *yeqayyem*, a standard equivalent of *yehayyeh*, "support," "nurse" (II Sam. 12.3; Ps. 33.19; Jer. 49.11 and elsewhere). For *we'ilo* we should read *we'illu.* The end clause is resultant where the Waw–Arabic *fa* "then, as a result, there is none..."

4.11: Symbolical for sexual congress (Rashi).

4.12: **For** *yitkefo*, read *yitkof*, error from a misplacement of letters. A triple cord: Qohelet quotes a Sumerian proverb or locution. (*See* p. 129.)

4.13: **Young man:** *yeled*, "child" in the Hebrew, does not quite catch the nuance in the context. The "child" possesses enough vigor to put through a palace revolution. *Talya* or *rabya* in Aramaic bear both meanings of "child" and "young man." To take care of oneself: *lehizzaher*, implying senility, so

Aramaic cognate.

4.14: The verse is difficult, arising mainly from the distortion in Qohelet's thought, a hysteron proteron process, and the verse obviously means: although the young man was born of humble origin in the kingdom, he emerges from the court revolutionaries to rule. Probably *malkuthah*, in Aramaic with the *He* ending was read *malkutheh*, "his kingdom." The word *hasurim* is problematical, the usual interpretation with *Bet* being "prison" with Alef in *ha-surim* omitted. It is possible, however, that the vocalization is not quite correct and that *ha-sarim/ha-surim* (cf. Jer. 6.28; Dan. 9.5.11) meaning "rogues," "villains," those of the lower classes (taking a cue from Rashi), or preferably pointing to an Aramaic word underneath, *'asirayya*, meaning as in Syriac (Payne Smith, p. 81, "conspirators"). The word *di/ki* means "who," not "because".; *mibbet* in the Hebrew really reproduces the Aramaic *mibbet=mibbe* from among, not from "the house." *rash=muskenu*, "commoner" rather than "poor man." (Cf. Meek's note p. 166, ANET, no. 44.)

4.15: Assembled: The people come together to witness a coronation, or to be told about the next in line for the succession.   the boy prince: *ha-yeled ha-sheni*, "the child," "the second," is surely peculiar but easily explainable on the basis of the extreme literalness of the Hebrew translation. The Aramaic read *talya tinyana/detinyana* but not "the lad who is second" but in the other idiomatic meaning of "the youth who is the vice-regent" (cf. Payne Smith, *Syriac Dictionary*, 616 f.). **Greeting:** Heb. *'im* is a mistranslated *lewath*, "to," not "with."

4.16: He: the Hebrew reads *haya* which makes no sense. The Hebrew translator should have read *hu'*. (*See* p. 106 f.) **Generation after:** the ones who come after. (*See* note at 1.11.)

4.17: Fools: the dull and the insensate who perform the ritual without thinking. A wicked act: The Aramaic *lema'abad bish*, "a wicked act," was taken by the Hebrew translator as *le* plus the infinitive. *Yod'im* is an inadequate translation of the underlying *hakmin* "recognize," "discern." The translator rendered it with the most common meaning. The verse carries the significance that Qohelet, with his oppressive guilt complex, feels that only through his psychology and experience can one know what an evil action and its punishment mean.

Chapter 5

5.2: Healing: The underlying Aramaic was *hilma* which the translator took as "dream" instead of "healing." **Pain:**   *'inyan* from *'inyana* for Qohelet does not mean "subject, matter, business" but as its verb suggests "affliction, pain." The connection with the preceding encompasses the thought: after one word of defiance, much (self-) punishment may ensue; and only after much pain, can one's turmoil be relieved. Downfall: The root is *qll* not *qwl*, "voice." Qohelet does not quite put his thoughts in order: the "fool" is the impulsive Qohelet (see p. 51, 71, 146). The ideas should run: the downfall of the impulsive comes through the profusion of words, and healing after much pain. Qohelet frequently puts aft what is fore, and "because" is simply the concomitant "and." (Compare Hoffman, F.J., *Freudianism and the Modern Mind*, p. 41 [reprint].)

5.3: Vow: Deut. 23.22 almost verbatim, the only passage from the Bible that Qohelet selects because of the significance of vows and oaths (to himself, *see* p.

39). The approximation of the Hebrew to Deut. may be the work of the translator or Qohelet himself. Defaulters: The underlying Aramaic should have been read as *satayya* rather than *shatayya*, "fools," which is not appropriate in context. *Satayya*, "deviants from the law, defaulters," are those who do not fulfill their obligations, as is evident from the context.

5.5: **Condemn:** the *lahti'* does not catch the nuance of the Aramaic *lehayyaba*, "condemn," the more apt and forcible expression. Messenger: a supererogatory reading of the Aramaic *sheliha*, the human messenger who collected debts owed the sanctuary (cf. Rashi). Forgetfulness: *shegagah* means "error" (JPS). Probably the underlying Aramaic had the word *shelutha* meaning both "error" and "forgetfullness"; the translator in his choice of rendition chose the first meaning instead of the second. A man would say in such remissness that he forgot about paying not that the sanctuary debt is in error.

5.6: **Are led astray:** the Hebrew translator confused two roots which were quite similar: *shegi*, "to err," and *segi*, "to be much," and the difference between the two would be a diacritical dot. There are alternative grammatical forms; *shegya, shegaya* and *sagi, shagayin* and *sagin*; the latter however is Palestinian/Galilean Aramaic Dalman, *Grammatik²*, *par. 42.* Magic incantations: the Aramaic was *miltha*, "*magic words.*" Alone: the English translation brings out the sense of the adversative *ki*, "but." *Ki* may also have the signification of *no* (cf. Brown, Driver, Briggs, p. 474).

5.7: The verse bears the implication: don't be puzzled about the widespread corruption you see in government because each corrupt official is on the lookout not only for himself but for his corrupt superior (to gain his favor); and beyond sight and comprehension there are still others in a chain of knavery and crime.

5.8: The form of the Hebrew verb is anomalous. It is simply a *faute de mieux* rendering of the Aramaic *mishta'bed/bad* "is subject to" and similarly the Qohelet Midrash to this verse (Soncino English edition, p. 138). "Field" means agriculture; it is good for a man to possess land even for the king, and Qohelet as a member of the royal court knew better than the rest of the population how much the king was dependent on agricultural revenues.

5.9: **Prizes luxuries:** *'Ahab b*...as a construction in the Hebrew is impossible and unexampled. The Hebrew translator misconstrued his Aramaic by separating his words incorrectly. The Aramaic ran *uman demehabeb segi'utha* (the verb is *pa'el*) but the Hebrew translator thought of the verb as *af'el* (there is but little difference in meaning, except that the Af'el is more frequent [cf. Payne Smith, *Syriac Dictionary*, 122] where the form is *maheb* [Payne Smith, *ibid*]). In dividing wrongly, the translator attached the additional *Bet* to *segiutha*, making for the impossible construction. *Segi'utha* is muchness in things, gaudy trappings, accoutrements, that one spends money upon in a lavish fashion, in general affluence. For the senseless *lo tebu'ah*, we should read with others *lo tebo'ehu* "will not accrue to him" i.e. will not have an income. Or in Aramaic *la 'atya leh*=it will do him no good, Payne Smith, 32. The verse now divides into two antithetic stichoi:

One who loves money will not have enough money.

On the other hand, the one who loves luxuries will have no income.

5.10: Basically, the verse has the meaning "when the good food increases, those who eat it increase," the Hebrew via the Aramaic going back to the Akkadian influence as found in the expression *a-ku-la ṭa-a-ba*, "eat the sweet food" (Delitszch, *Assyrisches Handwörterbuch*, 301a). We should read in the Hebrew *yitron/kishron*, and *bol'eha/be'aleha* as others have suggested.

5.12: Sore evil: the locution *ra'ah ḥola*, and so in 5.15, supposedly "a grievous evil" is a straddle which ancient translators indulge in, as for example, in the doublets of the Septuagint and the alternate translations of the Authorized Version. The phrase literally should not be translated "a diseased evil," not a happy expression, but as *bish bish* idiomatic to Aramaic "a great evil". The translator, in his dilemma, rendered the first *bish* as "evil" and the second as "disease," which meaning *bish* also has. He should have translated invertedly *ḥoli ra'*, and so in 6.2 where he translated correctly, with *ḥoli* first and *ra'* second! Guards his wealth: a typical Aramaic construction, the passive participle with the Lamed of Agent (M.L. Margolis, *Man. of the Aram. Lang. of the Babyl. Talm.* par. 58j). Bankruptcy: "For his hurt" as a translation is off the road. The opposite of *ṭobah*, "prosperity," is *ra'ah*, "bankruptcy," actually a mistranslation of *bishutheh*, Aramaic for "poverty." The man's money is lost in a bad investment as indicated in the following verse.

5.13: A son born: there is no connection about the birth of a son, either fore or aft. Qohelet, reminiscing about the bad venture, recollects his son as "a bad venture." The close proximity of the words "a bad venture" and "he begat a son" suggests the idea of the son "being a bad business." Compare too the philological analogy of *tolada/toladta* which may have momentarily occupied Qohelet's mind, which bears generally the concept of "child, son" and "happening, event." Compare Brown, Driver, Briggs, *Lexicon*, p. 410, Gen. 5.1 and 37.2 (accounts, events, history).

5.14: Penniless: there is a play on words, originally in Aramaic, but carried through in the Hebrew as well, where the Aramaic *'artil* means "be naked, bare" but also "poverty stricken" and so the Hebrew *'arom* meaning "naked" and "despoiled, poor," e.g., Ket. VI, 5 where the bride comes to the bridegroom's house without the customary outfit, *'arummah*, as her father conditioned it.

5.15: Satisfaction: *yitron's* meaning for Qohelet, p. 90.

5.16: Complaint: this is the required word and not "darkness." "Complaint" is synonymous and concordant with the other words of Qohelet's neurosis: agitation, illness, and anxiety. The Hebrew translator read *qibla* in the Aramaic as "darkness" instead of "complaint." *Ka'as*, which the Massorah assumes is a verb, should, against the accents, be read as a noun. The text reflects good Aramaic syntax: in such syntax, a preposition, either *b,l,m*, will carry through successive nouns without the additional particle. (Cf. Zimmermann, *JQR*, XL, 1949,88.) For the expression, *weka'as harbeh*, cf. Dan. 2.12. *benas uqzaf sagi*. The *Bet* there is prepositional; *nas* is the unaugmented form of *nesas* (cf. the longer form *nesis*, similarly *hat* and *hatat*). *See* B. Halper, *The Participial Formations of the Geminate Verbs*, ZAW, 1910, p. 42f. For Qohelet the word carries the connotation of *Angst*. *Holyo* is to be read as *holi*, the mental illness that distresses Qohelet. *Qezef* is not "wrath" but "fear," "anxiety" as in Eastern Aramaic. (Cf. BDB, s.v.)

5.17: **This:** The Hebrew has *hinneh*, "behold," is syntactically quite awkward. The Aramaic had the word *ha'* meaning "this" and "behold." The translator blundered in translating "behold." *Yafeh*="pretty," "nice," but the Aramaic equivalent *shappir* has the more accurate nuance of "most fitting, the best choice," e.g., Gen. 23.6 *mibhar/shefar*, Jastrow, *Dictionary*, 1620.

5.18: **Permitted:** literally "enabled." God awards to certain of His favorites a portion (as of a legacy for which one does not toil), and the favored one takes away his portion (*see* presently) and rejoices in it—all this is a reflection of a family scene wherein the father apportions gifts to the children for obscure reasons that the children cannot fathom. The Hebrew translator should have rendered *kol 'enasha/gabra'* indeterminatively without the article *(kol 'adam)*. *To win in this lottery*: Hebrew *las'et 'et helqoh* is an incorrect rendering of *lemintal lehulqeh*, Heb. *natal heleq*=to take one's portion allotted to one, as in an inheritance. (Cf. Deut. 10.9.)

5.19: This verse is difficult. The Hebrew word "remember" in the passage, and so in the translation of the Hebrew "He shall not much remember the days of his life" (RV), is peculiar. Probably the underlying Aramaic *la nahir lyome hayohi* was misinterpreted as "remember," which meaning indeed is found in both Talmuds of Jerusalem and Babylonia. (Compare the dictionaries of Levy and Jastrow s.v.) Much better would be the sense of "be bright." The Hebrew *'et* is a misconstruction of the *Lamed* of reference which the translator assumed to be the accusatival Lamed. Literally then: "it shall not be bright for him for the days of his life." The participle in Aramaic temporally may be future. The Hebrew *ma'aneh* does not make sense. The substrate Aramaic read *me'ayyneh*, "is eying him." The meaning of the verse now becomes: The days of a man's life are not bright for God watches him as he tries to enjoy himself. This is paranoid. *Ki* has asseverative force–"but," "however," "on the contrary," "on the other hand." (Compare D. Yellin, *Hiqre Miqra* I, Jerusalem, 1927, p. 10.)

Chapter 6

6.2: Aramaic *bish bish*, the first word meaning "illness," the second "evil," which the translator rendered syntactically correct here but incorrectly at 5.12.15.

6.3: **And live long years:** either a variant reading, or a smoother one for "and the days of his years be many," which was copied proleptically into the Hebrew instead of epexigetically. Note *shanaw* instead of the usual Hebraic *shenotaw*. The Aramaic form was unconsciously copied. No burial: Qohelet is fearful, on the one hand, of the desecration of his corpse by birds and beasts of prey, and on the other hand he is desirous of returning to the dark, still quiet of Mother Earth (the womb).

6.4: **From the womb:** literally "in nothing," the *Bet* as frequently in Hebrew and Ugaritic standing for *m*. Darkness: metaphor for the grave. Existence: - or remembrance. (Cf. Ex. 3.15, 2 Sam. 18.18.)

6.5: Hebrew *nahat*, "gratification[?]"—hardly the appropriate word, and certainly not for the abortion. *Nahat* reproduces the Aramaic *nahat*, rt., *nwh*, perfect, or perhaps in the *pe'il nihat* and is employed here in the idiomatic sense as in the phrase *niha* (passive participle masculine determinate) *leh le'nash*="better for a man," "better that a man should." It is also possible that *niha* in the Aramaic may have been read as a noun *neyaha*. (Compare *Qidd.*

20a, 'Arakhin 30b.)

6.6: The verse deals with Qohelet's fear of death. The first 'illu, "and even if." The sense of the passage then becomes: even if one did live long, and experience pleasure, still one has to face the eternal darkness.

6.7: Yet: lehod="also" and 2) "but," and the translator wrongly took the first meaning. **Appetite:** nefesh has a number of meanings, body, belly, appetite, soul. Appetite=desire.

6.8: Superiority: the substrate Aramaic would have been yater, participle active, used substantively (compare Levy, Dictionary for examples.) which the translator was hard put to render, reproducing lamely with a Hebrew participial formation, syntactically without parallel. Who: the Hebrew has the difficult ma le'ani yode'a. The translator mistook măn "who" for mān "what." Similarly 2.12 and the note there. He should have rendered mi le'ani yoda'... "who can tell a poor man [Qohelet] how to struggle against life?"—reading yoda' or yodi'a in the Hebrew. Is. 38.19; Num. 16.5. Life's problems: literally Life, hayyim plural abstract. Compare hayye 'olam, hayye sha'ah.

6.9: Loss: halak bears the meaning of "perish," "die," Arabic halaka, "perish."

6.10: Whatever exists now: the translator misread hu' again as hawa'. (See p. 106 f.) Most learned man: the Hebrew translator misread hakkim, "learned man," for hakim, the passive participle, "known." Nature: shem=nature, character, being, personality. Qohelet recognizes that a man's heredity is formed long ago, and one cannot change it. Forces mightier: either qere or ketib add up to the same sense. The meaning: no matter how learned the man, he cannot control impulses and instincts more powerful than his conscious self.

6.11: The verse is a banality in the usual sense: seeing there are many words that increase vanity, what is man the better? (JPS). The Hebrew translator mistook the Aramaic combination in his text mashgin masgin (or vice versa; the construction is good Aramaic: see T. Nöldeke, Syriac Grammar, par. 337; the subject may be pitgamin or even millayya though feminine) and was translated as if masgin masgin. He should have rendered "For misleading sorceries can increase frustration." The latter part of the verse means: what profit is there for a man in magic? Miltha=incantations, magic as in Aramaic. (Compare Jastrow, Dictionary, s.v. miltha.) Qohelet, despite his neuroticism, and the ubiquity of magic and sorcery in Babylonia, recognizes that magic is so much foolishness, and manfully challenges it. La'adam "for a man"=Qohelet. (See p. 53 f.)

6.12: Spend his days: Aramaic 'abad as well as Hebrew 'asah means "spend time." Play: Heb., kazzel, "to spend one's days as a shadow" is conceptually impossible. Most likely the Aramaic telal, "play, sport" in one of the forms, e.g., metallel (pa'el part. "was playing," Jastrow, p. 537) was confused with matlal, metala, "shade, shelter." To spend one's days in a sportive or playful fashion=without care. What follows is an ellipsis, a characteristic of Qohelet's thinking and neurotic feeling . . . so that he could spend his days as if at play! ellipsis: (but this is impossible) for who can tell what the future (consequence) will be?

Chapter 7

7.1: Fame: *Shem* does not mean "name" here but as frequently "fame, glory," (though fundamentally as in 6.10, i.e., the nature that a person is born with); for Qohelet, too, *shem*=existence; *shemen*=precious perfume (not oil, compare Prov. 27.9; Song 1.3; 4.10 and in 10.1). 1a carries a double meaning. For Qohelet, who neurotically is hopeless about the future, the day of death—unexistence—is better than the day of one's birth.

7.3: Sobriety: *ka'as* in contrast to *sehoq*, means without laughter. To laugh would mean to enjoy oneself, which Qohelet could not permit himself to do. How can he enjoy himself with such a burden of guilt, more imagined than real? A serious mien: Prov. 15.13 the exact opposite: a happy heart will make the face happy. Not so Qohelet.

7.5: Praise: not as in the Hebrew "the singing of fools" but the *praise* of fools in contrast to the rebuke of the wise men. The Hebrew translator again mistook a wrong meaning for the word in Aramaic: *shabah* signifies both "praise" and "sing."

7.6: Crackling of faggots: no heat and much smoke. This too is futility: In the loose syntax of Semitic languages generally, as well as in Hebrew, this part of the verse is not an observation on the first part, but a comment on the preceding verse (5).

7.7: The construction in stichos b seemingly is awkward but is good Aramaic order: *'et leb* is a mistaken retroversion of *leleb*, and is not a construct. *Mattanah* means "bribe," Prov. 15.27. In Aramaic, however, *matna* was taken to be a feminine whereas it should have been rendered as a masculine, say, *mattan* in Hebrew in agreement with the verb *wey'abed*.

7.8: Better the end . . . than its beginning: Qohelet's suicidal impulse. Chastened . . . Insolent: The Hebrew *'erek ruah* and *gebah ruah* (Is.66.2) or *shefal ruah* Prov. 29.23 Is.;57.15. Probably *ngd* I=be long and *ngd* II=beat, strike were misunderstood and the translator took the first meaning for his rendition. The second meaning is is to be preferred and he should have translated *nekeh ruah*, "chastened in spirit," the appropriate counterpart to "insolent in spirit."

7.9: Starts: Anger does not *rest* in the bosom of fools. It *starts* there, as the verb *bihel* implies. This is the reason for the admonition of not being quick to anger. The Aramaic *sheri* meaning "rest," has another meaning, "start," the required sense here.

7.10: How is it: not how was it, but "how is it?"—another example of how the translator confused *hu'* and *hawa'*, p. 106 f.

7.11: Especially: the Aramaic *yattir*, "especially," was misunderstood or read as a participle.

7.12: Lacking—lacking: The Hebrew translator mistook the Aramaic verb *btl* as *b + tl* "in the shadow of" and not making for any sense. The Aramaic verb *btl* means "unavailing," "of no effect." The latter part of the verse the translator misconstrued syntactically: he took the particle *de* to show a genetival relationship when he should have construed it as a relative conjunction introducing a subordinate clause. That is, the MT, which the JPS following the accents retails as "But the excellence of knowledge is, that wisdom preserveth the life of him that hath it," would be more correct in the Aramaic than the Hebrew. The Aramaic ran: *weyutran demandea'dehokmatha*, "The excellence of knowledge is *that...or because.*

7.14: **enjoy yourself:** *Heyey betob*=Aramaic *hewe betab* "enjoy yourself" cf. Tob 7.11 Syriac: eat drink, and enjoy yourself.

7.15: **Two things:** kol=two, as in 3.19 (Ginsberg).

7.16: **Laughed at:** there are two Aramaic roots, *zedi* I, "be wasted," "destroyed," and *zedi* II, "laugh at," "deride" (Payne Smith, *Dictionary* 473; Brockelmann 62; Jastrow, 1262). The translator chose the first, the more familiar. The second is more appropriate and pointed.

7.18: The familiar antithesis, here moralizing and philosophical, in that Qohelet cannot commit himself but falls back on the more basic psychologic impulse that the unconscious projects as the better recourse: Fear God and you will be safe.

7.19: **Wealth:** we should read with Perles *'osher/'asarah*.

7.23: **Acquire true wisdom:** *'ehkemah*, seems a reflection of the Aramaic *'ehkemah* with the He dageshed, "I will learn it," proleptically.

7.24: **Reality is beyond things as they appear:** the syntax of the Hebrew *rahoq mah she-hayah* is most peculiar; the Aramaic substructure, however, provides the correct clue: *rahiq min dehu'*, "Far more than what is" (reality). The Hebrew interpreted however *min*, "from," as *mān*, "what"; then again he read *hu'* as *hawa'*. His Hebrew should have run perhaps: *rahoq me'asher hu'*, "Far more than what is," i.e., *'asher hu'*=whatever is=reality, and has been so translated. Similarly, the translator did not recognize the second *'amoq* as being an Akkadian root having the meaning "deep" but also as found in the form *nimequ (emqu)*, signifying "wisdom."

7.25: **Revolved:** Qohelet cannot solve the problem of his life's meaninglessness and frustration. Read *belibbi/welibbi. Latur:* an Aramaism="meditate." (*See* note on 1.13.) The *hokma* here is his elusive lost love that he longs for, and which forecasts in the next verse the bitter snare of another woman, his wife. Stupidity of impulsiveness: or irrationality. The Aramaic probably had *siklutha deturfa*, but in a moment of thoughtlessness, the Hebrew translator rendered with the determinate in a genitival construction.

7.26: A key passage for understanding Qohelet's relation to his wife. He has criminal thoughts and death wishes toward her; the words "death" and "wife" are collocated together. She is full of traps (deception) and she is choking him. Qohelet, however, regards himself as luckless *(hote')*, and is caught in her clutches.

7.27: The feminine phrase *'amrah Qohelet* cannot be relieved by emending *ha-Qohelet*. The addition of the definite article to a name is unparalled and inexplicable. The translator saw the phrase as *'imrat kanshah*. The He of the determinate ending misled him to think of the verb as feminine and so we have the bizarre *'amrah Qohelet*. The retroversion to Aramaic, however, yields a different result. With a different vocalization, although the letters are identical, the verb should be read *'e/'imret* in the first person. *Kanshah* was wrongly taken as Qohelet's name; it should have been taken as the participle pendens with Mappiq He. *Maz'ati* of the Hebrew represents *mezet*, "be able." The passage originally ran:

hazeh den d'mezet 'imret
(kad) kanshah hada lehada lemimze hushbena
(See this, I am now able to assert, adding one thing to another, to reach a conclusion...a man I could find, etc.)

meẓi 'amar is good Aramaic for *meẓi lememar* (variantly *maẓe 'amar*), T. Nöldeke, *Syriac Grammar*, par. 337; *kanshah* with the Mappiq proleptically for "one," is dependent on the construction "I have been able to state"; the text probably also had the idiomatic but untranslatable *kad*. It is quite possible that *'askah* could replace *meẓi* as a synonym: the d' is idiomatic (cf. the Peshitta and the Syro-Hexaplar Vss). The sense of the passage reflects the impression that Qohelet seeks to urge on the reader that he added one secure conclusion to another certain premise to reach this certain summary of things and which Qohelet considered quite important, *viz.*, that he never found a woman he could trust, who would be faithful.

7.28: Among all that number: literally "in all those," "among those thousand." Qohelet suspects that Solomon, too, among his "thousand," the number of women in Solomon's harem, could not trust a single one.

7.29: Also: Hebrew reads *lebad*, impossible in syntax, but really a mistranslation of *lehod* "also" and "only," and the translator took the wrong turn. It was his intention perhaps to draw attention in particular to this last statement of verse 29. Wrongheaded schemes: the Hebrew *hiššbonot rabbim*, usually translated as "many inventions" whatever significance that may be, remains obscure. The Hebrew translator saw *husbenan saggiyin* and rendered accordingly. He should have read *shin* instead of *sin*, i.e., *shagin*, "erring misleading, wrongheaded" schemes.

Chapter 8

8.1: Correctly interpret events: literally interpretation of a thing, which is too indefinite. *Dabar* more likely signifies "event", e.g., *dibre ha-yamim*. *'Oz* is a noun, not construct and reflects either *teqof* or *huzpah*, Targum of Jonathan, Deut. 28.50, "fierceness, aggression." We should also read *yeshanneh*, "will transform," object *panaw*. (Compare Dan. 5.6 [emended].)

8.2: The king's countenance: the Hebrew should read *penei melek*, based upon the reconstructed Aramaic *'anpe melek* which the translator read as *'ani pi melek* with unconscious cerebration (and so H.L. Ginsberg). Don't be rash: borrowed from the following verse.

8.3: Don't swear to anything suspect: literally: stand not in an evil thing which both in Hebrew (and English) is most anomalous. Since, however, the immediate context deals with the caution of taking a serious oath, *'al ta'amod* conceals the Aramaic *la teqayyem*, "don't swear," which the translator failed to recognize, and took simply as of the root *qum*. Since he can do anything he wishes: either a variant reading to the same thought and phraseology of verse 4, or else an ellipsis to be supplied. Because if you do take oath, and the king's word and power is unchangeable, you will find yourself in the dilemma of being under oath, and powerless to carry it out.

8.5: The rules: *miẓvah*, a collective. End-time time for judgment: literally time and judgment. For Qohelet, time carries with it the omen of judgment, and so the following verse. The *hakam* is Qohelet.

8.6: The verse is to be taken pejoratively. When sins begin to accumulate and weigh him down, Qohelet is certain that he will be summoned to judgment. *'Adam* is Qohelet.

8.7: We should read *hayah*, "was," for *yihyeh*, following the Peshitta. The meaning of the verse is: Qohelet neurotically thinks that since one cannot know the (imagined) number of sins one has, who can know the severity of the judgment in the future, since Qohelet never knows whether he has made complete atonement.

8.8:   The *Waws* are comparative, as, e.g., Job 5.7: For man is born to trouble just as the [w] sparks fly upward. Divesting of armor: the Aramaic *shelah* means to divest oneself of armor (Payne Smith, *Syriac Dictionary* 589). The sense of the passage is that in the midst of the fray one cannot lay aside one's armor (Amos 2.16). The whole verse *vis-a-vis* Qohelet has the significance that impulses that surge within one can scarcely be controlled or put off, even as the day of death, even as one cannot control the wind. There is no surcease or quietus in this struggle, and finally one cannot escape one's guilt. The "battle" is the conflict of his emotions. The whole verse now hangs together. Emotion=*ruah* "spirit."

8.9: Breakdown: to his hurt lit.

8.10:   Given honor: in the Hebrew text, it is obvious that *wa-ba'u*, "and they shall come," is completely awry. The translator confused roots. He saw the Aramaic text *itta'alu* (Ittaph'al) or perhaps *'i'allelu*, rt. *'al* which had active signification, "they came," Jastrow, *Dictionary*, 1083 whereas the translator should have understood the form as coming from rt. *'aly* in the Ithpa'al, "be glorified, exalted" (Dalman, *Grammatik*,[2] 334). Holy place: the synagogue or sanctuary in Babylonia.

8.11:   The connection between verses 10 and 11 must be understood through the insertion of a transition, actually an ellipsis: how is it that the wicked are eulogized, how is it that he has not been punished? There are two "becauses" extending through the first half of verse 12. Is encouraged: *male' belebba* in Aramaic=encouraged (Payne Smith, *Syriac Dictionary*, p. 274). Transpose 11b and 12a.

8.12:   Yet lives: "days," "years" are understood, exactly in Aramaic *'agar* with *yomatha* either expressed or understood (Payne Smith, 328). Compare the following verse for the full construction. Although I do know . . .: this section of the verse is a part of the following verse. Qohelet again, with his neurotic doubt, equally entertains alternatives.

8.13:   And it shall not go well: a continuation of the latter part of the preceding verse. Disporting himself: either *ketalel* or *ketolela*=as one who revels, amuses himself, disports himself (see note to 6.12), was misinterpreted or read as *ketelala*, "shadow," which makes no sense.

8.14:   Paradox: *Hebel*; repeated twice in this verse with different meanings. Perhaps in the first *hebel* "iniquity, wrong" would suit the passage as well. The second *hebel* conveys Qohelet's sense of outrage.

8.15:   All this: literally: it. Combined: literally associated, accompanied.

8.16:   Qohelet's mind is constantly preoccupied with weighing decisions, of constantly investigating because of his persistent doubt. (Compare 9.1). Turmoil: We should read *be'innuyo*, "in his affliction," wordplay on *'inyan*.

8.17:   For what purpose: the Hebrew literally translates the Aramaic *bedil de*. The better Hebrew translation would have been *lema'an 'asher. He will not solve it:* an apodosis with the Hebrew *Waw* like the Arabic *fa* "...as a result, in the end, yet" would be satisfactory renditions.

Chapter 9

9.1: **Clarifying:** or investigating. Because of his doubt, Qohelet is always investigating, with difficulty in reaching a conclusion. Qohelet wishes to impress his reader that after much "thought" he has now come to a sure conclusion, and so in 8.16;7.25 and elsewhere. Doings: *'abadeihem*, i.e., the Aramaic word, was copied almost directly from the Aramaic Vorlage, instead of translating *ma'aseihem*. In their future everything is a blank: the Hebrew has *ha-kol lifneihem* which in the context does not make for sense. It is apparent that the Hebrew translator did not understand his text *kola qodomaihon: kola*. The first *kola* he should have read *kelah* which should have rendered "as nothing everything is before them," taking *kola* from the next verse. For *kelah* compare Dan.4.32 *kelah hašibin* (ms. variant *kela* with Alef). Observe the wordplay. The verse then bears the significance that man's future is as nothing, is a blank. In the statement that "man cannot know God's love or hate," Qohelet unconsciously recalls a family situation where the all powerful father dispenses favors and largesse to little ones without their understanding why. The lucky ones seemingly enjoy the favors; another son will be punished without knowing the reason.

9.2: The first *lakol* in the Hebrew is to be connected syntactically via the Aramaic with the preceding note. (*See comment supra.*) The word *latob* is to be deleted; it came in the Hebrew when the scribe had just written "for the good man and the evil one" and in the succession of the similar letter Tet wrote without thinking *latob*, anticipating, moreover, the *tob* a line ahead. The antithetic character of the verse is to be noted and moreover, that Qohelet shares with neurotics a fear of oaths, and in addition by the antithesis, regards himself as unclean, luckless, and basically evil. Because: read *ba'asher*.

9.3: **The evil:** Aramaic *bisha*, determinate which the Hebrew translator mistook and rendered without the definite article. Omit *bilbabam* as redundant to *leb*.

They shrug their shoulders about the future: The Hebrew text "and after them to the dead" does not make for a sensible sequence. The Aramaic reads. *w'ahorohi lemethayya*, "and their backs are turned to the events to come," i.e., they shrug their shoulders about the future. The Hebrew translator read *lemithayya/lemethayya*. The letters are identical.

9.4: Read the Qere *yehubbar*. The Hebrew expression with the so-called Lamed asseverative (why would this be the only example in Qohelet?) is actually a reflection of the Aramaic *bedil kalba*, except that the translator divided *bedil* wrongly: *bedi – l*. (Compare Dalman, *Grammatik*[2] 42b).

9.7: **On the contrary:** lit. Perhaps, *kebar* in the Hebrew does not mean "already," but is the Aramaic "perhaps." Verses 7-9 run parallel to a passage in the Gilgamesh Epic. See p. 91.

9.8: **White__oil:**this is to present a good external appearance. The white clothes are worn deceptively to conceal black thoughts; the oil to ward off demons and at the same time keep the hair from disarray; wild hair=wild thoughts which Qohelet wishes to conceal.

9.9: The advice is wistful; probably Qohelet is thinking of his early days of marriage. The caesura presents a variant reading. One text read: all the days of your futile life; another: all your futile days, omitting *hayye*. (Compare Zimmermann, *The Perpetuation of Variants in the Masoretic Text*, JQR, 34, 1944, 459-474.)

9.10: The Hebrew missed an idiom in Aramaic and translated too literally. *Bekohaka* is wordy, superfluous. The Aramaic was *'askaḥ ḥaila* or *mezi ḥaila*, idiomatic for "be able." The translator should have omitted *ḥailka*.

9.11; The race is not to the swift, nor the battle to the strong: a popular proverb. Qohelet, however, is outraged that men gifted with wisdom, intelligence, learning (to which he too pretends and does not hesitate to place himself) do not have bread to eat, nor wealth, nor favor (recognition) extended to men of learning, perhaps grace in speech, too. But Qohelet ends up with the familiar doubt and antithesis. There is the ellipsis: why be perturbed anyway. The fell time will strike at them all.

9.12: Evil hour: Read *'itto ra'ah* combined the two words having been inadvertently separated, perhaps *ra'ah* having been placed doubtfully between one line and the next (Cf. *'et ra'-ah* further on in the verse.) Read *ko meyukashim*: "So are caught..."

9.15: Happened: Aramaic *shekiaḥ* has the idiomatic use of "be present," "be at hand," which the Hebrew translator did the best he could with. The Hebrew should be corrected to *wayimmaẓe*, imper. *nif'al. Misken* as employed by Qohelet, and so apparently in Akkadian, means a citizen of the middle class. (Compare pp. 57, 146; Driver and Miles, II, 152.) Rescued: *millaṭ*, "cause to escape," "cause to slip away," is a none too good translation of *shezeb* which has also the meaning of "rescue." Perhaps *hizzil, hoshi'a* would have been better employed. (Cf. *sheyzeb/hizzil* Ex. 12.27; Deut. 32.39 Targum and MT as well as *sheyzeb/millaṭ* Amos 2.15.)

9.16: Brain is better than brawn: literally "Wisdom is better than strength," perhaps a popular proverb. Ordinary man: i.e., Qohelet, or perhaps "poor man" here. Qohelet retreats and qualifies this position in the next verse with an alternate reflection.

9.17: Acquiescence: Heb *benaḥat*, "quietly," but Aramaic *beniḥa, benihutha* "with ease," "with acceptance." "Quietly" is only assumed for the Hebrew because of the "shouting" in the next verse. In Aramaic the parallelism would contrast more effectively. Again, the familiar alternate reservation of Qohelet extends through to the next verse. Ruler: not the king but the vice-ruler or governor general at the twin capital at Seleucia on the Tigris. (See pp.126,130.) The hysterical shrieking of the governor at stupid underlings is a piece of living drama that Qohelet witnessed at the governor's court.

9.18: Weapons of War: Hebrew *kelei qerab* is an exact translation of Aramaic *ma'ane qeraba*. Miss . . . the target: the original meaning of *hata'*. (Cf. the lexica.) For Qohelet, to miss one's goal in life, as he conceives it is to destroy the joy and meaning of existence.

Chapter 10

10.1: A difficult verse. For *zebube mawet*, we should read *zebub ki yamut*. (Cf. Ez. 14.13 *'erez ki tehṭa'.)* The misconstruction of the last word in this verse has undone the sense of the rest. The word *me'at* is a misrendering of the Aramaic substrate *ze'er* which may mean little, or little child. The verse is divided into contrasts: on the one hand, it is true that a dead fly, small as it is, can putrefy perfumed oil; on the other hand, more precious than wisdom, than honor, is the foolishness of a little child. The manifest meaning is clear. Unconsciously the verse signifies: a disturbing thought (flies are thoughts) can undo one's whole life, can disturb one's whole emotional pattern; on the other hand, the wantonness of the penis (child = penis, Garma, *Interpretation of Dreams*, Gutheil, *Handbook of Dream Analysis*, p. 136 "the little one," and found elsewhere in the Hebrew Bible as *qotoni* I Kings 12.10) to enjoy sexual fulfillment for oneself, is more precious than esteem for wisdom or honor one can win from the outside.

10.3: The English translation assumes that *derek* means way=manner, fashion. (Cf. the lexica.) It signifies: the verb is impersonal and refers immediately to the "empty mind," and indirectly to the whole verse.

10.4: Can allay: a retroversion to the Aramaic reveals a challenging alternate to the MT: *marpe' yishboq hobin saggi'in.* 1) Don't resign you office, for resigning will leave behind great offences not cleared away 2) The translator took *marpe'* not as a verbal noun but as a noun, the verb *yishboq* as "leave," i.e., put to rest. Both interpretations are possible. *Yishboq*, moreover, means "forgive," which likewise should be admitted in the interpretation: For soothing will cause great offences to be forgiven.

10.6: Magnates: literally rich persons. Qohelet has awe for the rich.

10.8: The verse seems a metaphor on the political intrigue at court. Qohelet has seen carefully laid schemes revert punishingly on the heads of the contrivers; and others who would overturn the established order of things get "stung." Compare Ps. 7.16;35.7 and Prov.26.27) The language, however supplies on another level an unconscious caution: If one has a sexual fling, dire consequences may befall him, and one who infracts the conventional moralities (so the Midrash Qohelet to this verse, and compare Prov. 25.28) will be bitten. The Midrash takes the verse literally, and cites examples of actual attacks by serpents.

10.9: The verse is of a piece with the proceeding. "Stones" and "wood' are well-known symbols for the penis and the vagina respectively (Freud, *Interpretation of Dreams*, c. The Dream Work, Modern Library Edition, 371f.) and so the Midrash to Qohelet on the verse "A time to cast away stones" (3.5) avers: at the time when your wife is ritually clean, it is opportune to have conjugal intercourse.

10.10 From the point of view of the grammar, there are extraordinary difficulties. The general import seems clear: our English translation supplies the sense. *Barzel* is metonymic for ax, battle-ax, and a collective (Job. 41.19;Sam.23.7). The retroverted Aramaic *holala* (ax) plays upon *hailin*, i.e., Heb. *hayyalim*. The Aramaic ran: *wehailin mahe(y)l* which the Hebrew translated rendered as *mehayyel* as from *hyl* "strength." The *Mem*, however, is part of the root, to be read *mahel*, vocalic *Yod*, and means "weaken," "enfeeble, "discourage", (Payne Smith, 264.) The verse now makes admirable sense: If the battle ax be not sharpened, then it will weaken, i.e., handicap the strong, the soldiery; the better part of wisdom is to prepare the ax.

10.11: Without the charmer's control: so the sense; literally, with whisper, without enchantment, or incantation. Serpent charmer: literally man of words. Below the surface meaning is the unconscious reflection of Qohelet that sexual desire cannot be curbed, and breaks forth unrestrainedly, the invoking of law, custom, or morality is powerless to restrain conduct. Observe that enchantment carries sexual overtones. (Cf. Latin *fascinum*=1. enchantment 2. phallus.)

10.12: Run smoothly: literally full of grace. Verses 12 to 14a make observations that Qohelet witnessed at court where smooth talkers persuade and charm; "fools" stammer and are incoherent, distort and sour their pleadings at court. Qohelet himself quite likely suffered in this regard. He admired the erudite speaker who could present his case with finished wit and yet compactly. Verse 14a belongs with 13c in thought although Qohelet connected 14a *in situ* to make for syntactical connection via *sakal* with the following *kesilim*.

10.14: The verse seems isolated in thought. For the syntactical nexus, however, see the preceding note and what immediately follows.

Magic spells: Hebrew is *debarim*, reflecting *miltha*, *millaya*, meaning in Aramaic "magic spell, sorcery". Again by means of the same word as Qohelet's method is, Qohelet makes use of the preceding *dabar* for the syntax. Here again Qohelet resolutely repudiates magic and divination—"The fool multiplies magic practices"—for man cannot know what the future will bring. The verse also carries the distress that Qohelet feels about impending death (cf.5.19;6.12;11.8). This apprehension stems from the fact or feeling that he had perpetrated a serious crime now suppressed or forgotten, punishable by death, most likely of incest with his sister or mother, which he would like to blot out of his mind forever, but which he has fears of being disclosed or judged for.

10.15: In the Hebrew text there are four difficulties which when one turns to the Aramaic substratum is cleared up in an exceptional fashion. *'Amal* is masculine, but the verb is feminine; *ha-kesilim* is plural but the suffix of the verb is singular; on the other hand, 15b has a singular verb; what does the last part of the verse mean: "he knows not how to go to the city"? The Aramaic retroversion restores the sense. Hebrew *'amal* is masculine but *lei'utha* is feminine. However, the Hebrew translator in the midst of his rendering forgot two words later that he put down *'amal* as masculine, has copied mechanically the verb in the feminine from his Aramaic text. *Kesilim*=Aramaic *shaṭayya* which should have been read as a singular (same lettering); now the suffix of the verb is in concord. Furthermore, *yada'* singular, is correct. The latter part of the verse, *di la yada'lemezal lemethe*, which the translator misinterpreted or read as *lematha*=to the city, originally ran: because the fool does not know whether he is coming or going. The consonants of *lematha/lemethe* would be the same. (For the expression that he does not know whether he is coming or going, compare Targ. Isaiah 24:20.) The asyndeton is good Aramaic. (Compare T. Nöldeke, *Syriac Grammar*, par. 337.)

10.17: Moderately: Heb., "eat in strength," makes no sense. The Hebrew translator read *beḥusna*, "in strength" instead of *beḥusana*, "in moderation" (same letters).

10.18: Read *be'azlut*, the letters *ym* were written twice. Roof: literally rafters. The Aramaic had the word *kashorin*, "rafters," a play at *'azlut*, a root *ksr* being an antonym "skill" "industry." The Midrash thinks the verse applies to a woman, and interestingly so. The verse has sexual connotations. "Hand" is a familiar phallic symbol; "house"=body; the root *'atila* III, in Arabic means "stick fast *in coitu*," Lane, *Arabic Dictionary*, 2086, cited by Brown, Driver, Briggs, Lexicon, p. 782.

10.19: **Arrange a banquet:** The Hebrew which means "make bread" is mistranslation of an Aramaic idiom "make a feast"(Dan. 5.1). Heb. *ksf* means "desire, want" with a play on the word *kesef*=money. Supplies: the root *'anay* means "furnish, "supply, cf. Genseius-Buhl[17] s.v. Money is equated with love (compare E.H. Gutheil, *Handbook of Dream Analysis*, p. 203).

10.20: **Thought:** need not be emended. (Cf. "The words of your inner self do not speak [even] when alone" ANET, p. 49) Qohelet thinks that thoughts are "winged messengers" and can be revealed. Observe that *madda'*, "thought," in the verse at the beginning evolves to *qol*, "voice," at the end. Contrast the logical Ulpian's dictum, "No one is punished for his thoughts" (*Ad Edictum,* bk. III). Wealthy: Qohelet regards the wealthy with awe, because wealth represents power. *Hayyil*=wealth, power.

Chapter 11

11.1: The Hebrew reads the familiar "Cast thy bread upon the waters," which nevertheless is a most incongruous bit of advice. Moses Mendelssohn, Morris Jastrow and others see a suggestion for shrewd business venture, as indeed the sequence bears out. The Aramaic substrate supplies the key which had the word *peristak*, which the translator read as "bread," but as the context demands should have been read as "sail," "ship." Cf. Jastrow *Dictionary* s.v. 1232-33, and especially Ez. 27.7 and in the Targum.

11.2: **Country:** in contrast to the venture in seven or eight ships. Qohelet thinks (in a momentary contrapose to 5.8) of the plagues that beset agriculture, blights, locusts, fires, confiscation and wars. *Ra'ah* should be *ra'* as a rendition of *bisha* the masculine form, determinate, although it looked like a feminine form, indeterminate.

11.3: The latent content, and a reflection of the dilemma of Qohelet symbolically framed: his sexual organs fill with sperm, seek outlet and emit. He yearns for true love (lost) and fulfillment. On the other hand, he experiences impotence in the presence of a natural love object (woman) because of his distaste for his wife. (For the significance of the sexual symbols in the verse, see p. 22 f.)

11.5: **Breathing:** literally, way of the wind, i.e., spirit, animus, life force. Hebrew *derek ha-ruah.* represents Aramaic *'orah ruha*, word-play. The comparison and identity for Qohelet in the creation of the embryo and God's work is this: just as you do not know how the foetus acquires life, and yet you supplied the means and instrument in the most intimate fashion in the inner recesses of the womb for creation, so you cannot know what God does, in His creation far beyond you, for the whole world at large, the panorama of nature, and how it came into being.

11.6: **Seed . . . hand:** Sexual symbols with overtones of sexual opportunism. The Midrash to Qohelet, too, applies the verse to having children both in youth and old age. Qohelet is apparently thinking of his youth, and the need to take advantage of sexual vigor, and he now finds himself in a cul-de-sac of impotence and frustration. Similarly verse 9.

11.7 **Sun:** in a good sense of "enjoyment," in contrast to the forbidding sun, *passim* (compare 6.5).

11.8: Darkness: i.e., In the grave. What comes after: literally everything that will come.

11.9: But know this: seemingly a gloss but in reality an antithesis as it echoes again Qohelet's dismal contemplation of his own future, and the anticipation of the punishment that will come to him regardless.

11.10: Upset: i.e., agitated. Heb. *ka'as* i.e., Aramaic *rugza*, "agitation" (not vexation). Youth: we should read *bahruth* "youth"/*shahruth*.

Chapter 12

12.1: The proem is not with this verse but with 11.9. Your health: Hebrew: "Remember your Creator" which is difficult. "Creator" is out of character with the sequence in 1-7 dealing with the ill health and declining powers of old age. The Midrash to this verse implies a number of readings: your cistern, your well, etc., which Graetz assumes to be alternate readings. (See his *Kohelet*, p. 133.) It is evident, however, that by a simple change of vowel the translator misconstrued his text. He read *lebaryak* instead of *leboryak*, "your health." To be mindful of one's health is the theme of the passage from 1-7 before the evil days come. Days of illness: the translator read *yome bishutha* but interpreted *bishutha* as "evil" instead of the more suitable "illness" which the whole passage is about.

12.2: In the passage *'or,* "light" is superfluous with "sun" in the first stich. It appears that *negah*, meaning both "light" and "darkness," cf. *neshef* "early morning, sunset" and *'urta* "light, darkness," was mistaken in the passage, *negah* here=be dark. (Compare Payne Smith, *Syriac Dictionary,* s.v.) The verse now is restored to its proper couplet:

Before the sun goes a-glimmering
And the moon and the stars fade.

The sun, moon and the stars of the body are those which are "above" a man, in his head: thinking, talking, tasting, seeing, sensing, etc. The light of his body had been darkened (Math. 6.22-3). Clouds return: malaise and pains still persist.

12.3: Guardians of the house: if house=body, as per the usual equation, then the keepers of the body must be the hands and arms, and they tremble in old age, perhaps through Parkinson's Disease. Strong men: are the fingers on the hand. They become gnarled through age or arthritis.

12.4: Ease: Hebrew *qol* should be read as *qol,* "ease," rt. *qll* "be light," "be at ease," (Jer.3.9.) Becomes faint: the old man becomes hard of hearing. *Weyequm l* should be read as *weyiqmal,* "shall be faint," "languish." Musical notes: literally daughters of song. Decline: as one becomes older, one cannot reach musically the higher notes.

12.5: And one is terrified: read *yira,* sg./pl. as only one man is referred to. Read also *hat hatim* as two words, "he shall be afraid of dangers." (Compare Jer. 1.17; 30.10; Job 41.25; Gen. 9.2. For further explication of this verse, see p. 00-00) The latter part of verse requires some extended analysis. The Hebrew text has been questioned. It has been suggested that *weyanez,* "shall blossom," should be emended to *wiyna'ez,* "and it shall be contemned, derided," reading the Nif'al; *wetafer* to be read as *wetifer,* "shall blossom," on the basis of Aquila;

ḥagab, "locust," to be emended as *'agab* "love, desire." Now the verb *weyistabbel*, "be unbearable," supplies the key for the correct reading of the two verbs. "Be unbearable" in the Hebrew conveys distress, encumbrance, annoyance, affliction, a plague to one's being. Accordingly the other questioned verbs should be read in keeping with the same confines of meaning: *weyena'ez*, "shall be contemned," *wetafer*, "shall be unavailing." The verbs then would read concordantly: be despised...be unbearable...be unavailing...

It is also clear among the nouns that the caperberry and the almond comport in significance and function as aphrodisiacs, while *ḥagab*, "locust," is not. The usual Aramaic equivalent of *ḥagab* is *qamza* (so Lev. 11.22; Num. 13.33; Is. 40.22 in the Targums and the Peshitta) and one is tempted to say that *qamza de bara'* found in Syriac, supposedly *pastinaca agrestis* (=*parsnip*) accepted by Payne Smith, *Syriac-English Dictionary*, but questioned by I. Löw, *Aramäische Pflanzennamen*, 340, might have been the underlying Aramaic original. We need, however, a word closely associated with caperberry. This is *pirḥa*, a synonym of *nizpa* and *kipparis* (Greek), Aramaic *qapper*, the equivalent of *'abiyonah* "caperberry," Löw, 263. The word *pirḥa*, as a synonym of *'abiyonah* (so the authority Bar Bahlul, ibid, no. 201: pirḥa is *nizpa* which are the *qapper*; in another citation, he says that *qapper* is *pirḥa*, which most likely was in the text but the Hebrew translator did not recognize the word as a plant but mistakenly thought of it as a locust. (Compare Joel 1.4 in the Targum.) The translator should have considered *pirḥa* as one of the species of caper in Mesopotamia of which there are a number of varieties: *capparis spinosa* 2. *capparis caescens* in Damascus 3. *capparis parviflora* on the Dead Sea and the Sinai peninsula 4. *capparis Aegyptica* (Löw, 264). The caper, both in flower (Comp. Webster's International Dictionary,[3] s.v.) and berry, are used as condiments till this very day. Now the three nouns are in concord: almond, caperblossom caperberry. *Bet 'olam* is a euphemism for the grave (cf. *bet haḥayyim* "house of life").

  12.6: Verses 6 to 7 are a continuation of the sexual symbolism of verse 5. Silver cord: silver and gold represent the supremely precious things of life. The cord is that which binds or connects, and symbolically employed for the umbilical cord, signifies the connection with life (W. Stekel, *Interpretation of Dreams*, 407) but appears in dreams too as a sex symbol for the genital of the male (Gutheil, *Handbook*, p.136). Compare moreover, Latin *cordax*, Greek *kordax*, regarded as an indecent dance of old Greek comedy wherein the dancers passed a rope one to another with wanton gestures, (Liddel and Scott, s.v.) while others describe the dance as being performed with "grotesque paddings under a tightfitting garment with or without the phallus" (*Oxford Classical Dictionary*, p. 216). Golden bowl: Aramaic *gullah* meaning 1) bowl, 2) cloak, analogically like *keli*, 1) vessel, 2) clothes and so *m'ana* in Aramaic vessel and clothes. While *gullah* in the present context means "bowl," it is difficult to define sexually. If the bowl contains oil (Zech.4.2) and would have a spout for pouring, it would be a male symbol, required here, and so Rashi excellently but on different grounds identifies the *gullah* with the penis (*zeh ha-'amah*). But bowl is a bisexual word like bottle, i.e., an open container hence female. Jug in slang stands for mistress, pitcher a harlot(Partridge, *Dictionary of Slang and Unconventional English.*) In all probability, however, we are dealing with a bowl with a projective spout (Gutheil, p. 65); a pitcher too would be a male symbol (Gutheil, p. 139, fig. 39.) Read *yinnateq*, "will be snapped asunder," and vocalize too *weteroz*, "be shattered." Pitcher: with a spout, a male symbol (*See the previous note.*) Fountain: the female pudend. Wheel: so the Hebrew, or perhaps following the Ugaritic (Dahood) a type of bowl and so *Middot* 5.5; '*Erubin* 104a; or perhaps the whole works of the well generally (Jastrow, *Dictionary*, 244b *seq.*) Well: a familiar sexual symbol for the female. (Compare Prov. 5.15.)

12.7: **Dust:** Qohelet, with the usual deprecation of himself.

12.8: *See* note on 1.1 with the full discussion on the name Qohelet, and why ha-Qohelet is an impossibility.

12.9: A short biographical notice (verses 9-10) written by a biographer-disciple in Aramaic, but translated also into Hebrew. Kanosha: *hayah* is a mistranslation of the demonstrative particle *hu'* in Aramaic. (*See* p. 106.) Mature: Aramaic probably *histakkel*, "reflected," "observed". The translator rendered "be wise" inappropriately. The verse certainly should not be rendered: "And besides that Qohelet *was* wise, he also taught the people," etc. Pondered: *'izzen*, "scale," "weigh." has the semantic development of *pondero*, "weigh", then reflect, consider. Compiled: *tiqqen* has the meaning of "compiled" in later Hebrew. (Compare L. Ginzberg, *Geonica* I, 161.)

12.10: This verse was written as an apology by the disciple, who attempted to cover up Qohelet's deficiencies,who to the contrary, did not write pleasing themes (futility, death, self deprecation), nor an appropriate style (abrupt and frequently incoherent), nor true words (questioned by traditionalists and rationalists). Perhaps *yosher* is inappropriate with *katub* (l. *katob*) in this connection, and the translation from the Aramaic is off center. The Aramaic was most probably *kashirutha,* a frequent lexical equivalent of *yashar,* meaning "fitness," "aptness," "skill," therefore signifying not "upright" but an appropriate style for the subject matter (similarly Barton).

12.11: This verse was written by a second epilogist, orthodox, and a severe traditionalist, in contravention, point by point, to the assertions of the previous verse: As against matters of personal interest of Qohelet in pleasing themes as reported by the first disciple, this the contravener denies by saying, Oh, no, the words of the wise are like goads, immutable with set forms of the Mosaic tradition.

As against the skilled style, the words of the schools are like infixed nails (*see below*).

As against "true" experiences, one must follow the traditions, the "infixed nails" given by the scholars.

As against what Qohelet as a single individual sought to "find," the orthodox objector says were "given" plurally.

In fact, in verse 11 select Aramaic words are contraposed sharply against the words of verse 10.

As against *mille der'aya*, "words of delight, pleasing themes," one must follow the words of only one shepherd, Moses, *mille der'aya ḥad,* a direct counterthrust and wordplay.

As against the proposals of a *kanosha*, one must oppose the words of a *kenishta*, "assembly," i.e., the Academy, i.e., the traditional schools.

As against "the words of truth." *millayya deyazziban*, the words of the Academy teachings are *masmerin nezibin* or even *yezibin*, the one replacing the other synonymously occasionally. (Compare Levy, *Chaldäisches Wörter-buch*, Leipzig, 1881, 341.) (In translating "fixed nails" *netu'im*, which really means "planted" and about which the Midrash already queries whether one should not expect *qebu'im* as more proper, it is quite likely that *yezibin* was mistaken or read as *nezibin.)*

Ba'ale 'asufot composed in collections or masters of assemblies as ordinary translations go is most difficult. The Aramaic, however, clears the matter up: *more* (sic!) *kenishata*, "the teachers of the Academies." *yara* in the *Haf'el*, like the Hebrew means "teach," found in the Targums and the Talmudim. (Cf. Jastrow, *Dictionary.*) *'Asufot* as a passive form is merely a reproduction of the plural passive formation *kenishata*, the meeting place for prayer and for study. The Hebrew translator, however, misread *more* "teachers" as *mare* "masters" and is probably erroneous. Translate with the carryover from stich a: and as infixed nails are the words of the teachers of the Academies.

The "one shepherd" may be God or Moses. Yahweh is denominated as "shepherd" on a number of occasions (Gen. 48.15; Ps. 80.2;23.1) but on the whole the context seems to favor Moses. Thus, among the Babylonians in the regions of which Qohelet later lived, Hammurabi in the introduction to his Code is called "shepherd," e.g., Pritchard, ANET, 178: "The great gods called me so I became the beneficient shepherd whose scepter is righteous": "Hammurabi the shepherd," p. 164. Moses, of course, was the shepherd par excellence, designedly so that he should shepherd Israel. (In the case of David, the shepherd, the writer of Samuel made a word play at 2 Sam.5.2.) Moses at a later date is called "the faithful shepherd," *r'aya mehemna*, Ginzberg, L. *Legends.* V. p. 414. This denomination probably ascends to biblical times (compare Is. 63.11 [text is a bit obscure]). Like Hammurabi, Moses is called "shepherd" as a giver of law.

12.12: Mehemmah, stressed, is a meaningful emphasis to the preceding. Speculation pro and con: the usual translation "much study is a weariness of flesh" seems strange because Jewish tradition has always exhorted man to study (Deut.11.19; Ps.119.71). Here it must be the *idle speculation* that Qohelet indulges in. Quite likely that Aramaic document read *lahaga shage* (shin/sin), Aramaic *lahaga* "steam, vapor", *shage* "erroneous"/*sagi* "much" which in Hebrew should have been translated with the familiar *hebel* with the significance: much vaporing is a weariness of the flesh. As in English, vaporing=vapid remarks or speculation.

12.13: This verse and the next may be genuine, either from Qohelet himself with verses 9-12 interpolated, or else from the school of Qohelet. Note the confirmation of Qohelet's ideas in v.14. Will be understood: the Hebrew translator failed to recognize the temporal status of the participle in the Aramaic which ranges much more widely than in Hebrew, here the future. (Margolis, *Grammar*, par. 58.) Judge: the translation of the Hebrew translation of the Hebrew "for this is the whole man" makes no sense. The Hebrew translator read Aramaic *dayen*, "judge," as *den*, Aramaic for "this," *zeh.* The correction of the reading is borne out in the following verse: "For God will bring into *judgment."* For an exact parallel to the restored Aramaic, cf. Ps. 75.8 *ki 'elohim shofet.* The more normal construction probably would be with the untranslatable *hawa'* or *hu'*.

Translation

Chapter 1

The theme of the book: futility.

1. These are the words of Kanosha, the son of David, king in Jerusalem.

2. Futility of futilities! said Kanosha, all things are futile, the whole world is a futility.

3. What return does a man have for his toil which he labors at under the sun?

4. One generation dies and another generation is born, but the cosmos remains the same.

5. The sun rises and the sun sets; and he returns to his abode where he comes to rest.

6. The wind swirls to the south, then whirls to the north; round and round goes the wind and to its abode the wind returns.

7. All the rivers flow to the sea, yet the sea never fills up; to the place where the rivers flow, there they return.

8. What is the purpose of all this? A man could not end talking of it, nor could his eye be sated searching for it, nor his ear be surfeited with hearing about it.

9. What was will be, and that which has happened will happen again: there is nothing new under the sun!

10. A statement is sometimes made: Look at this! That's new! Perhaps it existed for ages before our time.

11. There is no remembrance of men long ago, and of latter ones too there will be no memory, even of those who will be to the very last.

The futility of searching for wisdom.

12. I Kanosha was a king over Israel in Jerusalem.

13. And I set my heart to search out, and meditate rationally about everything that has transpired under the heavens (–that evil business that God gave man to be afflicted with!).

14. I saw all the activities that are being done under the sun, and alas! everything was a frustration and a futile enterprise.

15. A defect cannot be made up;
And a minus cannot be made a plus.

16. I communed with myself, reflecting, Now I have greatly augmented a

164

store of wisdom, more than anyone before me in Jerusalem; and my mind has experienced much in the way of wisdom and knowledge.

17. So I applied my mind to weigh reason versus the impulsive, the irrational, although I knew that doing so is a delusion, too.

18. Because the more reason, the greater anguish, and adding knowledge is but greater distress.

Chapter 2

Futility of bodily stimulation.

1. I considered, thinking, "Come now! Let me try enjoyment, and experience pleasure." Alas! This too was futility.

2. Hilarity I consider stupid, and merriment? What good does it do?

3. In my mind I planned how to stimulate my body with wine (but my mind calculated with intelligence!) and give rein to impulse.

4[3b] Until I should reach a conclusion as to what was best for mankind to do under the heavens in the numbered days of their lives.

4. I kept busy with activities: I built houses, I planted vineyards.

5. I made me gardens and parks, I planted all kinds of fruit trees.

6. I constructed pools of water to irrigate timberland thick with trees.

7. I acquired men and maid slaves, as well as slaves home–born, together with possessions of herds and flocks, more than any that were before me in Jerusalem.

8. I also amassed silver and gold and the exotic treasures of kings and lands; I acquired male and female singers, and all the gratifications of men in divans and couches.

9. So I accumulated and amassed more than anyone else before me in Jerusalem (yet I remained in possession of my reason).

10. In sum, all that my eyes fancied I did not withold from them; I did not deny my heart any pleasure as my mind found satisfaction in all my work, and this would seem to be the destiny of all my toil.

11. Then I appraised all my activities that my hands had performed and the labor that I had toiled at to accomplish, and lo! the whole thing was a futility, a vain delusion, and a fruitless endeavor under the sun.

12. For who is the man who can follow in the footsteps of the king—to that which he has already accomplished? Then I turned to evaluate reason versus the impulsive, the irrational:

13. I saw that reason had a superiority over impulse just as light is superior to darkness.

14. Nevertheless, granted that the wise man has eyes in his head, and the foolish one walks in the darkness, yet I realized that one fate will befall the two of them.

15. Then I mused, "The fate of the fool will befall me, too; why then did I become wise the more?" Then I reconsidered and said, "This was senseless."

16. For there will not be a remembrance of the wise with the fool in the future; because days have passed already, and everything was forgotten. And so the wise man died with the fool.

17. So I hated life because the whole scheme of things under the sun was

most foul to me, for all was futility and a foolish delusion.

18. And I hated my labor that I toil at under the sun, that I must leave its fruits to a man who will take my place after I am gone.

19. And who knows whether he will be prudent or rash when he controls my properties that I toiled for and developed under the sun.

20. Then I reversed my thinking despairing about all the work that I toiled at under the sun:

21. For there is a man whose work is with intelligence, training, and industry. And then—he must turn over his property to another man, who has not labored at it all! This is an outrage and a great injustice.

22. Moreover, what does a man have of all his toil and ambition that he labors at under the sun?

23. And all his days are pains, agitation, and anxiety, and even at night his mind is not at rest. This too is a cause for rancor.

24. There is nothing better for a man than to eat and drink and sate his body with pleasure for the compensation he receives—and yet I saw that this could only be a grant from God.

25. For who can eat, and who can drink, and who can have sensation aside from myself?

26. Yet to a man well-favored before Him, He dispenses intelligence, knowledge, and happiness, but to the luckless He has given a drive to amass and accumulate, and then he hands it over to God's favorite! This too is an injustice and a delusion.

Chapter 3

Some compulsions that Qohelet must perform in his life plan.

1. For everything there is a time and tide in affairs under heaven.
2. A time to be born, and a time to die.
   A time to plant, and a time to uproot the planted.
3. A time to murder, and a time to refrain,
   A time to destroy, and a time to build,
4. A time to weep, and a time to laugh,
   A time to mourn, and a time to dance.
5. A time to throw stones, and a time to gather stones,
   A time to embrace, and a time to refrain from embracing,
6. A time to search out, and a time to give up as lost.
   A time to retain, and a time to cast away.
7. A time to tear, and a time to sew,
   A time to keep silent, and a time to speak.
8. A time to love and a time to hate,
   A time of war, and a time of peace.
9. What profits a man then in the work that he does?

The unchanging order of Nature; man's inner turmoil: his inferior status;

Qohelet's solution: pleasure in the oasis.

10. I have seen the scheme of things that God has given the sons of men to be

preoccupied with.

11. Everything he has made in its proper time. But as for the people of the world, he has so ordered their minds that no man should penetrate the core of existence which God made from creation to the end of time.

12. I know that there is nothing better for man than to be happy and enjoy himself in his lifetime.

13. And yet, every man who does eat and drink, and does enjoy himself from the gain of his labor—this is a gift from God.

14. I know that everything that God does will remain unchanged; one cannot add or subtract from it; and God did so pattern it that people should be apprehensive about Him.

15. Whatever exists now was in existence long ago; and whatever is to be already was in the past except that God shadows the guilt-ridden.

16. And moreover I saw under the sun: where law should be, there was but license; and where justice should be, there was but abuse.

17. I reflected: God will judge the good and the wicked, for a judgment time he has decreed on every thing and on every deed.

20. Every one goes to one place: all are of the dust, and all return to the dust.

19. For the fate of men, the fate of animals, the fate of beasts is one and the same; as one dies, so does the other; and there is a common breath to all. So the superiority of man over beast is nothing. All is but a breath.

18. Then I concluded: This goes to show that men are depraved by God, and that further they are as animals, they are as beasts.

21. Who knows whether the soul of man goes upward, or whether the soul of the animal goes downward?

22. So I maintain that a man should be happy in what he does now for that is his destiny. For who can bring him to see what will be after him?

Chapter 4

Human existence is not worthwhile.

1. Then I saw again all the injustices done under the sun; and lo! the tears of the oppressed and there was none to give them respite, and power was on the side of their oppressors and there was none to give them relief.

2. Therefore I praise the condition of the dead who have already expired than the living who are yet alive.

3. And better than they both is the one who has not come into existence, who has not seen this rotten scheme of things existing under the sun.

Work has no value.

4. I observed too all the toil and skill in industry—that it was man's jealousy of his neighbor. This too is an illusion and a stupid ambition.

5. The fool folds his hands, but then eats his own flesh.

6. Better is one handful of satisfaction than both hands full of tension and restless fantasy.

The lone man and his lack.

7. I marked yet another folly under the sun:

8. For example, a man without a wife, nor does he have a son or brother, yet there is no end to all his work, nor is his eye sated with his riches: "But for whom do I toil and deprive myself of pleasure?"—This is senseless and a sorry enterprise.

9. Yes, two are better than one because they have a mutual benefit in their undertaking.

10. For if one falls ill, the other can nurse his mate; but if the lone man falls ill, there is no other to bring him back to health.

11. Again, if two lie together, they have warmth; but how can one be warm alone?

12. If some one makes an assault, a pair will withstand the attacker; and "a triple cord will not easily be snapped."

Emptiness of royal pomp.

13. Better a poor but alert young man than an old and witless king, who does not know how to take care of himself anymore.

14. From among conspirators he emerges to be king, although in that very kingdom he was born of a commoner.

The vice-regent: the introduction

to the people or a coronation scene.

15. I witnessed all the throngs that assembled under the sun greeting the boy prince who was to take the king's place.

16. There was no end of people before all whom he stands; still the generation after will have no joy in him! This too is a frustration and a fraudulent show.

Conduct at sacrifice and worship.

17. Watch your step when you go to the house of God. To listen is better than to offer a sacrifice as fools do, who do not even discern what a wicked act is.

Chapter 5

The spoken word and its perils.

1. Do not be rash with your mouth, and do not allow your mind to break forth impulsively with a word against God. For God is above and you are below; therefore let your words be measured.

2. For healing comes after much pain, and the downfall of the impulsive in a rush of words.

3. If you make a vow to God, don't put off paying it. He extends little favor to defaulters; pay whatever you pledged!

4. It is better that you do not pledge, than pledge and not pay.

5. Do not allow your mouth to condemn your body while saying to the messenger it was forgetfulness; why should God be angry at your words, and

annihilate the life work you have accomplished?

6. Indeed, in the profusion of fantasies, delusions and magic incantations, people are led astray; fear God alone!

Corruption in the government.

7. If you see the oppression of the poor, and the perversion of justice and right in government circles, don't be exercised over the circumstances; for the one high up, looks out for the one higher up, and over them there are still others.

8. The advantage of land over everything is this: even the king is subject to agriculture.

9. He who is money-mad will never have enough money; on the other hand, he who prizes luxuries may have no income. Either is foolish.

10. With the increase of luxury goods, the consumers increase; but what can the eater enjoy the more except what his eyes feast upon?

11. Whether he eats little or much, the sleep of the laborer is refreshing; but the overloaded stomach of the rich man does not allow him to sleep.

The man who lived and lost.

12. There is a sore evil I have noticed under the sun: a man guards his wealth for...bankruptcy!

13. The money gets lost in a bad investment (meanwhile he has had a son born) and he is left empty-handed.

14. As he came forth penniless from the womb of his mother, so does he go back as he came; and he bears away nothing to carry on his person.

15. A sore evil is this: as he came, so he goes! Some satisfaction this that he worked for nothing!

16. Moreover all his days, eating is with complaint, much agitation, malaise and anxiety.

17. This is what I discovered as a blessing: it is best to eat and drink and enjoy life in whatever work one toils at under the sun, in whatever measured days of life that God has given him, for that is his life contract.

18. And yet—every man to whom God has given wealth and property and has permitted him to enjoy it; to win in this lottery and to be satisfied with his success—this is an award of God.

19. On the other hand, the days of a man's life cannot be bright very long for God eyes him when his heart is gay.

Chapter 6

The elusive happiness.

1. There is an evil under the sun, and it is most demoralizing to man:

2. A man to whom God has given riches, property, and prestige, and he does not need to deny himself anything that his heart desires, but God does not permit him to enjoy it but a stranger consumes it—this is an outrage; it is morbid, vile.

3. If a man beget a hundred children, and live long years, but does not enjoy happiness, and neither secures burial—I say, that an abortion is better off than he.

4. For from the womb it comes and in the tomb it goes, and its existence is blotted out in the darkness.

5. It did not see, it did not know sunlight; better off is the one than the other.

6. And suppose he lived one thousand years twice told, and even if he did enjoy pleasure...well...all go to the same place eventually.

7. All the labor of a man is for his mouth, yet there is no end to satisfying the appetite.

8. What superiority does the sage have over the fool? And for the poor man, who can tell him how to counter life's problems?

9. Better is the delight of the eyes than the loss of desire, although this too is a frustration and a will-o'-the-wisp.

10. Whatever exists now had its nature formed long ago; and the most learned man, because he is mere man, cannot struggle with forces mightier than he.

11. On the other hand magical sorceries can delude much; what gain is there for a man?

12. Who knows what good exists for man in his life time, the measured days of his vain existence so that he could spend his days as if at play! But, who can tell a man what his future will be under the sun?

Chapter 7.

Sundry Evaluations.

1. Fame is more delightful to have than precious perfume; but all told, the day of death is better than the day of one's birth.

2. Better to go to a house of mourning that to go to a banquet; because at home one will see the final stop to a man's life, and it will give the living some thoughts.

3. Better sobriety than hilarity for with a serious mien the mind will improve.

4. The mind of the wise turns to the house of mourning; but the mind of the witless veers to merry making.

5. Better to listen to the rebuke of a wise man than one should listen to the praise of fools.

6. For as the crackling of faggots underneath a kettle, so is the cackle of the stupid. This too is a futility.

7. A despotism can drive the man of reason into despondency, and corruption undermine the mind.

8. Better the end of a thing than its beginning; better to be chastened in spirit than insolent.

9. Do not become angry on impulse for anger starts in the bosom of fools.

10. Do not ask: how is it that the former days were better than the ones now? For you are not asking this out of due reflection.

11. Intelligence goes well with a legacy and especially to those who can

enjoy life.

12. However, if intelligence is lacking, then the money will be lacking, too; and intelligence is supreme, for alertness keeps a man alive.

13. Accept God's handiwork for what it is: for who can correct that which He created wrong?

14. When times are good, enjoy yourself; when times are bad, be philosophical: the one as against the other God made devisedly that man should not be able to forecast anything in his future.

The art of playing it safe.

15. I have seen two things in my indifferent life: there is the good man who dies early though good, and there is the monster who lives on and on in his villainy.

16. Do not be too good. Do not be too smart. Why be laughed at?

17. Don't be wicked. Don't be stupid. Why die before your time?

18. Better to hold on to the one and not let go of the other. Nonetheless the one fearful of God will come out safer than both.

19. Intelligence fortifies the resourceful more than the wealth of rulers in a city.

20. For no man is so righteous in the world that he should do but good and not sin.

21. Also—don't pay attention to gossip so that you will not hear that your servant cursed you.

22. Because oft-times you have been well aware that you have cursed others as well.

The vain search for wisdom.

23. I tested everything with reason; I thought I would acquire true wisdom, but it remained beyond my reach:

24. Reality is beyond things as they appear, and deep is wisdom—who can fathom it?

25. So I revolved in my mind to experience and to reflect: on the one hand to seek wisdom and the reason of things, and on the other hand to weigh the evil of folly and the absurdity of impulsiveness.

26. However, I did find (more bitter than death!) the woman who is like a trap, her thoughts snares, her hands chains; whoso pleases God escapes her, but the luckless gets caught.

27. This too observe: I now am able to say, adding one thing to another to reach a certain conclusion:

28. (Because at first my mind still sought, but did not find...) one man out of a thousand I found trustworthy, but a woman among all that number I did not find.

29. Note this also that I discovered: God fashioned men aright but they strive after wrongheaded schemes.

Chapter 8

Correct demeanor with the king.

1. Who is like the intelligent man? and who can correctly interpret events? The intelligence of a man gives his face a radiance, but ill-breeding can alter his face.

2. Mark the king's countenance but don't be rash to utter an oath of consequence.

3. Avoid it; don't swear to anything suspect, (since he can do anything he wishes).

4. Because the king's word is all powerful, and who may say to him: what are you doing?

5. One who observes the rules will not suffer any untoward thing but there is an end-time for judgment as every thoughtful man anticipates.

6. Because for everything there is a time of reckoning when a man's sins hang more and more heavily over him.

7. He does not know now what his situation was before; so who can tell him what will be afterwards?

8. No man can so master his emotion to overcome it; just as there is no control over impending death; and just as there is no divesting of armor in life's conflict, so there is no escaping the burden of one's guilt.

Justice and injustice: Qohelet's suggestion.

9. All this I saw and kept in mind: of activities that are done underneath the sun: how one man tyrannizes over another to his utter breakdown.

10. And so too I have seen scoundrels brought to burial, and they were given honor, and people made a procession from a holy place, and then they were eulogized in the city how rightfully they acted! This is revolting.

11. Because sentence against an evil action is not executed quickly,

12. Because an evil doer may sin a hundred times and yet lives on full many a year,

11b. Therefore the impulse in man is encouraged to do evil.

12b. Although I do know on the other hand that it shall be well with them that fear God so that they continue to fear Him,

13. And it shall not go well with the wicked, and he shall not prolong his days disporting himself, because he does not fear God.

14. There is this paradox that occurs in the world that there are good persons who incur the retribution of the wicked, and there are the wicked to whom there accrue the rewards of the good people. I thought: this is the world of the absurd.

15. Therefore I extol pleasure. For there is nothing better for a man under the sun than to eat, drink and make merry; and all this should be combined with his work during his life span that God allotted him under the sun.

16. When I gave my mind to speculation, observing the trouble that is inflicted upon the world of men, because even by day and by night a man cannot enjoy sleep in his turmoil,

17. And I pondered the Divine order how man cannot solve the riddle of existence under the sun: for what purpose should a man work? In the end he will not solve it! Even if the most learned man should seek to know it, he will not solve it.

Chapter 9

Inexorable fate and the formula for happiness.

1. All these observations I kept in mind, finally clarifying: the good and the wise, and their doings are in God's power; His love and His hate men cannot foretell; in their future everything is a blank.

2. Because one fate comes to all: to the good man and to the wicked, to the clean and the unclean, to the one who sacrifices and to the one who does not, to the favored and the illfavored, to the one who binds himself with an oath as well as the one who is apprehensive of an oath—

3. This then is the evil in everything that transpires under the sun: that there is one fate to all; therefore the minds of men are large with villainy and vice throughout their lives, and they shrug their shoulders about the future.

4. Nonetheless, he who has a hold on life has hope because a live dog is better off than a dead lion.

5. At least the living know that they will die, but the dead are not conscious of anything. Life's prize comes to them no more. Their memory is forgotten.

6. Their love, their hate, their jealousy perished a long time since; they do not have any role to play in the future, in anything that is happening under the sun.

Conduct of life.

7. Come now! Eat your food with gusto, and drink your wine with a merry heart. On the contrary, perhaps God favors your actions!

8. Let your clothes be white at all times, and don't be sparing with the perfumed oil on your head.

9. Enjoy living with a wife you can love all the days of your (futile!) existence which He has allotted you under the sun, for futility is the destiny of your life, and whatever reward you have struggled for under the sun.

10. According to the resources you have, explore the utmost! For there is no doing or planning, no learning or thinking in the other world where you go.

Skill and heroism but no reward.

11. I saw too under the sun that "the race is not to the swift, nor the battle to the strong"; yes, but nor is there bread for the wise, nor wealth for the men of intelligence, nor favor to men of learning! Even so... For all of them that fatal hour will strike.

12. For man cannot foretell his evil hour. Just as fish that are caught in a net, and as birds that are snapped up in a snare, so are men trapped in a mortal hour when it drops upon them unawares.

13. I garnered another experience under the sun, and I thought it significant.

14. It was a small town, with but few men in it; and there marched against it a formidable king. invested it, and constructed great bulwarks against it.

15. A poor but wise man happened to be there, and through his strategy rescued the town. However, no one ever remembered that poor man!

16. So I thought: Brain is better than brawn; however the wisdom of the

common man is derided, and his words are not hearkened to.

17. The words of the wise are listened to with more acquiescence than the shouting of a ruler at fools.

18. Wisdom is better than weapons of war yet one miss of life's target can destroy much good.

Chapter 10

1. A dead fly will make the perfumer's oil rank and putrid; on the other hand more precious than wisdom, more than honor is the foolishness of a little child.

2. The mind of the wise man turns to the right way, but the impulse of the dimwit veers to the left.

3. The empty mind of the fool is shown by the shiftless way he walks and it signifies to everyone that he is a fool.

Folly in High Places.

4. If the anger of the ruler flare up against you, do not resign your place; for soothing talk can allay serious offences.

5. There is an evil under the sun which I observed: it is like a mistaken policy on the part of a ruler:

6. Stupidity is enthroned in high places while magnates occupy a low station

7. I have seen the low-caste up on horses while princes walk as slaves in the street.

A miscellany of proverbs.

8. He who digs a pit may fall in it; he who breaks through a wall may be bitten by a serpent.

9. He who quarries stones may be injured; he who splits wood may endanger himself.

10. If a battle-ax be blunt, not having been sharpened before, it may handicap the soldiery; the better part of wisdom is to sharpen it.

11. If a serpent strike without the charmer's control, then there is no point to a serpent charmer.

The grace of the wise man and the gabbling of fools.

12. The words in the wise man's mouth run smoothly but the lips of the dolt swallow his words.

13. The onset of his talk is inane and he finishes with stupid incoherence.

14. The fool makes frequent use of magic spells. But now—a man cannot tell what will be in the future, and who can foretell him what will be after his death?

15. The toil of the fool wears him out because he does not know whether he is coming or going.

16. O hapless country! Hapless when your king is but a child, and your

nobles feast in the morning:

17. O happy land when your king is independent, and your officials eat at the proper time, moderately and not in debauchery!

18. By neglect the roof will fall in, and the house will leak through idle hands.

19. People will arrange a banquet for a merry time, and wine is the elixir of life. Money however supplies the wherewithal.

20. Even in your thought do not curse the king, nor in your bedchamber curse the wealthy; for a bird of the air will carry your voice and a winged messenger your utterance.

Chapter 11.

Risk capital, but average your risk.

1. Set sail your ship upon the sea for you will retrieve it with the passage of time.

2. Divide your venture into seven or eight parts for you do not know what catastrophe will befall the country.

Action and consequence: the future cannot be discerned.

3. If the clouds be filled with rain, they will empty themselves upon the earth; if a tree falls to the north or to the south, on the spot where the tree falls, there it lies prone.

4. He who waits for wind-currents will not scatter seed, and he who watches the clouds will not reap.

The mystery of creation.

5. Just as you do not know how breathing comes to the embryo in the burgeoning womb so you cannot understand the works of God who has formed all creation.

6. Mornings scatter your seed; evenings do not slack your hand; for you do not know which will thrive, the one or the other, or whether both will flourish.

Bitter-sweet happiness: what should a young man do?

7. Still...daylight is sweet...it is a pleasant thing for your eyes to see the sun...

8. However if a man live many years, let him be happy in them all; let him be mindful of the days of darkness for they shall be without end. What comes after is a void.

9. Young man, be happy in your youth, and let your heart be gay while you are young; follow your passions and your roving eye, but know this! God will hold you to an accounting for everything.

10. Keep your mind from being upset and do not let illness hang on untended. For your childhood, your youth are—pouf!

Chapter 12.

Old age and its miseries.

1. Be mindful of your health in the days of your youth before the days of illness arrive and the years have caught up, wherein you will say "I do not desire them any more" :-

2. Before the sun goes a-glimmering, and the moon and the stars fade, and the clouds return after the rain,

3. At the time when the guardians of the house become unsteady, and the strong men become gnarled, and the grinders become useless because they are few, and the viewers at the windows be dimmed,

4. Ere the two doors to the outside are stopped, and the ease of grinding flags,
Ere the twit of a bird becomes faint, and musical notes decline:

5. Before one is terrified of a height, and fearful of pitfalls while walking, and one shall despise almonds, and caperbuds will be noisome, and the caperberry be useless; for man has set out on the road to his long, long home, and the mourners will turn round and round in the streets,

6. Before the silver cord is snapped, and the golden bowl is shattered; and ere the pitcher is broken at the fountain, and the wheel falls broken into the well:

7. And the dust return to the earth as it once was, and the spirit to God who gave it!

8. And so concluded Kanosha, "It is all utterly futile! The world is without meaning!"

9. (*First voice*) The more mature Kanosha became, the more he imparted his knowledge to the people; he pondered, studied and compiled many maxims.

10. Kanosha sought to compose pleasing themes, a proper style, yet true to the facts.

11. (*Second voice*) The words of the wise are as goads, and as well-infixed nails the words of the teachers of the Academies given by one shepherd.

12. Beware of more than these, my son! There is no end in acquiring books, and speculation pro and con wears out a man.

13. Postscript: everything will be understood at the last. Fear God and keep His commandments since He is a judge of all man.

14. For God will bring in judgment every action—even in secret— whether good or evil.

NOTES

1. Comp. his *Totem and Taboo. See* further E. Jones, *Life and Work of Sigmund Freud,* II, 332 ff.

2. Studies in these fields have swelled to immense proportions as the various journals in psycholanalysis and psychiatry attest. Stimulating to the Biblical student would be the studies of E. Jones, *Papers on Psychoanalysis* (reprint, 1967); T. Reik, *Ritual* (English) 1946; O. Rank, *Art and the Artist,* 1932; G. Roheim, *Eternal Ones of the Dream,,* 1945; Idem, *Gates of the Dream,* 1952 (reprint); Carl Jung, *Collected Works:* Bollingen Series.

3. Comp. G. A. Barton, *Ecclesiastes,* p. 28; and similarly, E. Podechard *L'Ecclesiaste,* 1912 who diversely finds "a wise man, a pious man" etc. and K. Galling *Prediger Salomo,* 1940 who predicates 37 separate sentences, O. Loretz, *Qohelet und der Alte Orient,* 1964, pp. 135–217, 71 *topoi.*

4. Comp. L. Edel, in his article "Hawthorne's Symbolism and Psychoanalysis" in *Hidden Patterns* by L. and E. Manheim.

5. *See* p. 25 and comp. the Midrash Qohelet to the verse. A similar observation is offered for 10.8 where the verse reads: "whoso breaks through a fence, a serpent will bite him" where the Midrash explains: who bursts the bounds of the Torah (conventional morality) a mishap shall befall him.

6. Comp. Liddell and Scott, *Greek English Lexicon,*[9] *s.v.*

7. For other meanings of *'amal* as "profit, benefit", comp. p. 88.

8. Comp. 3.10 with the word-play and the later *'innui* "torture."

9. R. Gordis, *Koheleth—the Man and his World,* 78.

10. A. S. Peake in his article in J. Hastings, *Dictionary of the Bible,* I,640.

11. Comp. *Encyclopedia of Aberrations,* E. Podolsky, M.D. ed. p. 528, *Distortion of Time Sense.*

12. Qohelet shares in common much with such personalities as Brahms, who employed much of Qohelet's words and thoughts in his Requiem, and Schopenhauer with his pessimism, asceticism, contempt for women, and feeling for disaster, and on the other hand with but little identification with Omar Khayyam as Morris Jastrow in *A Gentle Cynic* would have it. Anyway, Omar Khayyam is much more Edward Fitzgerald than the Persian poet, as recent studies have showed. Comp. further E. Hitshman, *Great Men,* p. 38.

13. Comp. Stekel, *Compulsion and Doubt,* 264.

14. Comp. Emil A. Gutheil, M.D., *Handbook of Dream Analysis,* 97f.

15. *Collected Papers,* 1949, II, 368; III, 99; IV, 359.

16. E.A. Gutheil in his Introduction to W. Stekel's *Compulsion and Doubt,* p. 12.

17. Gutheil, *Handbook,* 325.

18. For the *Bet,* comp. Brown, Driver, Briggs, *Hebrew and English Lexicon,*

p. 90 sub V. In the manner in which Qohelet thinks however, the subordinate clause is frequently to be understood as co-ordinate. Comp. F. J. Hoffman, *Freudianism and the Literary Mind*, 1959 (repr.) p. 145.

19. Comp. Meg. 13a: A woman is not jealous (or envious) except with regard to the *yarek* of another.

20. Comp. *Tanḥuma*, ed. Ḥoreb, p. 34; Rashi to Gen. 6.11; A.B. Ehrlich, *Randglossen*, I, 32.

21. For the similar usage of the word *ṭaḥan*, comp. Sotah 10a, and Ber. Rabbah, 48.20.

22. Comp. *Standard Dictionary of Folklore, Mythology and Legend*, I, 38.

23. *Ritual and Belief in Morocco*, I, 582.

24. "Grease the wheel" was nineteenth-century slang for coitus. Comp. E. Partridge, *Dictionary of Slang and Unconventional English*,⁵ 948.

25. In the Mishna, Ketubot 7.10, a situation is described wherein a woman thought she would marry a man even though he had a disease (e.g., a skin disease) and then after marriage argued for a divorce because she could not tolerate him. R. Meir would grant the divorce. The Sages said, she remains married to him except in the case of *mukkeh sheḥin* (apparently leprosy) *mippene shememaqqto* "because she weakens him through sexual intercourse," i.e., she aggravates his disease by weakening him. Similarly *Berakot* 57b: Three things give one a taste of the sublime life in the world to come: Sabbath, the sunlight, and intercourse...and the inquiry is put: but doesn't sexual intercourse weaken one? The Hebrew-Aramaic word is *khš*.

26. Impotence in dreams is frequently represented by a fall, Garma, 100.

27. *Bekol 'eileh* means "in all that number," with *'eleph* understood from *a*.

28. Stekel, *Compulsion and Doubt*, 446.

29. *Ibid*, 543. Stekel discusses a patient who sustained the most severe trauma of his life which brought on his neurosis when his mother married for the second time. In literature, F. L. Lucas cited Baudelaire as a well known instance. His old father died when he was six. For almost two years he was intensely happy with his young mother. When he was forty years old, he still remembered that brief sunshine in his life: *ca été pour moi le bon temps*. A distinguished soldier, Gen. Aupick asked the mother's hand in marriage, and she accepted. Baudelaire thought this was outrageous of her: "when she has a son like myself, she should not have remarried." On the wedding night, it is reported, he threw the key out the window. When he was nineteen or twenty, the tension burst. At a dinner party, his step-father reproved him for some improper remark. Baudelaire advanced upon him saying, "This requires correction and I will have the honor of strangulating you." The General slapped his face. Baudelaire had a nervous breakdown and had to be shipped off for a voyage to Mauritius. Comp. F.L. Lucas, *Literature and Psychology*, 1951, p. 39.

30. Stekel, *Compulsion*, 300 and Index under "Authority."

31. Mary Higgins and Chester M. Raphael, *Reich Speaks of Freud*, 1967, p. 127: "The genital functioning in a person is an expression of his life energy. If that is disturbed...he doesn't function...and he hates."

32. The psychiatrist, S. Tenenbaum *"A Psychiatrist Looks at Marriage"*, 1968 has even reduced a propensity to impotence by the hostile feelings engendered in the relations between husband and wife. He reports that the

anger of a husband against his wife resulted in impotence.

33. *Midrash to Qohelet*, Soncino ed. p. 237 and 211.

34. L. Ginzberg, *Legends of the Jews*, VI, p. 14 and 36.

35. *Mel'o Ha-ro'im*, Notes to the tractate *Berakot* folio 57.

36. In his *Casebook of a Crime Psychiatrist*, 176.

37. Stekel, *Interpretation of Dreams*, 272.

38. Stekel, *Compulsion*, 112–113, 188 and Index s.v. Annulment; E.A. Gutheil, *Handbook*, 427 and Index s.v. Annulment.

39. Comp. W. Robertson Smith, *Religion of the Semites*³, 451 *(Notes by Stanley A. Cook)*.

40. *Stekel, Compulsion*, 137.

41. It will be recalled that a betrothal was a serious matter: violating a betrothed woman was punishable by death (Deut. 22.23) and in talmudic times a broken troth required the formality of a divorce.

42. Stekel, *Compulsion*, 246.

43. It is not likely "error" or "neglect"; a man will usually say apologetically, "I forgot about it," a well-known characteristic of human behaviour. In the words of Ernest Jones, "Most of those who have filled secretarial positions have been astonished to find the difficulty there is in collecting subscriptions as they fall due, and the ease with which people with otherwise good memories "overlook" such matters. It is far from rare for them to falsify their memory and to assert firmly that they have already paid..." *Papers on Psycho-analysis*⁵, repr. 1961, p. 29. In a similar vein, comp. Midrash Rabbah 8.2: In time of trouble, people vow; when relieved they seek to escape fulfilling the vow. Read perhaps *pashti* (Theodor's ed. *shafti)*; Tanhuma's reading *shamṭi* is probably to be preferred and is supported by ms. authority.

44. Comp. Freud, *Totem and Taboo*, 1952, trans. by James Strachey, p. 85f.

45. Stith Thompson, *Motif Index of Folk Literature*, 1958, II 334 and Index Vol.; E.A. Westermarck, *Ritual and Belief in Morocco*, Index, s.v. Evil Eye.

46. Stekel, *Interpretation of Dreams*, 427.

47. Comp. *neta'* "children," "plants," Ps. 144.12; Jer. 2.21; Is. 5.7; 17.11 and *zera'* "seed," "plant," "semen." Comp. further Midr. Qohelet, ed. Soncino p. 294, 295.

47a. In a letter to Southey, Lamb wrote: "I was at Hazlitt's marriage, and had like to be turned out several times during the ceremony. Anything awful makes me laugh. I misbehaved once at a funeral [9 August 1815]." It is well known that Charles Lamb had some psychological disturbance, "an inconquerable impediment" in his speech, his confinement in an asylum in late 1795, and similarly his sister Mary's periodic confinements after she had stabbed her mother in the heart, *Encyclopedia Britannica*,¹⁴ art. "Charles Lamb."

47b. Stekel has argued that he was able to discern a homosexual component in every case of compulsion, *Compulsion and Doubt*, 367.

48. For a summary of the views of Minkowski, Fisher and Merloo, *see Encyclopedia of Aberrations*, ed. E. Podolsky, M.D. Art. Distortion of Time Sense, pp. 528ff. One authority claims that anal personalities are very much the same as their attitude towards money, agitated by their use (and abuse) of time. They alternate with being parsimonious and generous with time, miserly to the fraction of a minute, at other times prodigal to heedlessness. Our authority, Harnik (*ibid* p. 529) avers that the ability to measure time is rooted in anal

eroticism. In the toilet training of a child, for example, the regularity of defecation, he says, how often it should take place and when, how long and in what stated intervals it is to take place, how protracted or deferred, would give the child the first sense of time rhythm, of sequence, regulation, short or long periods of time.

48a. Proust declares that "Each one of us is not a single person but contains many persons who have not all the same moral values," *Remembrance of Things Past,"* X, 157, English Trans. Knopf, 1913–27. Is this the id, ego, and super-ego of Freud?

49. *Compulsion,* 426.

50. *Ibid,* 430 (condensed).

51. A,E. Gutheil, *Handbook,* p. 425.

52. i.e. his frisky "animal ego"; Gutheil, op.cit. 221 and especially p. 442 where the dreamer identifies himself with the dog.

53. La Rochefoucauld, *Maxims,* no. 26.

54. Cf. Gutheil, *Handbook,* p. 132.

55. me'ayyeneh "is watching him." *See* comm. *ad loc.*

56. *Comp. Garma, A. Psychoanalysis of Dreams,* no. 29, p. 78

57. *Basic Writings,* 1 vol., p. 577.

58. Reading *bol'eha.*

59. A. Heidel, *The Gilgamesh Epic and Old Testament Parallels,* 1949, p. 155.

60. Stith Thompson, *Motif Index of Folk Literature,* sec E 412.3.

61. Tobit 4.17: "Pour thy bread" should read as "Pour thy wine." Comp. Zimmermann, *Book of Tobit,* comm. *ad loc: lehamrak/lahmak.*

62. Jer. 9.16; 13.30; 22.18; 2 Chron. 35.25.

63. J.B. Pritchard, *Ancient Near Eastern Texts,* 90.

64. Stekel, *Interpretation of Dreams,* 192.

65. Comp. Leon Edel in "Hawthorne's Symbolism and Psychoanalysis" in *Hidden Patterns,* ed. by Leonard and Elanor Manheim, p. 98.

66. Oil was needed to break the spell of demons, the spreaders of disease, James 5.14; *Sanhedrin* 101a.

67. So 2 Sam. 11.4. One could deduce from the verse that there were few acts of sexual congress, or perhaps even one as the commentator Levi ben Gerson suggests at v.5.

67a. 2 Sam. 3.2 f.; 1. Chron. 3.1 f. and *ibid* v.9; 2. Sam. 20.3. *Benei pilagshim*=sons and daughters of concubines.

68. The name Shelomoh may be interpreted as an intermediate form, a reduction from an original form **Shelomon,* cf. the Aramaic form *Shalman* Hos. 10.14, and I would not hesitate to adduce the Greek from *Solomon,* but the posterior Nun fell away as in so many instances, comp. *'abaddon* Psalms 88.12, Prov. 15.11 and *'abaddo* with *He, Qere* with *Waw* Prov. 27.20; *Salmon* Ruth 4.21 and *Salmah ibid* v.20; *Megiddo* and *Megiddon* Zech. 12.11 The *He* of *Shelomoh* is orthographic, standing in for *Waw,* hence a dipthong, cf. *yitro/yatron* in Syriac representation and so *yitran,* Lagarde, *Bildung der Nomina,* p. 52. **Shelomaw,* to continue with its development became **Shelomai/Shelomi* (Num. 24.37), and feminine *Shelomit,* ev. 24.11. —On the form *Shelomot, see* no.70.

69. Conversely, to expel a demon it is essential to know his name. Comp. the

episode where Jesus required the name of the demon possessing the mad man of the tombs, and Mk. 9.38; 16.17; Lk.9.49.

70. Cf. art. *Names* in Hastings, *Encyclopedia of Religion and Ethics*, and the Additional Notes of L. Ginzberg in the suppl. vol. of the A. Kohut's *Aruk*, 425b. The form *Shelomot*, 1. Chron. 24.22; 26.26, does not derive from *šlm*, but is of two components, *šlw mot* "safe from death." *šlo* originally *šelaw* meaning "at peace," "quiet," "safe," is construct to *mot*, the construct having the signification of "safe *from.*" For this usage of the construct, cf. for example, Is. 32.2, *seter zerem*, "a covert from the storm," Davidson, *Hebrew Syntax*, 1902, p. 31. This interpretation is in line with the notion that, like Shelomoh, it is a substitute for a name, if the preceding child died. He is to be "safe from death."

71. It was quite unusual for a king of Egypt to give his daughter in marriage to a foreigner. Thus when the king of Babylon sought the hand of the daughter of Amenhotep III, the Babylonian king was rejected on the grounds that, as the Tel-el Amarna letters report, "from of old, a daughter of the king of Egypt has not been given to anyone" (i.e., to an outsider). Herodotus, III, 1. implies that the king of Egypt refused to give his daughter to Cambyses, king of Persia. The only foreign ruler known, besides Solomon, who wedded an Egyptian princess was Niqmad, king of Ugarit fourteenth century, B.C.E.). Comp. "Views of the Biblical World" II, p. 206 ed. by B. Mazar, et al., Ramat Gan 1960.

72. Stekel, *Compulsion*, c.14.

73. idem, *Interpretation of Dreams*, p. 14 in the Introduction by Gutheil.

73a. *Tafat*, I Kings 4.11 supposed meaning "to drop," Montgomery, *Book of Kings*, 125 following Noth, does not seem likely. The root would be *ṭfa*, *ṭfe*, found it is true in the dialect of Babylonian Aramaic having the sense of "increase," but not entirely impossible, cf. the Aramaic names in the chapter, *'Abda, Ba'ana* (two persons, these names are on coins of N. Syrian origin, Montgomery, *Book of Kings*, 125) and the meaning "increase" in the prosperous climate of Solomon's reign would be of a piece with *Rehab'am*, "may the nation expand," *Yerab'am* "may the nation increase."

74. *Compulsion and Doubt*, 327, 359: "Neurotic fathers have neurotic children."

75. In the dialogue, for example, that Re has with Isis, there is the sentence: "...[my name] was hidden in my body before I was born...may my name come forth from my body into thy body..." (ANET, 13.)

76. *Compulsion and Doubt*, p. 7.

77, Comp. H. Donner—W. Röllig, *Kanaanäische und Aramäische Inschriften*, 1962, III, 49.

78. The way our biographer, 12.9, describes him as a lecturer is suggestive. The root *kenash*, "gather," *Kanosha*, "harvester," "sweeper" intimate jointly his role. In Eastern Aramaic, *kenasha* means "school," Payne Smith, Dictionary, 219 (cf. *kenishta*, the latter mostly "synagogue"). As the bearer of the name *kanosha*, the changeover from, say, "sweeper" to "lecturer" was undoubtedly prompted by the two meanings of the word 1. sweeper and 2. schoolman, lecturer that he associated in his mind.

79. Quoted by Gutheil, *Handbook*, 94.

80. And so in Shakespeare: "And think it no addition" (advantageous circumstance) Othello, 3.4. In some instances, *yoter* represents *yattir* in Aramaic "especially" as in 7.11.

81. *Ancient Near Eastern Texts,* 67, A.E. Speiser's translation.

82. E. Jones, *Essays in Applied Psychoanalysis,* II, 1951, 281.

83. It is well known how Hera was impregnated by the wind and gave birth to Hephaistos, and how in the legends and traditions of the Catholic Church the conception of Jesus was brought about by the Holy Ghost's breathing in Mary's ear, e.g., St. Augustine: *Virgo per aurem impraegnebatur,* E. Jones, *op. cit.* 269.

84. E. Jones, *ibid* p. 266f.

85. *Idem,* p. 278.

86. *Ibid,* 270; Sandor Ferenczi, *Further Contributions to the Theory and Technique of Psychoanalysis* (English), p. 305.

87. G.B. Gray, *The Forms of Hebrew Poetry.*

88. A separate monograph could be written on the otiose character of the Hebrew *ki* in Qohelet. In a number of instances, *ki* merely reproduces the functionless character of the Aramaic particle *d.* Comp. Payne Smith, *Dictionary* s.v. and so in 6.11, 12. Moreoever, *ki* doesn't always express a causal relation but is employed as a function word, and sporadically redundant as the English "for." *See* Webster's *International Dictionary*[3] s.v. and Brown, Driver, Briggs, *Hebrew Lexicon,* art. *ki* and especially 474b; sometimes as our "Why, of course," or "and so...," merely expletive as 7.6.12.13. The most likely reason is that the unconscious is not aware of space or time, i.e., simultaneity is a substitute for the usual causal sequence of events. Freud predicates that the unconscious annuls contradictions, nullifies stress or displaces it, voids outer reality by an inner psychic reality, makes for condensations and episodes, are neither ordered in a temporal sense nor are subject to change with the passage of time. Comp. Hoffman, *Freudianism and the Modern Mind,* 145; Stekel, *Compulsion and Doubt,* 203; Freud, *Collected Papers,* IV, 120.

89. Comp. JBL, LX, 1941, 159 (Enoch); JQR, XLII, p. 387; XLVIII, 1957, 236f. (Story of Susanna); LI, 1960, 107f (IV Ezra) LIV, 12f. (The Three Guardsmen (Additions to Daniel); LVII, 1-27; 101-135 (Book of Wisdom); *Studies and Essays in honor of Abraham A. Neuman,* 1962, p. 580 (Apocalypse of Baruch); *Journal of Theological Studies,* vol. XL, no. 158 p. 151 ff. (Textual Observations on the Apocalypse of Baruch).

90. JBL, LVII, 1938, 255f. (Daniel); *ibid* LVIII, 1939 (Daniel); JQR, LI, 1961, p. 198 (Daniel) JQR, XLII, 1952 f. (Chronicles).

91. The use of letters for numerals is tolerably early. Attic inscriptions discovered in Greece, dating from 454 B.C.E. to about 95 B.C.E. have an elaborate system of initial numerals i.e. Gamma, an old form used for *pente*=5, *Delta* from *deka*=10; *Xi* from *xilioi* was 1000. In the time of Solon (ca. 594 B.C.E.) according to the report of Heroianus, they were already incorporated in Solon's laws. They were combined with Semitic marks undoubtedly, One /=1, two //=2 to mark units up to four. The Babylonians and Arameans had already been using these abbreviations, m=100 for *me'ah, laph ('eleph)* for 1000 (cf. M. Lidzbarski, *Ephemeris* II, 388). In the fifth century B.C.E. we have boundary stones marked with Greek letters with the signification of ordinal numbers. Likewise the beams of the great altar of Pergamos as well as some oracular tablets of Dodona display markings of numbers with letters. Moreover, the works of Homer were divided by the scholars of Alexandria (c. 280 B.C.E.) into twice twenty-four books with the Greek letters of A-Ω, corresponding to the twenty-four letters of the Greek alphabet. For the Jews the evidence is more scanty. They did have in

their Bibles acrostic poems in alphabetical order (Ps. 25, 34, 37, 111, 112, 119; Prov. 31.10-31; Lamentations 1-4) ascending to the prophet Nahum of the seventh century B.C.E. and the inflexible order of the alphabet implies a numerical chain. We must depend on coinage although the Jews with their short span of independence could issue but few specimens. The so-called Hasmonean coins have been questioned, and are assigned to the Bar-Kokba Revolt, Cooke, *North Semitic Inscriptions*, 355–56. The first Hebrew coins that may be definitely dated are those struck by Antigonus-Mattathias 40–37 B.C.E. They bear the legend *mattithyah ha-kohen ha-gadol shanah a'(leph)* and *shanah b'(et)*, meaning the letters are employed for numerals. Any evidence that may be adduced seems to be later: the so-called Atbash, cf. S. Krauss, *Griechische und lateinische Lehnwörter*, p. 171, that is the substitution of Aleph/Taw, Beth/Shin and supposedly found in Jer.25.26 *sheshak=babel; leb qamai=kasdim*, 51.1 may or may not be late. The LXX at 25.26 knows nothing about *sheshak=babel;* in the second the translation "upon those who live among the Chaldeans" (leb qamai) implies the Atbash and so the Targum. Interesting too is the equation of *Menahem=Zamah* as a name for the Messiah where the letters add up to 138, Yer. Ber. II 5a but this is late, post Destruction. Similarly, the 318 that Abraham mustered to fight the kings in Gen. 14.14 is a numerical cryptogram for Eliezer (Ned. 32). Among the Arabs of Morocco, there is a striking custom of taking a man's name and that of his mother, and adding up the letters numerically, and then to insert them into a leather bag to be worn as an amulet, Westermarck, *Ritual and Belief in Morocco*, I, 144.

Provisionally, as the term "gimatriya" is probably the Greek *grammateia*, indicating the Greek origin and provenience in the Hellenistic period, and although the Jewish sources seem late, it will be safe to say that these permutations and combinations of numbers and letters were operative in the pre-Christian era. At Rome, Julius Caesar and Augustus made use of cryptography (substituting vowels letters for consonants and vice versa) in their writings, comp. E.M. Thompson, *Handbook of Greek and Latin Paleography*[3], for disguise. Thus *Kansha=Shelomoh=375* would be nothing unusual. Much of the material in this note is indebted to the article of Solomon Gandz, *Hebrew Numerals* in the *Proceedings of the American Academy for Jewish Research*, IV. 1933, 53.

92. For the different halakic notices on Syria, cf. *Ab.Zar.*1.5; *Ḥallah* 4.11; *Sheb.*6.2.5; *Ohol.* 17.7.

93. Josephus, *Bell. Jud.* 3.2.4.

94. *The Cambridge Ancient History*, XI, 269.

95. F. Zimmermann, *Book of Tobit*, p. 20.

96. Idem, *Book of Wisdom*, *JQR*, LVII, 132.

97. J. Reider, *Book of Wisdom*, 1957. The emended readings in the text are based on the following:

Prolongation: the Greek translator misread his Aramaic *'aruka* as "healing"; the word is good Aramaic, cf. Levy, Kohut, Jastrow, Dalman in their Dictionaries and especially Ps. 147.3 in MT and Targum, and 2 Chron. 24.13. The Greek translator should have read the word as "length, prolongation."

Dissipated: the Greek reads "weighed down by the heat thereof" which is puzzling. The Greek translator read *mitteqal* as if from *tql* meaning "weigh" whereas he should have read the form as derived from *qll* "abate, diminish, lessen." This confusion could only occur in Aramaic.

Earnestly...creation: The Aramaic evidences a wordplay, *beṭalyutha beṭila'it* "diligently in youth," Brockelmann, *Lexicon Syriacum*[2], 66; Payne Smith, 41; Zimmermann, *Book of Wisdom*, 26.

Sweets: The Greek reads "perfumes", difficult and incongruous in the text. The Aramaic had probably a form *besima* meaning "perfume" indeed, but also "sweets" or even "wine." Cf. op. cit. 26.

Splendor: The Greek reads "flower," but the text is difficult. "To let not a flower of spring pass us by" makes little sense. The Aramaic root *zemaḥ* was taken to mean "growth, flower" instead of the more appropriate "shine, splendor," cf. appropriately Is. 4.2 MT and Greek. "Let not the splendor of spring pass us by" makes for the more apposite sense.

I
Works in Psychology and Psychoanalysis
Select Bibliography

The standard Edition of the complete works of Sigmund Freud in 23 vols. ed. James Strachey is basic. Franz G. Alexander and Sheldon T. Selesnick, History of Psychiatry is useful and illuminating. The American Handbook of Psychiatry 3 vols ed. Silvano Arieti[10] 1969 gives broad coverage. The list of course could be immensely extended. The following have been of service in the present study:

BOOKS ARE CITED WITH THEIR ABBREVIATIONS
OR CATCHWORDS.

Adler, A., The Individual Psychology of Alfred Adler, Selections, ed. Heinz L. and Rowena R. Ansbacher, 1956.

Brill, A.A., Basic Principles of Psychoanalysis 1949.

Erikson, Erik H., Identity and the Life Cycle 1959.
　　　　Young Martin Luther 1958.

Ferenczi, Sandor, Sex in Psychoanalysis trans. E. Jones, 1950.

Garma Angel, Psychoanalysis of Dreams (repr.)

Gutheil, Emil A., Handbook of Dream Analysis (reprint) 1966.

Hitschman, E., Great Men ed. Sydney G. Margolin.

Jones, E., Essays in Applied Psychoanalysis 2 vols. 1951.

Jung, C., Works, in the Bollingen Series:
　　　　Symbols of Transformation 1956.

Podolsky, E., Dictionary of Aberrations (contains reprints from various Journals) 1953.

Rank, O., Art and the Artist, 1932.

Reik, T., Ritual, 1946.

Stekel, W., Disorders of the Instincts and the Emotions 10 vols (reprint) 1966-
　　　　Compulsion and Doubt (reprint) 1967.
　　　　Interpretation of Dreams (reprint) 1967.

II

Dictionaries

Levy, Jacob Levy, Neuhebräisches and chaldäisches Wörterbuch über die Talmudim und Midraschim, 4 vols 1876.
Chaldäisches Wörterbuch über die Targumim, 1881.

Kohut, Alexander Kohut, Aruch Completum, 1878–92.

Jastrow, M. Jastrow, Dictionary of the Targumim, the Talmud Babli, and Yerushalmi and the Midrashic Literature 1886–1903.

Dalman, G. Dalman. Aramäisch-neuhebräisches Handworterbuch zu Targum, Talmud, und Midrasch 1901.

Partridge, Eric Partridge, A Dictionary of Slang and Unconventional English, 5th ed. 2 vols. in 1, 1961.

Lewis and Short, A Latin Dictionary 1958.

Brown, Driver and Briggs F. Brown, S.R.Driver, C.A.Briggs, Hebrew and English Lexicon of the Old Testament.

Gesenius-Buhl Wilhelm Gesenius' Hebräisches und Aramäisches Handwörterbuch über das A.T., 17 ed., rep. 1949.

Payne-Smith, J. Payne-Smith, Compendious Syriac Dictionary, founded on the Thesaurus Syriacus of R. Payne Smith. 1902.

Brockelmann C. Brockelmann, Lexicon Syriacym[2] 1928.

G. Delitzsch, Assyrisches Handwörterbuch 1896.

A.L. Oppenheim *et alii*, The Assyrian Dictionary Chicago.

E.E. Lane, Arabic-English Lexicon, 8 vols.

J.G. Hava, Al-faraid, Arabic English Dictionary.

III

Texts and Versions

Biblia Hebraica ed. R. Kittel, textum masoreticum curavit P. Kahle, 3–4 ed. A. Alt et O. Eissfeldt, 1949.

Peshitta, Peshitta ed. Lee, 1823.

Targum, Targum to Qohelet in standard Rabbinic Bibles.

Yerushalmi, Talmud Yerushalmi, Krotoschin 1966.

Babylonian Talmud, Vilna Ed. 1928.

   B. Meẓ.—Baba Meẓia

   Meg.—Megillah

   Pes.— Pesaḥim

   Ta'anit

The Babylonian Talmud ed. Soncino ed. I. Epstein.

Midrash Midrash to Qohelet ed. Ḥoreb 1928.

Midrash ed. Soncino vol. 8, Ruth and Ecclesiastes.
Josephus   Works, ed. Niese.
    Loeb Classics

IV

Grammars

Margolis   M.L. Margolis, A Manual of the Aramaic Language of the Babylonian Talmud, 1910.
Epstein   Y.N. Epstein, Babylonian Aramaic Grammar (Hebrew: *Dikduk Aramit Bablit*) 1960.
Levias   C. Levias, A Grammar of Babylonian Aramaic (Hebrew: *Dikduk Aramit Bablit*) 1930.
Dalman   G. Dalman, Grammatik des jüdisch-palästinischen Aramäisch, und Aramäische Dialektproben, repr. 1960.
Gesenius, Gesenius' Hebrew Grammar ed. E.F. Kautzsch tr. A.E. Cowley. 1910.

V

Commentaries

For commentaries and literature on Qohelet, the reader may be referred to the full literature in R. Pfeiffer *Introduction to the Old Testament*, 1948 and the more up-to-date O. Eissfeldt, *The Old Testament*, an Introduction, trans. by Peter R. Ackroyd, 1965, from the 3rd German edition, R. Gordis, Koheleth and his world,[2] 1955; R.B.Y. Scott, Proverbs. Ecclesiastes, 1965. The following commentaries have been cited in the present study:

Graetz,   H. Graetz, Kohelet 1871
Barton, Barton G.A.   Ecclesiastes 1908
Levy, L. Levy,   Das Buch Qohelet 1912
Wildeboer, G. Wildeboer,   Fünf Megillot: Koheleth.
Galling,   K. Galling   Prediger Salomo, 1940.
Ginsberg, H.L. Ginsberg, Studies in Kohelet. 1950.
    Kohelet (Hebrew) 1961.

VI

Special Studies relating to
the language of Qohelet, specifically Aramaic

F. Zimmermann, *Aramaic Provenance of Qohelet*, Jewish Quarterly Review, 36, 1945, 17–45.

R. Gordis, *The Original Language of Qohelet*, JQR, 1946, 67–84.

C.C. Torrey, *The Question of the Original Language of Qohelet*, JQR, 39, 1948, 151–60.

R. Gordis, *The Translation-Theory of Qohelet Re-examined*, JQR 40, 1949, p. 103f;
        Journal of Biblical Literature, 71 (1952) 93–109.

H.L. Ginsberg, *Supplementary Studies in Koheleth*, Proceedings for the Academy for Jewish Research, 1952, 35–62.

M.J. Dahood,   Qoheleth and Recent Discoveries, Biblica 39 (1958) 302–318.

VII

Other Literature Cited in this Study

ANET   Pritchard, J.B.   Ancient Near Eastern Texts Relating to the Old Testament, 1955.

Heidel   Heidel A.,   Gilgamesh Epic and Old Testament Parallels.

  Driver, G.R. and Miles, J.C.   The Babylonian Laws 2 vols. 1960.

  E. Westermarck,   Ritual and Belief in Morocco 2 vols. (repr.)

Cowley   A. Cowley,   Aramaic Papyri of the 5th Century, 1923.

Stith Thompson   Motif Index of Folk Literature 6 vols. 1955.

J. Low,   Aramaeische Pflanzennamen 1881.
      Flora der Juden. 1924–34.

SUBJECT INDEX

A.

Akkadian Literature 128; Alexandria 124, 126; Angst 68, 148; Annulment 35; Antioch on the Orontes 126, 138; Antitheses 42, 142; Aramaic Language (Eastern) 125; Aramaic translation in Q.'s Hebrew 98-122; Aramaic words in Q 100f.; authority, shattering of moral, 31, 76.

B.

Babylon 126; conditions in, 128; Bath sheba, 74-75, her connivance 75; Book of Q, incoherences of, 96.

C.

cathexis by writing 81, 87; compulsions, c. 2; 48; confusion of hu' and hawa' 106f.; cryptogram of Q 119f; curses 41; cycle 62; cyclothemic tendency 62.

D.

date of Q 131; disciple-translator 87, 162, and his orthodox opponent 162; dog 54; doom 48; doubts 42, 71, 96.

E.

Egypt 124f; ego and counter-ego 51, 58; ellipsis 94, 156; Elephantine papyri 104; eyes 62; evil eye 40.

F.

father 61.

G.

Gilgamesh epic 35, 66, 70, 91, 128, 155; government corruption 147.

H.

Hawthorne 70,
HE as orthographical mark 136; heart 50; heptad in Q 135; horror vacui 65.

I.

identification of Q with Solomon 136f.; illhealth 68; impotence c. 4; 28; inclination, good and bad 50.

189

WORD INDEX
I HEBREW
A.

'abiyonah 23; 'adam 57; 'aḥer 75; 'amal 12, 88; 'ammah 22; 'ani 138; 'asah tob 101; 'asham 56.

B.

bait 22, 25; basar 22; beged 70; bor 24.

D.

dabar 90; delet 22.

E.

'et 47-49; 'eber 22; 'ezba 22.

G.

gullat 24, 161.

H.

ḥakam 51, 90; halak 26; haras 9; harag 9; ḥobeq 27; ḥokma 6.32, 72, 89, 90; ḥote' 56, 109.

I.

'inyan 2, 68, 88, 138.

K.

kasaf 63, ka'as 28, 89; kesef 24, 63; kesil 51, 71, 90.

M.

melek 1, meshalim 81, mishlaḥat 102; misken 57.

N.

napaḥ, nippuaḥ, nepiḥa 93; nasi' 1.

P.

peh 26.

Q.

qahal 85; qeber 55; qol 23.

R.

ra'ah 62; ra'ah tobah 62; reihayyim 23; re'i 94; rekeb 23; ro'eh 129; ruah 58, 91, re'ut ruah 93.

S.

sehoq 89; shaqed 23; shekab 23; shem 151; shemesh 60; shiddah 139; Shelomoh 180.

T.

tahanah 23; tob 83, 109.

Y.

yad 25, 27; yarek 22; yezer 48, 50; yitron 90, 101.

II ARAMAIC

A.

'abad 150.

B.

bedil de 102; bish bish 110; boryak/baryak 112; b + tl 150.

D.

dibra 101; danah 114; dira/dura/dara 114, 137.

G.

gerar 115; gumaz 102.

H.

Hawa' betab 101; hu'/hawa 106; hu' 100; hebel 154; hab 56; had 118; hawwar 128; Hilfai (and associated forms) 74; hilma 146; husana 111.

K.

kanash 85, 115, 136; Kanosha 86, 115, 136; kebar 100, 141.

L.

lahag 103; lehem 102, 111.

M.

măn, mān 140; mashlamanutha 74; mahel 103, 157; mata' 117; miltha 90; meshalahta 102; misken 57.

N.

nah 125, 149; na/e hir 149; negah 113; ngd 151.

P.

peras 111.

Q.

qayyem 153; qibla 148; qll 160.

R.

ra'ayonah 140; ra'aya 94; re'ut 93.

S.

shegi' 147; sehor sehor 115; serah 109; shalah 111; shekiah 156.

T.

tab 114; tinyana 146; tur 100.

Y.

(min) yad 103; yehu/yehewe 103.

Z.

zedi 152.

AKKADIAN

akala tabtu 129; qata nadu 129; lu-ub-bu-bu zubatuka 128; nemelu 130; nimequ 129.

ARABIC

fasl 48; hin, hain 44; qismat 48.

ETHIOPIC

lahem 144.

LATIN

funis, funiculus 24.

GREEK

mitos 24; mullas 23; mule 23; mullos 23.

NAME INDEX

A.

Abaye 71; Achan 10; Antiochus III, 130; Aquila 160; Baudelaire, C. 143, 178; Arieti S. 89; R. Ashi 33.

B.

Bacher, W. 21, 128; Bar Bahlul 161; Barton, G. A. 20, 177; Ben Yehudah E. 93; Bleuler, E. 12; Brederek, E. 118; Brussel, J. A. 35; Brockelmann C. passim.

C.

Charles, R. H. 98; Chesterton, G. K. 16; Cooke, G. A. 183; Cowley, A. E.; Chloris 92.

D.

Dahood, M. 21; Dalman, G. 74, 104, 105, 118, 127, 145, 154; H. Donner (jt. author) 136, 180; Dostoievsky 143; Driver G. and Miles, J. C. 57, 130, 138, 156; Delitzsch, Franz, 100; Delitzsch, Friedrich, 100, 148.

E.

Edel, L. 70, 170, 180; Ehrlich, A. B. 101, 178; Eissfeldt, O. 20, 124; R. Eleazar b. Pedat 84; Emerson, R. W., 37, 68, 122.

F.

Fisher, 179; Flora 92; Freud, S., 12, 14, 21, 22, 38, 42, 51, 60, 62, 70, 93.

G.

Galling, K. 77; Garma, A. 21, 27, 180; Ginsberg, H. L., 20, 21, 53, 56, 71, 103, 152; Ginzberg, L., 162, 178, 181; Gordis, R., 25, 135, 157, 177, 182; Gordon, C. H., 88; Graetz, H. 120; Gray, G. B. 182; Gutheil E. A., 16, 21, 22, 62, 94, 96, 159, 177, 180, 181.

H.

Halper, B., 142, 148; Hammurabi 118, 129, 163; Hazlitt, W. 179; Herford, E. T., 45; Harnik, 179; Higgins, M. (jt. author) 178; Hillel, 127, 128; Hitshman, E. 177; Hoffman, F. J. 141, 146, 182.

I.

Ibn Ezra, A. 36; Ibn, Janah, Y. 21; Ibsen, H. 143; Innocent III, 25.

J.

Jastrow, Marcus, passim, Jastrow, M., Jr. 177; Jephtha 37f.; Jones, E. 60, 170, 182; Josephus, 125, 183.

K.

Kafka, F. 143; R. Kohen (Midrash) 25; Krauss, S. 183.

L.

Lamb, C. 179; La Rochefoucauld, F., 60, 180; Levy, L., 111; Loretz, O., 177; Löw, I., 161; Lucas, F. L. 178.

M.

Margolis, M. L., 112, 121, 141, 148, 163; Mazar, B., 180; Merloo, A. M., 42, 179; R. Meir 85; Minkowski, 46, 179; Montgomery, J. A., 110, 180; Moses 129, 163.

N.

Nietzsche, F. 70; Nöldeke, T. 150, 158.

P.

Partridge, E. 24; Payne Smith, J. M. passim, Peake, A. S. 177; Pffeifer, R. 124; Podechard, E. 177; Podolsky, E. 174; Powell, H. H., 121, 127, 136; Pritchard, J. B. 84, 163; Proust, M. 180.

R.

Raba 171; Rank, O. 60, 138; Raphael C. (jt. author) 178; Rashi 20, 21, 22, 25, 33, 178; Reider, J. 183; Reik, T. 60; Roheim, G. 177; Rostovtzeff, M. 124, 127.

S.

Seleuceus, I. 126; Schiller, F. 48; Smith, W. R. 179; Stekel, W. 12, 31, 35, 38, 41, 60, 65, 68, 70, 76, 95, 177, 180, 182; Strindberg, J. A. 143.

T.

Tcherikover, V. 126; Tenenbaum, S. 178; Thompson, E. M. 183; Thoreau, H. 122; Torrey, C. C. 113, 121, 122.

W.

Wells, H. G. 64; Westermarck, E. A. 23, 183.

Y.

Yellin, D. 144, 149.

Z.

Zeitlin, S. 127; Zephyrus 92; Zimmermann, F. 144, 148, 155, 183, 184.